SPURS ON THE BOOT

FIRST MEETING OF HITLER AND MUSSOLINI

The author appears at the left

SPURS ON THE BOOT

Italy under Her Masters

BY

THOMAS B. MORGAN

LONGMANS, GREEN AND CO.

NEW YORK · LONDON · TORONTO

1941

LONGMANS, GREEN AND CO.
114 FIFTH AVENUE, NEW YORK
221 EAST 20TH STREET, CHICAGO

LONGMANS, GREEN AND CO., LTD.
OF PATERNOSTER ROW
43, ALBERT DRIVE, LONDON, S.W. 19
17, CHITTARANJAN AVENUE, CALCUTTA
NICOL ROAD, BOMBAY
36A, MOUNT ROAD, MADRAS

LONGMANS, GREEN AND CO.
215 VICTORIA STREET, TORONTO

SPURS ON THE BOOT

First edition June 1941
Reprinted July 1941

PRINTED IN THE UNITED STATES OF AMERICA

CONTENTS

CHAPTER I

BUNDLES OF COMBAT

The first World War was over. No one knew it then but the peace tainted and even tinted the air, the earth and the sky for the next World War. We can see it all now — many things decayed, many things red, many black, many brown, from the Caspian to the North Sea at least. Anything could come out of it and did — Communism, Fascism, Naziism and the Second World War.

Victors, and thinking they should be somewhere in the money, the Italians were the first disgruntled. They were not getting what they wanted in Europe, Asia or Africa. But, with all the vast lands passing from one power to another, they set their hearts on Fiume, a smiling though unimportant town of 50,000 along the Adriatic. It was Italian, they said. They had asked for an orange whereas in other parts a gold mine gaped for ownership. They cried for the orange.

The place was noted more than anything else for the quality of its shrimps though it once was an Austrian naval base, and possessed a torpedo factory and an airport. The Italians wanted the town not alone for its naval base, its torpedo factory, its airport and its 50,000 souls but for everything else including the shrimps. The allies refused to give it to them.

Then and there, Fascism was born.

Fate willed that your reporter should witness its genesis, obstetrics and adolescence. In Milan, Benito Mussolini just an editor then, gathered several score of political vagabonds in an upper chamber in a dark and spooky structure on Holy Sepulcher Place. In that Stygian seraglio, he promised that if they followed him, some day they would rule the world. It was March, 1919.

He called the Italian government names. He called Prime Minister Victor Emmanuel Orlando names. He called King Victor Emmanuel the Third names. They were not getting Fiume for Italy. The hope was the future. The future was in the hands of the vagabonds — if they followed him. The vagabonds were ex-Socialists, ex-Communists, ex-Populists, ex-Nationalists and ex-Monarchists. Wandering, they were in search of a haven. Now they had found it.

One single unbreakable duty was imposed — they must be bound together and to him, Il Duce. To us a thing bound is a bundle; to them, it was a *fascio*. But they were not just a dead bundle. They were a fighting bundle, officially *Fascio Italiano di Combattimento*, Italian Bundle of Combat. Each one of them was called a *fascista*, a fascist.

Their emblem was the Lictor's rods of the Roman Emperor, *fasces* in Latin, a fascio of rods tied with thongs, symbol of force. Mussolini's was a fascio of men tied to him. The United States has a similar emblem, the fasces alongside the motto "E Pluribus Unum," especially on a dime.

From Milan, the vagabonds scattered, starting other *fasci* (plural) in Rome, Florence, Genoa, Turin, Naples, all over the country. Little attention was paid to their fiery artifices. They were "just a bunch of boys." It was just a phase. But they circulated, they organized. In Rome within a month we knew that something had happened.

"Down with America" was what they were shouting. We did not want their shrimps. Your reporter boiled. And worse, he showed it. Involuntary as it all was — down we went. A club on the head by an impregnated youth had transformed our legs into wet soda straws. In due time, we got up. More of this would clog the narrative but you can tell what was going on.

The American Embassy was guarded by cavalry, infantry and artillery. A merry and martial sight these soldiers made. They were living at that very moment on American wheat, American beef and American salmon. We risked betrayal by that salmon. When the Mussolini youth attacked our embassy with epithets and deadly threats, the Italian cavalry, infantry and artillery bravely drove them off with swords, muskets, bayonets, machine-guns and cannon. They liked our bread and beef.

The bundles of combat paraded the streets, morning, noon and night. They sang dirges as if a battle had been lost. Everything went well when they sang. They chanted for the return of the "unredeemed brethren" of the shrimp center.

Intermittently, a screech "Long live Fiume" would clatter above the singing like a pneumatic riveter above the traffic. That sound stirred the mob and each one became a riveter. The screams were moistened by tears. It was a heavy strain both on the eyes and the throat. Soon the sounds degenerated into a wheeze. Before the

vocal cords finally gave out, there was one last dying
effort. "Down with America" they groaned. Then
there was a wait until the vocal cords came back.

American consulates throughout Italy were guarded
and so were the consuls. The sight of the coat-of-arms
of the United States whether on consulate window or
embassy door brought epithets and deadly threats. But
the coat-of-arms could with difficulty be touched. It
would complicate matters. The populace, too, was
living on American wheat, American beef and — salmon.

In Trieste mobs attacked a Y.M.C.A. headquarters
established there to provide amusement for both Italian
and American soldiers and sailors. The headquarters
kept its flag flying and bricks and bottles were thrown
against its folds. A frenzied Fascist youth climbed a
pillar against the building in an attempt to seize the
flag and tear it from its fastenings at a window. A big
U. S. marine was leaning on the window as the Mussolini zealot reached for the edge of the banner.

"Get back," growled the marine, "or I'll push you
back."

Cries of joy came from the street just as the boy got
his fingers on the sacred cloth. The marine's blood
boiled, too. He gave the Italian a straight jab in the
face so powerful that the lad was stunned, lost his grip
and fell to the ground. The mob simmered. More
bricks and bottles went up against the window until not
one single pane was left whole. The flag stayed
guarded by the faithful marine until sunset when, with
simple though solemn ceremony, he performed a lower-
ing of the colors as he reverently grasped its folds to

prevent the emblem from even touching the window sill.

And all this clamor against us was caused by Fiume. The town was not much to us. President Wilson trying to do the right thing for everybody had collided with Italian ambition. The Italians had many things coming to them by treaty. Getting so burned up over the shrimp center, they let a lot of rich German colonies, including the East African gold mine, slip through their fingers. But President Wilson had said no. It was not an Italian port, he claimed. That was right. The Italians argued that the population spoke Italian. That was right, too. The two claims could not be satisfied. Therefore, it was, "Down with America" in Italy.

Now, leaping at the head of the movement as if he took the baton of command from Mussolini was Gabriele d'Annunzio, self-baptized the archangel and self-styled "the Announcer." Temporarily, he eclipsed the leader of Holy Sepulcher Place. International figure, he was adorned with the aura of a great popular war hero. It was natural that he should steal the show.

A poet by trade, he was known also as the unfaithful lover of Eleonora Duse, idolized Italian tragedienne. Tiring of her, he had tossed her unconcernedly aside. Outside of Italy, the sympathy was with la Duse. In America of those days, it had made him a "no good" poet. The Italians, however, had forgiven the amorous episode as of something happening in the course of all love and did not hold any of it against him. He had previously skipped the country for debt and had lived in France. He came back to serve king and country.

Who would have the brass to dun him now? Instead of extortionate creditors, he met cheering patriots.

He was fifty-two when he decided to be a soldier, and though he had borne arms only nominally before, he seemed somehow to have a natural aptitude perhaps not so much for the soldiery itself, but for dramatizing heroism and getting promotions. He was good at speechmaking. In fact, he had often been found in the dugouts haranguing assembled warriors on the beauty and poetry of dying, a theme which always upset the officers because they tried to instil in the minds of their charges the beauty and poetry not alone of living but of fighting for their lives.

His chief claim to usefulness as a soldier was that he was carried as an observer on aerial reconnoitering trips. Each pilot entrusted with taking him aloft virtually shivered in his shoes at the prospect. The poet had a knack of getting out of so many scrapes and escaping death while the pilot often met it. The aviators thought it small wonder he could declaim on the beauty and poetry of dying since he was so elusive to the call.

In the air, he was always a problem. His plane would meet an Austrian plane, but instead of allowing his own pilot to maneuver either to shoot the Austrian down or to retire to the rear as the situation warranted, the poet would orate and gesticulate against the perfidy of the enemy as a nation.

"Rascal! Coward! Scoundrel! Our invincible arms will crush you to withering dust," he would challenge in the skies.

The words either evaporated in the altitude or were

drowned by the rumble of the motors. The Austrian, if he were looking, could only see a pair of scraggy arms, placed in the attitude of defiance. To the Italian pilot, however, it was another story. The planes of 1916 were delicate craft at their best. A gesticulating and oratorical passenger was often as much as an upset in mid-air.

The poet had, of course, perpetrated many exploits which were spectacular. Some, perhaps, were more spectacular than useful. In those days, it was considered something of a miracle that he had flown from Padua to Vienna in a bombing plane. There he dropped pamphlets on the Viennese to tell them that their cause was lost, though their own hungry stomachs as well as their own famished army were telling them the same thing and telling it even more dramatically.

But the deed for which he had won the gold medal for valor was the accomplishment of the unique military task of delivering sealed bottles containing admonitive though non-explosive pamphlets by sea. With Costanzo Ciano, father of Count Ciano, son-in-law of Mussolini, and Luigi Rizzo, a young naval officer, he set out from Venice in command of four sub-chasers. They crossed the Adriatic and zig-zagged into the Gulf of the Quarnero at night. In the small harbor of Buccari they found the Austrian fleet but they could not enter because the crafty and inhospitable enemy had laid a heavy net across the entrance. Instead of dispatching a score or more torpedoes, the customary procedure on these occasions, they dropped the sealed bottles as if they were fulfilling the humane duty of delivering the morning milk.

And now the poet was to be the chief attraction in the Fiume turmoil. He was brought to Rome to whoop up the already whooped-up populace. It was all somewhat reminiscent. The poet had shaken his clenched fist at the Austrian airplanes. Before the multitudes, he could shake his clenched fist at America, too.

Returned soldiers, students and women patriots joined the bundles of combat in a consuming ardor over the poet-soldier. The first big rally was scheduled for a Sunday morning in the Augusteum, then Rome's biggest music hall. But all day on the previous Saturday, the singing parades kept a feverish public smoldering. Shrieks of "Down with America" came out again from exhausted throats. Sunday morning could not come too quickly. Scorched were the patriots.

For me, as a cunning and not too sacerdotal newsman, it would help if I secured an advance copy of the poet's speech so as to be able to handle any flaming epithets without unnecessary shock to the great American public. I went to his hotel to see this conjurer of fiery Italian passions. He could not be seen. I called again and again.

A score of soldier sycophants were waiting on him. First one and then another told me that the "Announcer" was writing his speech. How could he give me a copy? Toward dinner time, the sycophants left. I remained alone to patrol the corridor.

Your reporter caught the Announcer going from one room to another. He wore a flowing red silk robe with golden figures — greyhounds and snakes, perhaps to inspire him as swift and evasive. The robe was wrapped closely about him. This exaggerated his scrawny body. He would have been truly Mephistophelian were not his stature unhappily dwarfish. He was not more than five feet four. Crimson slippers embroidered in gold concealed his feet.

His head was completely bald. His chin bore a most impoverished beard as if it were unfertile for the growing of hair. His face was anemic and drawn, imposing the wonder that any woman had ever been attracted by it despite the far-flung reputation he enjoyed as a truly great lover. His left eye was reposeful; his right had been lost in a flying accident, replaced pathetically by a glass eye. He walked with a cultivated finishing school step — a poet walking in the garden. He was not a soldier stepping out. He was a *poet*.

We were alone.

"As an American newsman, Colonel," I blurted so bluntly that he started as if it were a holdup, "I have been trying to see you all day long. You have been busy."

"Yes, I have been busy," he returned in exquisite French when he had regained his breath. He seemed happy for this break from the day of receiving and writing. "Come in."

I entered the room behind him and closed the door. It was filled with flowers. A slightly stifling though pleasant aroma buoyed the place. I breathed it in again a little perplexed. Four uniforms hung in a half-open closet. On a dresser was a very large jewel box, the size of a brief-case. It was filled with thirty or forty medals all arranged according to some scheme of his orderly. He noticed that my breath had been taken.

"Won't you sit down," he said with a wave and a smile. His voice was high-pitched though persuasive, a purely conversational voice.

"I always like to see Americans," he continued as he sat up straight on a divan and drew the robe about him to insure that he would be covered and spare me the discomfiture of a shock. "I saw the American regiment on the Italian front. Splendid soldiers. They were superb soldiers."

"Of course, we liked them," he continued. "It was good for our people to see them. But Wilson, what has he done? Why should he treat us like this after so much Italian blood has been shed in a common cause? Surely! Surely! We know that the American people do not support him in this. All Italy loves America. We love the American people. But, we must have Fiume."

He paused, but it was a rhetorical pause. Conversation was an art for him. He began every new spurt with a natural "Of course!" or a mild interjection or a softly spoken rhetorical question. He continued to smile all the time. Occasionally, he would adjust a monocle to his single eye. Then both hands would rest on the silken covering over his horizontal right calf which he had crossed on the left knee. He hugged it to the body but was careful to keep it covered.

"America, how wonderful! You know that I always

liked your poets, too. Walt Whitman, he was my favorite. Do they read him much?" he mused.

"Not enough," I answered. "He is a truly American poet."

"Yes, yes," he continued quietly. "He has such freshness, such virility and such truth. I like a poet who gets next to the people. Life is the great thing. To depict it is another. One has got to live it to be able to depict it."

And he went on with the poets just as if our visit was a nice social call. And I enjoyed it though I had come to get his speech. He lamented the lack of American sculptors, painters and musicians. He said they would come. He admitted we had done much in architecture and more of that was to come also.

Then he went off on motion pictures. He wanted to write a great heroic scenario. We know that he could have done it had he set his mind upon it. The very first great scenario written was his own *Cabiria*, a movie milestone.

The little scrawny man kept his leg crossed over his knee and continued to talk as if he were a character in a play. It was all so pleasant, all so interesting. How could I bring up the profane typewritten copy of a speech for the newspapers. He never used a typewriter anyway.

Finally he rose from the divan.

"You must come again," he said.

I could see that he intended me to leave. But I had not yet asked for the speech. I would not get back in to see him very easily. The visit was thrilling enough for the reporter, but of no consequence to the Associated Press unless I should get that speech.

"There is just one thing, Colonel," I blurted again in distinct contrast to his suavity. "Could I have a copy of your speech?"

He continued to smile, but turned half around almost away from me. It was plain that this was a new situation to him — a man wanting a copy of his speech, when speeches were made to be delivered. They, too, were art to him.

"Copy of my speech?" he repeated slowly, somewhat surprised and hurt that I had introduced the earthiness of newspaper technique into an artistic performance.

"Do you want to publish it now?" he asked, still confused.

"Oh, no," I explained. "It is just to get it ready for the newspapers to be published after you speak."

"Then why now? There will be plenty of time to get it after I speak. Come and hear me."

Outwardly pleasant but inwardly irked, he shook hands bidding good-bye and bowing most ceremoniously.

Well, on Sunday the Augusteum was packed and many thousands could not get in. Cabinet ministers, the mayor of Rome, generals and plenty of other stage trimmings were on the platform. The vast audience sang the dirges and just as in the parades interspersed them with shrieks of "Long live Fiume," concluding with the usual finale of "Down with America."

When the poet entered to take his place in the center

of the stage, the crowd exploded. Cheering rocked the building. This wild enthusiasm for a hero contrasted with his sorry physique. He lacked the traditional military bearing but he *was* a hero.

He wore a grey-green uniform. A very high white military collar close about the neck made him keep his head up. White was the color of the aristocratic Novara cavalry regiment in which he was a lieutenant colonel. This may seem to contradict his status as an airman, but in those days the officers were called from all branches of the service since there was no separate air arm. A small metal badge of outspread wings on his left breast, the insignia of a flyer, showed that he had deserted spurs for wings. But, to be on the safe side, he wore both.

Finally, silence permitted his first words.

"Popolo di Roma," he shouted straining his thin and streaky voice. But high pitched, it carried throughout the vast edifice. They were stirring words and almost identical with those of Coriolanus, Caesar or Mark Antony in other ages. They recalled centuries of history, of triumphs, of Roman holidays and of Roman dominion.

It was enough for a second ovation. The wonder was that such an impoverished voice could command the audience. But soon it was evident that it was not the voice but the cadence. His rhythm held the listeners enraptured. It was poetry. At times, he rose to climactic heights. For an hour he kept them trembling with emotion.

He mingled his attacks on Wilson with patriotic

platitudes done with modulated challenges and dramatic rhetoric. He had performed the artistic, too. He scored America as un-spiritual. The war president, he flayed. His language was so strong that Orlando forbade its publication.

"Wilson is a horse-faced fool devoid of intelligence," he said.

"The United States is a nation of trade-mongers and its god, the almighty dollar."

"Anglo-Saxon puritanism is nothing but a flagrant hypocrisy."

"Where are their poets and their heroes? They possess neither the genius nor the heroism of Latin blood."

"Where are the ideals of a nation whose god is money? We live to keep alive the flame of heroism and the immortality of the hero."

The overwhelming climax was reached when he defied England, France or the United States to prevent the annexation of Fiume to Italy. He took a solemn oath with upraised hand that Fiume would forever be Italian.

"I solemnly swear," he proclaimed amidst the ebullient fervor, "that Fiume will be annexed to Italy if I have to give my last drop of blood."

Applause rocked the hall. "We will follow you," "We will obey," "Down with America," they re-echoed. Larynxes were lost only to be found again. Patriots counted on his word. It was another victory for him.

In the mingled wave of hate and patriotic fervor, the bundles of combat received their first great boost. Exsoldiers, professional patriots and fiery students joined.

They worked themselves into a consuming ardor on getting Fiume for Italy. The poet travelled the land. He pepped the hopeful spirits with the purity of Italy as against the wickedness of America in particular and mankind in general. He was the high priest of Fascism, the voice crying in the wilderness.

Plodding in his office still unknown was the not less fiery Mussolini, his rabble-rousing talent still to be exploited. He was thirty-six. His star had not yet begun to rise. He was tightly binding each bundle of combat with the thongs which the poet spun from the sorrowful though highly convenient tragedy of Fiume.

For his newspaper, *Il Popolo d'Italia,* he wrote several columns a day stirring the soul and wrenching the heart on the plight of the unredeemed, who hardly without his knowledge were receiving millions from the Italian government to shed bigger tears and cry louder that they might be annexed to "their Motherland." His literary skill and relentless tenacity fired his Fascist fledglings with dutiful though not unselfish devotion. He held for them the hope of fulfillment of their hitherto abortive political ambitions.

He told them it was an uphill fight. They must, above all, be bound in the bundle, be Fascist. He had the will and they the faith in his will. They perceived Fascism as a fine vehicle. They could get somewhere.

But, they knew also that their greatest obstacle to political riches was the power which the Communists and Socialists wielded in Italy at that uncertain moment. They knew, because many of them were either unceremoniously removed from the radical ranks or had retired with proletarian dignity. Reds and Fascists were parties of action. Both were revolutionary. The Reds, however, controlled a virile Italian working-class mass and were the strongest political party in the country. It was a long haul.

Desperation for existence, the gamble on events, a hunch on Mussolini and a certain measure of faith compelled the fledglings to plunge all. Perhaps they would rule Italy some day.

CHAPTER II

CARUSO, COMMUNISTS AND CARABINEERS

Born in March, Fascism was naturally not grown up in July. Hence, Communists still talked back to the police, and told officials, high and low, what they had better do or refrain from doing. They did not want to take charge of the government. It was too much of a bother. They preferred to be ornery. It was fun to disobey and to get others to disobey. Since Italians in general, not unlike the Irish in proverb, were perennially "agin' the guvvermint," Utopia had partially arrived.

In all the towns, large and small, the radical Reds strutted in the squares laughing everything off. When a squadron of Red youth sacked a store and handed out the wares somewhat without fear but not without favor to the motley proletariat, budding commissars chuckled. It was dividing-up. When trucks of industrial concerns were commandeered and the products of the factories bagged, they snickered. "Comes the revolution," they said. When officers of the army and navy were jostled, they averred it was too good for them and nothing to what they would get from the hopefully awaited Red guards. They did have a good time and so did the populace. They were the people's friends; the government, their enemy.

I was sent to cover a first-class dividing-up in Florence. Somehow this flagrant taking from those who had and flinging it to those who had not, looked definitely out of place in this city of placid marble statues, graceful centuries-old churches and lordly palaces. The contrast between an ordered past and the disordered present made me ponder on whether the Florentines had changed altars. But, they had had periods of turbulence, too, in between long periods of peace, and this was one of the periods of turbulence incited by the spirit of the times.

The flower of Red youth worked without system unless one could call the efficient mulcting of a merchant's store a system. The young men cleaned these shops cleaner than a wishbone. One could not discern, however, how they chose the victims. Ten gangs of from twenty to thirty men worked the city. Each such nucleus was followed by hundreds of human albeit indiscriminate beings. When the gang invaded a store and had with loud talk, threats and unmistakable nudges reduced the owner to but passive resistance, the hundreds surged at the entrance.

Their numbers prevented all from getting in at once. The first in would load up with all that the limits of a rather necessary mobility would permit and very reluctantly leave the rest. The last to get in theoretically had little choice but it so happened that while the first had a maximum of selection they had a minimum of time. The impatience of those outside did not allow too much indecision. Consequently, some of the best things remained. It made little difference that the late arrivals were forced to pick over the wreckage of the previous waves. They sorted until they found something they wanted.

The gay though irregular procedure caused me to wonder where the law and its guardians were. Eventually, my curiosity was satisfied. Despite the general civil uproar, a superb company of the law and its guardians, in their gaudy Napoleonic uniforms of red and black with red pompoms on their hats, in leisurely fashion marched down Via Cavour. A brave but suspiciously agitated captain with drawn and shining sword stalked at the head — the Royal Carabineers.

And they were marching to restore order on the complaint of one mulcted drygoods merchant while nineteen others were being similarly dispossessed. I followed them. On the spot, I saw their effort to enforce the law "equally for all," as the Italians as well as the French say. Many beneficiaries of Communist bounty were rushing away with boxes of lace, bolts of cloth, dresses, furs, plumes, scarfs, stockings or whatever they could appropriate. The sight of the captain and his men quickened their pace. A few timid hopefuls who had not yet entered the store and were guilty therefore only of intent joined the fugitives fearing that the red pompoms could ferret the conscience. Most of the vandals, however, not yet glutted with booty, remained and continued their depredations only just slightly apprehensive of captain and cops.

The commander ordered his men to break ranks; which seemed a pity when they looked so prim. He wormed his way into the store followed by his company in file. The red pompoms quivered. They had penetrated well into the main room when the captain asked for space, lifted high his sword and shouted, "Out." Mysteriously but satanically struck, the mob begot panic and made for the doors. Much of the grabbings were dropped on the spot. The exodus was laborious, bruising and clamorous.

Within a few minutes, sword and pompoms were left in complete command. The captain called for the merchant, who bowed in gratitude though he was now hardly a merchant at all for the store was half empty. The sword was brought to a precise salute. A full flourish then skillfully placed it in the scabbard. Merchant and captain shook hands. The company was reassembled. Pompoms were adjusted. The sword came out of the scabbard again. "Forward, march" was shouted and the parade resumed.

When the picturesque cortege had turned the corner, out from the most inconceivable recesses poured the proletariat anew. They had only been in hiding. There was a general dash for the store. In five minutes, the status quo ante had been resumed. This was order in Florence in July, 1919.

Inconveniently, an earthquake shook the whole of Tuscany; remorse shook the populace. Guilty, they discerned an act of divine retribution, themselves singled out for heavenly wrath. Instead of the victimized stores, it was the churches which were crowded that night. The earthquake did no damage in Florence except to jolt the larceny from its complacency. Even the Reds could not laugh off an earthquake. It was too gloomy a foreboding.

Reports from the country districts showed that the earthquake was serious. A hundred dead and five thousand homeless was its toll. By force of circumstance, an armistice was tacitly declared between Communist and capitalist. Taking advantage of the truce I now began scouring the country. The news center had changed from civil to terrestrial upheaval.

No automobiles were available for the round-up. Wartime rules still in effect deprived me of motor locomotion. It was a high-seated shay which carried your reporter around the saddened land. The driver, unconcerned with havoc, pointed out the numerous places of interest with a cold abandon, as if I had been a tourist and there were no earthquake at all. The dead had been collected and put into any building left standing. Somehow it always happened to be a stable. Since soldiers were plentiful, the government sent whole regiments to put up tents and distribute food. For those who remained living, the physical suffering was not great because the weather was mild.

But my driver was allergic to suffering anyway. Whenever we passed a commissary tent where the survivors with or without injuries received their daily rations, he railed at them as unworthy sluggards and sighed to himself that no free living ever came his way. He worked for all he got, he complained. Finally, he turned about on the seat.

"Look! Look!" he marveled at me. "And without paying a cent. Without paying a cent."

While out in the country, I learned that the Communists had held a dividing-up at the home of Enrico

Caruso, the great Italian tenor. This, too, was in the Florentine hills, but in a different direction from the earthquake. I went there by train.

I left the train at Signa Lastra, and, directed by an obliging and not altogether disinterested cab driver was shown the tenor's villa way up on the steep hillside. It required two stout legs, lots of breath and no thought of time to get there. Here was where the interest and deference of the driver was rewarded. I took his transport, paid him handsomely but saved the legs, the breath and the time.

There was a wall perhaps a mile in circumference enclosing the estate. I had no difficulty in getting welcome. I was a newspaperman. The guardian rushed from the lodge to the house and I was told to come in. I walked up the drive and there on the veranda found the tenor himself in shirt and slippers. He showed me around the house. Though his wife stumbled into us a couple of times he did not introduce me. She certainly looked as if she wanted to know who I was. She was Dorothy Benjamin and we were compatriots. An appreciative recognition passed between us though we were confused. Since Caruso was from the south of Italy where women are but men's playthings, I could not figure whether he thought the wife unworthy of the guest or the guest unworthy of the wife.

I told him what I heard about his being visited by the dividing-uppers. It was true, he said, but he seemed unconcerned for the moment about it. What seemed to interest him more than the division of wealth was a room he was preparing for little Gloria, his infant

daughter.   He led me there and showed me a great al-
cove where he had projected a *Presepe*.   This was a
Neapolitan institution in which the birth of Christ was
depicted by small figures which the children collected
from time to time.   Gloria was to get a most populous
Presepe.   Besides the main figures of the Infant, Mary,
Joseph, the ox and the ass, it had angels, stars, shep-
herds, sheep, wise men, camels, peasants in costume,
palms, singing children and a heavenly host rejoicing
in the historic scene.

I appreciated the *Presepe* and was lavish in my esti-
mate of its artistic and educational properties.   This appreciation seemed to close the subject.   The topic of
the most modern technique in dividing-up as it had
been practiced on the world's greatest tenor was then
opened.

"Yes, they have been here," Caruso moaned lamen-
tably, as his great physique reposed in an armchair.
"The committee asked me how much olive oil I had.
I told them I had seven barrels in the storehouse.   They
thought that that was a lot and said that five of them
they needed and would take.   And, just like that, without any argument, they said that two barrels of oil were
enough for me until the harvest came in.   That's how
they did it."

Your reporter listened.   The virtuoso sighed.   His
sadness was interspersed with little fits of anger.

"And then they asked me how much wine I had," he
continued.   "I called my man and my man said that we
had thirty-two barrels.   That was of fine Chianti wine.
The committee heard him say it.   Right away, the head

man said that they would take twenty-seven. Five barrels were enough for us until the new vintage, they told me."

"How can you keep the place going?" I interposed.

"They expect me to keep the place going on what I make from singing," he remarked, raising even his speaking voice to a pure C. "And that was not enough. They asked me how many automobiles I had. I said there were three in the garage. They needed two of them, somehow. I protested. They told me that one was enough for me. They took the two cars and that same afternoon sent up trucks and men to carry away the oil and wine. Yesterday they sent up for my last car. I have nothing now to carry us into town."

He was downcast. He had been generous with Italy in the money he earned from his singing. He thought the police were to blame.

"I will leave Italy forever," he finally concluded dejectedly.

His expressive face portrayed the sadness of frustration. It was plain to me that what seemed like overemphasis on the *Presepe* was just something to take his mind off the disappearing fortune which the Reds at that very moment were trying desperately to wrest from his possession. He had built it through hard work. It was true that they had only taken wine, oil and automobiles up to that point but he was fearing that they would return for wheat, cattle, furniture, works of art or whatever touched their fancy. While he would not be destitute had they taken all, yet it had shaken his faith, robbed him of his quiet in the Tuscan hills after years of operatic toil and changed a way of life to something his simple though ardent soul was wholly incapable of understanding.

I sympathized. I smiled again to the signora. He shook hands with me. I left and trudged down the walk thinking how many innocent men and women were always caught in the meshes of civil strife. And this was very, very mild.

I arrived again in Florence. Everyone was safe and sound. I was just in time to perceive that the remorse for past sins which the earthquake had created had worn off. Saved from worldly catastrophe, the populace deserted the churches to resume their riotous living with the Communists. The truce had run forty-eight hours. It was like the expiration of an ultimatum. Avid eyes and watering mouths were awaiting a more voluptuous dividing-up. The city seethed again.

The truce had evidently allowed the Communist high command to draw up a more co-ordinated battle plan. This time there was a zero hour for a proletarian "over the top." The gangs became squadrons centrally controlled. The whole city was blanketed with a crude but serviceable intelligence system, serviceable enough against the pom-pommed carabineers. Seven o'clock on the following day was the zero hour for the coup-de-main. They did not want a coup d'état. They wanted the riches.

Generously before seven I was present at the marketplace and so were the Communists. Promptly at the zero hour the doors opened. The Marxian hierarchy immediately took charge. Orders were shouted by slim and officious men with red bands on their arms. When carts and trucks came in, the hierarchs came forward and with peremptory gestures proclaimed, "That's ours."

Just as in the preliminary skirmishes before the earthquake, there was confusion. Gesticulating farmers foamed in rage. But the orders were authoritative. The quaint Florentine guards, as traditional as the city itself but distinct from the carabineers, had assumed the guardianship of the law. They looked on wondering whether they should act as mediators or just let those who understood this new distribution take charge. It was easier to let the new and virile men command.

That part was very nice to watch. The farmers did not know what was happening though they were reasonably sure that they were going to be left without payment. On the other hand, it was a festive day. It was festive to see the eager eyes satisfied with free vegetables, wine, meat, butter, cheese and all those luscious edibles which a Florentine market generally dispenses. It all went on until ten o'clock when the prefect, who is the responsible ruler of an Italian city, got down to his office. Even he was not unduly perturbed but just the same ordered the Florentine guard to put a stop to it. They had no trouble in that now because distribution had been so complete that all that was left for this unaccountable police to do was to close the doors of the market.

The storekeepers spared from the first levy now squirmed over what was expected from them after this appetizing requisition in the market place. They did not open their stores. Communists paraded, viewing the closed emporia where fine shoes, clothing, dress goods, furniture, pastry, everything was waiting. The air was charged. Crowds surged through the thoroughfares getting more incensed at the barred and locked stores. They complained that nothing was being done to liberate the merchandise and "make it available to the people."

Bigger and better gangs, huskier and hungrier proletarians and stronger and sterner carabineers were around. All were dickering for something. This was to be all-out, all-Florentine assault. As a sort of warming up skirmish, a police commissioner organized a charge of carabineers mixed with plain-clothes men to clear a square. They did not have the primness of the captain and his company now. This was business. But as fast as they cleared one square, the crowd surged into another. Commissioner and commissar played capitalist and Communist hide and seek.

Hide and seek continued all morning. The police conceived it as order if they could keep the crowd running. Without any particular connection with the plan, a company of soldiers in wartime olive-grey paraded. The crowd suspended the running and cheered the war-worn veterans. They made common cause with them more especially to show their disdain for the comic-opera tactics of the pompoms.

Finally, the colonel of carabineers resplendent in abundant silver and gold as well as red arrived in the great square, Piazza Vittorio Emanuele, in a luxurious open car to assume command in the face of such a threatened disaster. Sitting in the car, he viewed the soldiers fraternizing with the mob. He was exasperated. Lesser officers approached and saluted. He gesticulated in anger and proclaimed that the honor of the king and the safety of the state were in jeopardy.

"I want iron discipline," he said, clenching his fist. "I will get it. I am in command. Order, unbreakable order must be restored."

The officers listened and saluted again but wondered what miracle was going to restore order. They willingly surrendered to his genius since they regarded it as a herculean task to stop the appropriation of butter, eggs, potatoes, drygoods, shoes without a major military operation. The colonel was therefore forced to act, to do something whether it had any chance of success or not. He, too, carried a sword. He stood up in the car. He frowned at the chaotic multitudes of veterans and populace. He turned to left and right. His officers watched him. The crowds ignored him. He was wild in rage. He snatched his sword, lifted it high over his head and in a strained raucous voice, shouted,

"Away! Away! All of you! I want peace." He was still ignored. Confusion persisted. The sporadic chasing from square to square made it worse. Heroism was in vain. He was dejected.

Carabineers were drawn up at one end of the square. He ordered them to fix bayonets and then deploy. The crowd stopped and looked on as if it were a military drill. To them, it was still a playful holiday. The carabineers were ordered to advance. The crowd was not moving back. Somewhat precariously, the populace dared the carabineers to stick them with bayonets.

The carabineers could not stab anybody in cold blood. Some joked. Some sweated.

The colonel saw that it did not work. The square was as chaotic as ever. He refused to see any fun in it. While he thought he had been leading his men in the advance as a true hero against the unarmed mob, he now took his position behind them as a true colonel of carabineers.

"Load your rifles," he cried out.

That, too, the crowd watched. The rifles were all loaded. He looked over his line of carabineers.

"Fire and advance," he screeched.

Irregular volleys punctuated the air, turning the holiday fun into whitened terror. This *was* a charge. Slowly, the carabineers moved forward and discharged more irregular volleys. Panic seized the multitudes. All rushed for the side streets. Cries of children and shrieks of women mingled with the rap of the firing. A machine-gun was brought in and added its clatter to the terror of the rifles.

The square was cleared.

I was carried by the panicked avalanche into a street parallel with the square. The carabineers were still behind the crowd forcing the mobs from the center of the city. Firing continued.

"Get back! Get back!" shouted the carabineers.

Advancing, they finally reached the street where I was marooned. The firing was continuous. Panic increased. The mobs had scampered into every available doorway. I gained an apartment house entrance. When I got in, the janitor slammed the doors. There

were a score of us inside. Everybody railed at the carabineers. "Scoundrels, cowards, and public hangmen,"
it seemed that they were.

After all had recovered from the momentary fright,
your reporter discovered he was trapped. Here was the
biggest riot since the disorder had started and I could
not send a dispatch. If I ventured outside the door, I
would be shot down. The telegraph office was on the
other side of the square. Why had I rushed this way
instead of taking a street where I could at least reach the
telegraph office? What was the use of having this dramatic story if I could not get it on the wire?

The firing was furious for forty-five minutes. Then
it came in intermittent volleys as if they were rounding
up the gang. Finally, it died down. I told the terrified
janitor to let me out. He at first refused. He said I
was treating life lightly. They called me crazy. I
must, must send the dispatch. Finally, I induced the
janitor to open the door enough to let me out alone.
Grudgingly, he complied. The street was deserted.
There were still intermittent shots from the square. As
I advanced, clinging close to the wall, more volleys were
heard. I expected to reach the square in a moment and
find a hundred or more dead bodies there.

Hugging the side of the building, I gained the corner when a bayonet jutted out from the adjacent street.
A moment later and I was face to face with a cara-
bineer. He raised his rifle.

"Dietro (Back up)," he cried.

I turned about and ran back toward the doorway.
Volley after volley seemed to come from that cara-

bineer's rifle. I wondered whether I would ever reach that door. I knew that as long as I heard the shots I was alive. I reached the door and hammered frantically for admission. They just barely opened it. When they saw me, they let me in as if I belonged there. They asked me how many were dead. I told them I could not get to the square. It must be terrible, I thought. That was all I knew. I was there for another half-hour while the firing continued. Finally there was a dead calm.

The dead calm was only a few minutes old when the door was opened. All burst out on the street as if the absence of firing were a scheduled sign. Other doors on the block were opened, too. People came from everywhere now. A storm might have passed over the place and they were now coming out for the sunshine. No carabineers were to be seen. Everyone seemed to take it that the fight with the police had to be, but the fight was over now. It was not fair to hit when the fight was over.

I ran over to the telegraph office and sent three flashes :

"CARABINEERS CHARGE CROWD WITH FIXED BAY-ONETS."
"CARABINEERS BATTLE RIOTOUS MOBS TWO HOURS."
"CARABINEERS MOW CROWDS WITH RIFLES MACHINEGUNS."

The three bulletins told the story. That would bring a banner in New York. I had to go out now and get the number of casualties. That was the important thing. I thought there must be fifty to a hundred. I saw no ambulances loading corpses. The square was filling up and people were congregating in the cafés. Within half an hour, the usual evening gaiety reigned. Nothing seemed to have happened. I met an Italian newspaperman and asked him the number of casualties.

"Five badly wounded," he replied.

"That's all, with all the shooting?" I inquired.

"No one was shot," he said. "The five injured were fighting amongst themselves."

"What, no one hit with rifle shots?"

"No, no!"

"That's a miracle."

"No miracle. Everybody was just a little excited. That's all."

"But it was a two-hour battle!"

"That's nothing. Just a little noise. The colonel put on the act. He had orders to be energetic but prudent. He was energetic in the shooting, prudent in killing no one. That's all. He saved his job."

I collapsed.

I went to Venice to recover.

CHAPTER III

EVERY BULLET HAS ITS BILLET—SOMEWHERE

In a state of semi-collapse, His Excellency the Honorable Carlo Schanzer mopped his brow one July afternoon.

"Toil in summer is torment," he gasped.

Your reporter agreed and added:

"Especially in summer."

His Excellency gave a sickly laugh but was still tormented.

He was foreign minister at the time, and an unheralded diplomatic snag about some island Italy wanted had replaced loafing with labor, and labor in summer is not an Italian custom.

The hot months may inspire but certainly they do not stimulate exertion. They are supremely adapted for *dolce far niente* and *dolce far niente* is supremely adapted for them. Schanzer was right. Schanzer made it official.

But, in those immediate post-war summers there was torment whether one worked or not. Everyone was restless. Everyone wanted something else. Dividing-up had become a summer custom. A reckoning was to come. Then, no one knew when. Certainly there was nervousness, jitters, anxiety and torment but—no toil.

The Communists were getting along with their extra-legal distributions. It was not a complete success. The

33

dispossessed were disgruntled at this type of peace on earth and this particular kind of goodwill to men. The bundles of combat were also heard from but they were still adolescing, not yet ready to assume the mature status of Caesarian legions.

I squeezed out that little midsummer rest after Florence without getting it chalked up against vacation. A murder trial, unusual for a foreign correspondent, whisked me to Bologna. Antonio Cocchi, a thirty-year-old Italian mechanic, after stabbing a sixteen-year-old American girl, Ruth Cruger, in New York, had escaped to Italy. He had sawed her body apart and had thrown the pieces into a cellar. An enraged public had demanded retribution. An old Roman law protected Cocchi for no Roman could be extradited. Cocchi sought refuge in the ancient law and was tried in Italy. He was sentenced to thirty years, a sentence from which no criminal ever returns, they say. This is only to show you what I was doing the rest of the summer.

After the trial, I went to Venice again but this time on regular vacation, which, while welcome, inconveniently forbade an expense account.

Your reporter was living in happy ignorance of bolsheviks and bundles. One balmy evening, stepping onto the wharf from a gondola, I could not miss a newsboy's barks with something sensational about D'Annunzio. I warmed. I burned. I bought a paper.

"Gabriele d'Annunzio Has Seized Fiume," is what the headline ran in arrestingly black characters.

It was September 13. The vacation was over. There was no dinner. I packed.

Fiume had been held by the inter-allied command. A battalion of British Tommies, a battalion of brown French Annamese and several companies of Italian infantry were quartered in the town. Strange but true for so far away, the United States was represented by the cruiser *Pittsburgh* under the command of Admiral Philip Andrews. The British also kept watch with the cruisers *Cardiff* and *Ceres*; the French, with the battleship *Condorcet*.

To go against this formidable accumulation of force, a disgruntled Italian major, Reina by name, had presented the poet with his own battalion of Sardinian grenadiers, tall of stature and copious in strength. It was imperative that preparations be perfect especially since one battalion, tall and strong though it was, was to meet battleships, cruisers, admirals, Annamese and Tommies. The odds were overwhelming. Preparations *were* perfect. At the very moment when the Italian commander within the town winked, poet and battalion slipped in without the loss of a single Sardinian. Fiume was taken.

It was natural that the brave and honest winker should confess ignorance of the entire affair even though there were plenty of little signs to breed a perhaps too hasty suspicion that he knew it all the time. The British commander viewed the situation with alarm and insisted that it was all wrong. The winker consoled him :

"Leave it to me. I will straighten it out."

He did. The poet with his brave and cheering battalion paraded down the main street to show British,

French and Americans that he had fulfilled his vow of getting Fiume for Italy. It was advertised thereafter as an expedition, a bloodless coup-de-main. The Sardinians were decorated as heroes with bronze medals and ribbons of blue, yellow and cerise, the colors of the martyred town.

The stroke was hailed by a garrulous press and a gullible public as one of those great military achievements in which the strategic element of surprise played its part. It was something no one would think of. They said that the world had been caught napping. It was temporarily forgotten that Italy was supposed to be an ally of the British, the French and the Americans. For Gabriele it was an ideal expedition. Soldier, poet, dramatist, strategist, patriot and adventurer were combined in the same hero.

But after poet and battalion got in, the gates were closed again. No others could enter or leave. The Italian government loudly promised that they would smoke, starve and storm him out. They threw a kind of blockade about him, a kind of blockade by land, by sea and in the air. It was a blockade for everybody but the Italians.

Your reporter had to get in. I received orders to interview D'Annunzio.

I must run the blockade. It looked too risky by sea — too many hazards, storms, patrols and the sea itself. There were no planes unless you pilfered one from an Italian military hangar and knew how to pilot it. I would try by land. The blockade could not surely have a solid ring of soldiers around the town. There must be woods to grope through at night. Certainly all the roads would be patrolled but if I tried a nice dark and enveloping wood, I might steer myself into the town without being seen by a sentry. If I found someone who knew the lay of the land, it would be rosy. I did not expect to get shot anyway since the big war was over and this was not war. It would be inconvenient, though perhaps not perilous, to meet an over-zealous guard who disliked Americans especially if he found one trying to penetrate the lines. It would always be too bad if you could not prove yourself an Italian.

This was all by way of mentally exploring the possibilities. I took the train to Trieste to make my soundings. Fiume was sixty miles beyond. Facing the reality, I found that the American consul offered no encouragement to my wild ideas. But while he was short on enthusiasm for the risk, he was long on a desire to get all the information I collected — should I return. As a correct and impartial diplomat, he was against D'Annunzio as a rebel but he was highly in favor of being party to my contraband providing it would not soil his diplomatic hands.

I tried the Italian High Command. Here I found a well-rehearsed indignation, much more dramatic than righteous in that I had requested safe conduct from the "regular to the irregular command." How could I dare ask them for an official pass from the loyal Italian troops to the rebels? In tragic disdain they refused the pass and withheld both encouragement and advice. Instead they countered everything with a warning that should any communication with the rebels be attempted, I would be placed under arrest and conducted under escort outside the territorial limits of the occupational forces.

Disconsolate, I sat at an outdoor café in Piazza dell' Unita to take counsel with my wits. I seemed to have neither counsel nor wits and in melancholia found no consolation. The piazza was crowded and little groups of youths were shouting "Long live Fiume," "Long live D'Annunzio." There was not much of "Down with America" now because the poet had seized Fiume.

A somewhat mature man, accompanied by a woman came searching for places. Every table was occupied. Since I was alone, at a table for four, he asked that he and the lady be permitted to join me. I showed a certain reluctance, but chose discretion in preference to valor in this town where one of the boys had tried to tear down an American flag. He and the lady took seats at my table. I was annoyed. What happened, however, was one of those rarest of occurrences. Had it been fiction, no one would have believed it.

The man noticed I spoke Italian with a foreign accent. What next? He asked me my nationality. I told him. Immediately he spoke English.

"Wilson has made a great mistake," was the first thing he said.

I neither agreed nor disagreed. I was still annoyed that he had disturbed my unhappy loneliness. But he continued as if undismayed by coldness. Somewhat boldly inquisitive, he asked me what I was doing in Trieste. Annoyed, I was brave. I told him the truth. I was on my way to Fiume to interview D'Annunzio.

"I will get you there," he breathed to me confidentially and suddenly, as if springing to duty.

He startled me. He was eager. It was as if we had been two wanderers and had found one another. He had discovered an outlet for his patriotic fervor. He was doing something for the Fiume cause. To me it was one of those thousand to one shots which so often come into a newsman's life; that is, if he surely could get me past the blockade.

We exchanged cards. I was pleased to meet Signor Ernesto Besso, actuary of the Italian General Insurance Company. It sounded so solid. Reciprocally, this leading citizen seemed enthralled with the handshake of a correspondent *della* Associated Press of America. Madame Besso joined in the honor I was bestowing on Ernesto but remained almost oblivious to the good luck he was bestowing on me. All the honor was going one way; all the good luck, the other. He was to get busy right away to squeeze, sneak or smuggle me through the guard line. Complacently ignoring my previous aloofness, I turned from cold to tepid, to warm, to ardent. Now, they were "a bit of all right." I raised him to supreme civic distinction. He was as good a Triestine as the man from Samaria, a good Samaritan.

We arranged to meet the following evening in Piazza Dante, a smaller square a block or two away. Before leaving, he advised me to travel without baggage. It suited me because I had to get in, secure the interview and return to Trieste to put the story on the wire. Since Fiume was blockaded, one could not send a cable from there.

Could it be bona-fide? It was worth the gamble. Next evening at five-thirty, Signor Besso was as good as his word. He was accompanied by two other men. Instinctively your reporter wondered whether it was a plant. We were all introduced. One was D'Annunzio's liaison man with Mussolini. We breathed. Though it was daylight, it was spooky. They talked in whispers. Was it dynamite? I was being taken into their confidence. Slowly but stealthily they uncovered to me the steps I was to take. Bit by bit they warned me against false moves. The talk was so low at times that all sounds were sibilants.

I understood everything perfectly. I was not afraid now. I was on the scent. Surely it was clandestine but it had to be clandestine if anyone was to get into Fiume. Slyly, the third man drew from his coat what looked like a flashy military cap. I was puzzled. He gave it to me. Was I to masquerade as an Italian officer? It was always dangerous to put on any military uniform which did not belong to you. I could be shot as a spy. What good was a hat, anyway?

The third man spoke. My fears were assuaged. Slowly, he described the purpose of the hat. Out from the terror of military peremptoriness emerged the genteel announcement that it was the headgear of an Italian passenger brakeman. They had told me the secret of the D'Annunzio tunnel, pipe-line or underground from the mainland to the town. The cap was the *passe-partout*.

The instructions were these. I must take the train.

Again, I should take no baggage. I must befriend the trainmen. The train would only travel to the line of blockade. There every passenger must disembark. I must not wait for that. I should get out of the train at Ruppa, the station before the rebel frontier. There, I was to put on the brakeman's hat. I could borrow, if possible, a trainman's lantern and wave it important-like. Then, I should board the engine.

I left Trieste at six-fifty that evening. When the tickets had been collected, I began the friendship with the trainmen. It worked. They understood. It was all so patriotic for them. They, too, seemed to have forgiven Wilson since D'Annunzio was in Fiume. Arriving at Ruppa, I got out, put on the brakeman's cap and was given the lantern. I waved it majestically and headed for the engine.

The engineer was leaning over the cab. There were other dim forms there. He gave us all a nod of approval. It was much more appreciated than a long and unintelligible greeting. I could always nod well. The fireman told me to hide in the coal as the military police might find too many brakemen on the train. Without saying a word I slid down into the coal. The train started off.

In a few minutes we were at the frontier. I could hear the uncoupling of the coaches. I could hear carabineers challenging persons on the track. I could only hear. The place had the air of that life and death business associated with the military. I pressed harder against my black bed thinking thereby to hide better, a chameleon in the coal. I could hear so much military talk and snappy orders that I knew if I were caught I would be taken for a spy.

I always thought of the worst. The old anger for America would be aroused. I had no one to tell if I were shot or anything happened. I could not record that I died a hero's death for the press. They could put me out of the way and no one would know it. Such fatal ingratitude in the profession was worse than death.

The engineer was sticking his head out of the cab all the time. Finally, he got the order to pull out. At the first puff of the engine and the first feeling of movement, I was much relieved. We gained momentum. The locomotive rattled to what seemed a terrifying speed. The two other stowaways who also evidently knew the system were easy themselves now. We all got up from the coal. They began to talk to me. I answered with "yes" and "no."

Presently the engine began to slow up. The engineer gave a playful Toot! To-toot! To-toot! Toot-to-to-toot-toot! We finally stopped. Here was a spacious modern station. I looked out and there before me was the sign, "Fiume." All silence was off now. Everybody was gay. Thinking it was worth it, I handed the engineer what I thought was a fifty-lire note. He looked at it and suddenly burst into the most prolific evidences of joy. We climbed down from the engine. I touched the soil of Fiume. It was Fiume all right. The sign was on the station. I had made it. Signor Besso was a good Triestine.

It was midnight and peaceful in this city of world

strife. A few of the poet's military police were patrol-
ing the station. They asked for no papers. I went
with my two companions of the tender to the Hotel
Testa di Ferro. I was there but I still must interview
D'Annunzio.

The next day, I started out to see the hero. I examined my pocket-book to make sure that I had money
enough to carry me through the orderlies and sycophants.
One five-hundred lire note was missing but an extra
fifty was there. I understood the reason for the engineer's expressive joy.

The streets were truly gay. Companies of very peppy
Italians paraded. They sang. They rejoiced. Nothing was wrong.

I called to see the poet. It was difficult but skipping
all that, I interviewed him. I felt as if I knew him.
He was dressed as a colonel but I had known him in a
red dressing robe. He was nice and seemed to know
me, too. The interview was important because it was
timely and exclusive. It was not so much in what he
said. He had said those same things about Fiume being Italian and all that before. It was its spontaneity
which gave it life. My breaking of the blockade and
getting in to see him while others had not yet met
Signor Ernesto Besso made it great — no self-aggrandize-
ment intended.

I am just letting you in on greatness which is more
talked about than achieved. Melville E. Stone, then
general manager of the Associated Press, made a special
report on "my heroic exploit" to the pompous and even
important directors of the great organization which I

had the necessary honor of representing. I was one of
Melstone's "boys." "I had risked all for the story," they
said.

But, in spite of Melstone and the directors, from that
moment, Italy kept Fiume. The poet now played on a
world stage. Now he shook his bony fist at England,
France and America. They called him mad but he
still challenged. In Italy, it was the greatest boost for
the bundles of combat. It was a common cause — D'Annunzio and Mussolini.

And it was here that all those knick-knacks which became the sacred trinkets and sacramental trimmings of
Fascism were devised. The opaque and unceremonial
black shirt chosen by D'Annunzio because it was cheap
and seldom needed a change, became a shiny and highly
ceremonial full dress. He invented a hyena howl "Eia!
Eia! Eia! Alala!" which was adopted as the Fascist yell,
a necessity for the organized or unorganized claque if
one ever becomes a hero, an orator or both, and must
be applauded. He inculcated a devil-may-care spirit
in his legionnaries and perpetrated on them a war-cry
which was more lethargic than combative, a convenient
spirit if you preferred playing war to fighting it. "Me
Ne Frego" (I don't give a damn) it ran. It was adopted
as the official Fascist motto. It is just history now.

The cult of martial music amongst the devil-may-care
found its lofty though hardly symphonic expression in
a playful and unwarlike march, "Giovinezza" (Youth).
The poet requisitioned the song — words, music and
royalties — from an old Swiss theme and melody.
Though he had but one battalion officially, there were

a dozen bands, each one playing this single tune. All the day long to the great consternation of the usually peaceful inhabitants of the town, trying to converse in their homes and in the cafés, the blaring trumpets obligingly accompanied them no matter what hour of the day one wished to open his mouth. This became the official Fascist song and in the maturity of the movement was enacted into law as a national anthem. One stands with bared head, today.

Black shirt, yell, motto and song were the free and generous contribution of the poet to the foundation of Fascism. Here it received its official investiture with the emblems and tokens which today they call its traditions — here in Fiume of Italy.

Fascism was now on its way. It proclaimed that its brave men D'Annunzio and Mussolini, the dual commanders, had secured "the far-off outpost" to the motherland. The noble though somewhat cloudy enterprise gained adherents for the movement throughout the country. Mussolini collected the funds. D'Annunzio set up a kingdom, lived a princely life, took on the royal prerogatives, printed the postage stamps and minted the coins with his image. The battleships, cruisers, destroyers, Annamese and Tommies had left so that the Italian government might have a free hand in ferreting the rebel out. Instead, he dug himself in.

But what was more than a side show was occurring concurrently with the Fiume episode. It seems incongruous that one nation could stage two such performances at the same time, but Italy can always put on a show. Why not two, if necessary? The Florentine dividers of wealth had only skimmed the surface. In the summer of 1920 came the Red Guard. They brought a strategic plan, — occupation of the factories, control of the means of production and distribution, Red technicians as commissars, and Communism in the saddle. They overpowered the police at the Fiat automobile plant in Turin and planted machine-guns at all entrances. They seized steel mills, textile plants and chemical works around Milan. They took over the shipyards and harbor at Trieste. Academically, they had a revolution. Anyone who owned a factory was worried.

And here we will note for the sake of the record that Mussolini also dabbled in this scheme of seizing the factories. It looked as if he were just a bit concerned that the Reds were going to take over. If they succeeded his game was up. He attempted to drive a wedge between them. Fascists were installed in a little plant near Como. At that moment, he announced that the bundles of combat were revolutionary, were anti-monarchist and republican.

Fights with the police were frequent. Giovanni Giolitti, then seventy, was head of the Italian government. He sent regiments everywhere to keep order. They did keep the kind of order which is standard with the Italian police but the Communists held the factories. Three or four workmen were killed. Everything was boiling again — lots of soldiers, lots of wild Reds, lots of singing the "Internationale" and lots of waving of the red flag.

Now, I had travelled all these cities but the one event which outranked all the others was the attack on a new

American consul at Trieste, Joseph Emerson Haven.
He was a ponderous and jovial man and had a truly
meritorious career in our Consular Service. He liked
Italians and previously had been consul in Catania and
was only now being transferred from Turin to this new
post. The State Department had chosen him especially
for Trieste because of his tact — to handle the delicate
situation of hostile Italo-Yugoslav relations. The Yugoslavs wanted Fiume, too.

But in Trieste, the Communist-Fascist fight was rag-
ing as much as Italo-Yugoslav malevolence. Following
a new consul's practice Haven called and left his card
at the government bureaus, the post office, the newspapers, the chamber of commerce, the clubs, the harbor
master, all and sundry, so that no one would be offended.

He was preparing his last round one very pleasant
afternoon when the late Lincoln Eyre, correspondent of
the old *New York World*, walked into his office. Both
were amenable and amiable men. Eyre mentioned that
he had been ordered by his editor to call at the offices of
Il Lavoratore, a Socialist organ, the only newspaper in
Europe to publish the manifestoes of the Third International. The *World* wanted that number. Haven
said that he had not yet left his card at *Il Lavoratore*.
Since Eyre was going there, they would both go together.

Just outside the consulate, they ran into me and I
decided that I, too, would like a copy of the manifestoes
of the Third International. We all went together. It
was into a section of Trieste away from the waterfront.

We found the offices of the newspaper rather deserted. In that regard, your reporter recalled that the

Socialists of Trieste were staging a big demonstration in the public gardens that day in honor of Comrade Lenin. Nevertheless, from an obliging underling, we secured the copies we required. Eyre wanted to know what the manifestoes said. He sat down with Haven at a reception table. The consul began translating. Your reporter grew tired of this long literary effort and left. I was winding through the streets, when a bang! bang! ominously like a couple of bombs came from the direction of *Il Lavoratore*.

I rushed back. The building was being attacked by Fascists. They were throwing bombs. The inmates closed the front doors. The Fascists tried to surround the place. People were scampering everywhere. The Fascists commanded the street. You could not tell at whom they were shooting. It might be anybody.

Haven and Eyre were caught in the building. They joined the panic of the inmates and rushed to a rear door. It led out into a small yard completely shut in. Beyond the back of the yard, the land rose in terraces up the hill. It was on the edge of the city.

Eyre was lanky and lithe. Haven was corpulent and clumsy. Eyre scaled the back fence and started up the terraced gardens with the scores of other fugitives. Haven could not scale the fence. He was caught in the enclosure. He *was* caught.

The Fascists continued firing at anybody and everybody. But the big man was held immobile in the little yard. He was a target. It was proof enough he was a Red for he had emerged from the building. He was dressed well, looked more capitalist than Communist.

This made no difference. A beautiful target! A beautiful target!

Four Fascists rested their elbows on the fence. Great disturbances were going on all around. Slowly they started emptying their revolvers on the giant but wilting frame of Haven. He put up his hands and desperately cried out:

"I am the American Consul. I am the American Consul."

They took it as a Socialist ruse. They continued their aim. Any second, Haven expected death. He was weak, hot, cold, crazy. It was seconds. It seemed hours. The shots were unending and yet none hit him. He knew one bullet was enough. Automatically, he kept shouting and protesting and gesticulating. The marksmen continued. Finally, their chambers were empty. Relief! Relief! They had fired twenty-four shots. Haven was still standing.

He hollered louder while they began reloading. Excited, Francesco Giunta, their leader appeared. He gave a cry "To the Park! To the Park!" The four marksmen turned. Without a word, they followed. They were off to break up the Socialist demonstration. Everyone left the scene. It was all silent now. Haven collected himself. He came out of his cock-pit. He walked alongside the building to the street.

When I found him, he was still carrying a cold sweat.

I met Tommy Ybarra, now a radio man. We found Haven. He had escaped twenty-four shots but his first thought was his career. Would the State Department understand? The State Department did understand but the *New York Times* wrote an editorial wondering why he had been there. They perhaps thought he should have played favorites with the newspapers of a foreign town.

Next day, your reporter accompanied Haven to the government building to protest the attack. We were received by Vice-Governor Crispo Moncada, who afterwards became Mussolini's chief of police. Listening to the vivid deliverance from death, he was unmoved. He was unimpressed. When Haven had finished, this bloodless little man sneered.

"Don't scold them," he muttered unconcernedly. "They were in such a hurry."

We could not tell whether he meant the marksmanship or the mistaken identity. Perhaps, he meant both.

CHAPTER IV

OUT OF FIUME INTO ROME

Three revolutions were in the making. Pleasant and unpleasant passages at arms pockmarked the Italian peninsula. *Primo,* the poet organized "The League of the Oppressed" to overthrow the unoppressed. Everyone must change places. *Secondo,* the Reds challenged anybody who owned anything. They, too, wanted a reversal from the bottom to the top. *Terzo,* the Fascists having passed their change of voice just wanted a change of bosses. They did not care how so long as they were the bosses. At times, it was difficult to know who was fighting whom and for what.

In the *lull* of battle, the government flirted with Mussolini, Mussolini flirted with the poet and the poet flirted with the Reds; in the *heat* of battle, it was the Fascists against the Reds, the Reds against the government and the government against the poet. Everything was triangular in those days. It suited the poet. He was temperamentally triangular.

The pleasant passages at arms caused him to smile, the Italians to fuss and fume and world statesmen to frown. He was the author of the pleasant coups. No one was killed. Night assaults, piracy on the high seas and mutinies in the Italian navy and merchant marine were his chief specialties. For one thing, he did not like the saddle horses bequeathed him by the evacuated British and French and decided on a foray into Italian

remount stations to obtain bays, blacks and chestnuts, a
pleasure to ride and a joy to look upon. He equipped
and dispatched but two score legionnaries in barges.
One dark and moonless night, they stealthily hugged
the coast until they reached the remount station at
Volosca, just a mile beyond his Fiume frontier. They
overpowered the sentries, rushed in and walked twenty
magnificent mounts onto the barges and then sailed back
to Fiume. The Italian government raged and sent him
an ultimatum. He tore it up and laughingly remarked:
  "Tomorrow, there will be war between Fiume and
Italy."
  The newspapers of the world announced the war in
big front-page banners. His delight was so much the
greater with both the front pages and the bays, blacks
and chestnuts, a pleasure to ride and a joy to look upon.
There was no war.
  He raided peaceful merchantmen on the high seas.
This naturally singed the beards or scraped the stubble
of dignified ministers of state. He was a blasted pirate.
When luxuries or even wheat were needed, he would
send ten or a dozen of the faithful who had sworn to
live and die for him to Trieste. There they signed up
as seamen on some heavily laden cargo-boat going to
Egypt or India or anywhere.
  When the poet received word that the steamer had
left with his death-and-glory boys aboard as seamen, he
ordered units of his navy — destroyers and sub-chasers —
to put to sea and intercept the abundantly loaded craft
as it passed down the Adriatic coast. Challenged, the
captain of the merchantman was asked to surrender. If

he refused, the twelve loyal men and true pounced upon him and took command of the ship. In any event, the helpless skipper could do nothing since the cannon of the Fiume navy were leveled at him from without and twelve revolvers from within.

The freighter was then fittingly escorted into port where the brave crews of destroyers and sub-chasers were enthusiastically acclaimed for having succeeded in another heroic exploit. Accompanying the cheering was general rejoicing that a boatload of luxuries or flour or whatever it was had relieved a threatened scarcity. The pilfered booty was consumed without the slightest remorse even though the better class of Egyptians and Hindus were anxiously waiting for dresses, shoes, jewelry, sweets and even automobiles.

But, there were unpleasant passages at arms, too—these between Red and blackshirt. Mussolini had written much about terror and about sharpening wits and weapons. He called it "sacred violence." He introduced the punitive expedition. Since he did not seem to be against the government in those days, the government winked an eye. The trucks which the Reds formerly requisitioned with such authority were now the luck of the Fascists since the industrialists had become strong enough to say "no." The Reds walked, more often ran.

The punitive expedition was a truckload of Fascists armed variously with clubs, knives and revolvers, dropping unexpectedly in a workmen's district. It was perhaps provocation enough for them to see a workman, for without asking whether he was red, white or blue, the urge to use the club, the knife or the revolver overcame their otherwise peaceful demeanor since they were very nice boys at home, quite often sons of the nobility. The consequence was beaten heads, bloody wounds and death for the workmen.

On their part, the Reds who had continued their challenge to the owning class to the point of anxious foreboding had also a record of sanguinary ugliness behind them. They, too, had had their provocations. Enraged at a flaming epithet leveled at them, they had massacred nearly the entire city council of Bologna just as that august body was ready to undertake a serious discussion of the problems of the city including the urgent necessity for the maintenance of public order. The Reds, too, had made a martyr of a sixteen-year-old boy in Florence, Giovanni Berta, who trying to escape some Red onslaught had clung to the girders of a bridge over the River Arno. The Reds chopped off his hands. He fell into the river and was drowned.

The official score of the "sacred violence" was never computed but estimates of newspapers at the time said that the Fascists were away ahead with a total of ten thousand Reds put *hors de combat* while the Communists, Socialists and pinks had only bagged three thousand of the rising and militant bundles. Both estimates were exaggerated.

In the very midst of this thrilling and yet unpoliced internecine strife, Prime Minister Giolitti signed a treaty with the Yugoslavs recognizing the autonomy of Fiume, which signified that the Italians while releasing their grip with their hands still held on with their feet. And it meant much more, too. D'Annunzio must be smoked out. Giolitti told him to get out. He refused. It was Christmas, 1920. The Prime Minister ordered Marshal Caviglia, who commanded the troops surrounding the lair, to start making the smoke. There was another ultimatum. This time it was business.

The bombardment started on Christmas Eve. Your reporter was faced with the dilemma either of staying in the town without communication with the outside to witness what was certain to be the poet's heroic death or of standing by the attacking forces and getting the day-by-day progress of hostilities. Since the A.P. wanted it day by day, I stayed with the marshal. The action lasted five days and it was no fake war. The marshal's job was to save as many men as possible while getting the poet to say "Enough." After all, they were all Italians. The poet did not seem to count the cost that way but proclaimed once more the beauty and honor of dying. It was for that reason we thought he would die — his last heroic stand.

On the fourth day, a six-inch shell struck the palace squarely amidships, nautically speaking, and only missed the poet by a split second as he was passing from the main salon into his bedroom. It made him ponder. It made him ready to say, "Enough." The next day, he issued a proclamation, since his brave deeds must be in writing, saying that Italy was determined to destroy Fiume. To save bloodshed, he would withdraw regretfully and leave the "oppressed" to their Italian conquerors. This heroic little caprice had cost a hundred lives, about evenly divided between marshal and poet.

He had done it again, dying bravely while elusively keeping alive.

He asked to be allowed to stay in the town to get his affairs straightened out. Caviglia agreed. The straightening took three months but with strict military chaperonage. When he left all was silent — no bands, no banners, no booms of cannon. He was trailed by a caravan of twenty-one trucks containing all his documents, his wearing apparel, books, manuscripts, photographs, furniture, presents and works of art. A villa on Lake Garda was assigned him and a bountiful grant of money allowed. He retired into seclusion to see no evil, hear no evil and speak no evil. There he spent the rest of his life, seventeen years.

The poet removed, Mussolini now assumed undisputed command. The Fascists united in one cause, one direction and one leader. They became a political party and organized elaborate parades to show their strength. The populace watching the parades were ordered to uncover their heads when the fascist standard with the motto, "I don't give a damn" went by. They began holding annual conventions like the Liberals, the Republicans, the Democrats, the Populists, the Socialists and the Communists.

It was not surprising that whatever the Reds did, the Fascists condemned, and vice-versa. Things moved to a climax in 1922. Weapons, fair and foul, were dished as well as brandished. A quart of castor oil per radical became a favored Fascist arm. To be contrary, the Reds countered with another general strike. This blackshirt weapon, however, was allergic to strikes and worked with greater vehemence since the more general the strike, the more frequent the purge. It is hardly necessary to say that while the Reds accused the Fascists of bad taste the Fascists countered that they meant no harm since a general obstruction was quite as bad as a general strike.

Your reporter was convinced that Mussolini would have preferred to be leading the general strike rather than the purge. Properly organized, there was more riot and rebellion behind the strike. He craved that revolutionary drama. There being only two sides in a strike, he was forced to take the opposite side. He tried to break the strike. Suffering and hunger, however, did a much better job. He claimed the credit.

And here is where we get an insight into his method of action. To him, issues are vehicles. Not always has he championed a principle because of conviction. The aim is to gain power. Wherever the road to power lay, there also would he find the issue. He had tried it with Socialism but the Socialists had kicked him out. Expelled, he embraced nationalism. Winning followers, he invented Fascism. Incorporating what D'Annunzio had contributed, he claimed it all his own.

Before he was forty, he had tried belonging to everything in politics, each shade naturally in its turn. He had been a rampant internationalist; now he was a flag-waving chauvinist. His political acrobatics had found him a Communist, a Socialist, an Anti-Clerical, an Anti-Monarchist, a Republican, a Pacifist, a War-monger, a Monarchist, a Conservative, a Populist and much more, but conveniently not all at the same time. In all this, his abundant mob theatricals had worked miracles. Commercially he would be one of those who could sell a bicycle to a man without any legs. The supreme talent of making his followers believe that he was ready to shed his last drop of blood for any cause he espoused hypnotically subjected them to his will.

Now, he was vehemently against the general strike. It suited. He gained support from industrialists, businessmen, bankers and landlords. Besides, the very thing played into his hands. The Italian government at this crisis was presided over by Luigi Facta and was the weakest and most vacillating in decades. It could not handle the situation. Mussolini assailed them with a charging militancy.

The annual convention of the Fascist party met in Naples in early October. Using what usually worked, his talent for picking the right moment, in full convention he issued a challenge—either the government would be peacefully turned over to Fascism or the Fascists would take it by force. He was out for revolution. He was banking on the terrible confusion of a weak government, a general strike and a Socialist opposition which had refused to take over the responsibility to rule even after it had been offered to them.

The Fascists were supposed to number a hundred thousand—a lot of men. On October 25 Mussolini is said to have issued his order for general mobilization. All these forces were to converge on Rome in four columns corresponding to the cardinal points of the compass. This was hardly necessary since an old Latin proverb prescribed that all roads lead to Rome. The plan of battle, the hundred thousand, the march, the squadrons, the quadrumvirs, the legions, the standards, all had a most militaristic threat, though to feed a hundred thousand men, much less arm them, required not an inconsiderable amount of supplies and of organization, a sum of money and the sublime courage for the eventuality that it might be called treason. Clubs were obtainable from trees so clubs were the adopted weapon. They served just as well as rifles since the adversaries did not even think of descent to such a primitive instrument of combat.

Your reporter has examined all the mementoes, orders, photographs and souvenirs, pleasant and unpleasant, of this decisive period but never could find this order for mobilization. I asked Arnaldo Mussolini, the brother of the Duce, where it was, since he was in charge of these sacred and historic relics in their newspaper office.

"Who knows?" replied the rotund and gentle Arnaldo, shrugging his shoulders. "It's disappeared."

Of course, this disappearance was a pity though no one cared. The document would have demonstrated that Mussolini was brave enough to plot a revolution, face the charge of treason and defy the firing squad. Posterity unfortunately has been cheated. Inquisitive historians have maintained that either it was never issued or that Il Duce, modest to a fault, had destroyed it with his own little match. Besides, it would have been embarrassing had the plan failed, for some officer of the crown would have found the action contrary to peaceful obedience of the king's laws. History loses a priceless document while the rare and precious quality of dictatorial humility goes unrewarded.

Facta decided on a proclamation of martial law to counter the threat of Fascist mobilization. On October 27, he prepared the decree for the king's signature and dispatched the text to all the prefects so that it might be posted up for everyone to see. Many saw. But during the night the king had taken counsel with his liver and did not sign for martial law. Instead, he decided to ask Mussolini to head a new government. So that day, October 28, 1922, is renowned for two great events, the improvement of the royal liver and the invitation of Il Duce to form a cabinet.

Sporadically, the beclubbed legions were gathering. Italo Balbo, known in America as the commander of the Italian squadron which flew to Chicago in 1932, drew up a plan of campaign for the taking of Rome. He had confidence that he could do it on a shoestring and 15,000 soldiers of the Rome garrison who were expected to make common cause with him. It was his first guess. Events made a second unnecessary. Balbo ordered the converging of the four columns. But there was no hundred thousand. Had there been more than twenty thousand, the remaining eighty thousand would have perished with hunger since twenty thousand is a lot to live by pilfering their way to victory in times of peace.

Mussolini was in Milan while Balbo might have been getting into trouble. Il Duce enjoyed the king's invitation, which came by phone. He replied more quickly than I can tell. He would be in Rome by the early train the next day. The legions were going afoot so that he would beat them into the city. Even the general strike had been settled. Consequently, he took a deluxe sleeping compartment and merrily snored his way to the Eternal City. Aldo Finzi, an aviator who ran a bicycle shop as a fitting avocation for statesmanship, accompanied him as one of the first loyals.

Arriving in Rome, fresh from the sleep on the luxurious ten-hour ride, he was met by Fascist cronics and accompanied to the Hotel Savoia, a modest little place, to which he always had the habit of going since previously he could ill afford a higher price. At eleven that morning, he was received by the king. He accepted the joyous task of forming a ministry. He had done the trick. He was prime minister. Certainly, it could have been no easier. Then he ordered the March on Rome.

Though he held the baton of power, he regretted that it had not been by force. He craved above all the pyrotechnics of revolution. Undismayed, he called this a revolution. But the regrets for the form were overwhelmingly submerged in the substance — the power he wielded.

The Balbo legions converged at Monterotundo, some seven miles from Rome. They were trucked to within a mile of the city and re-formed. Mussolini in blackshirt, and red, white and green sash headed the parade and some twenty thousand marched down the historic Corso Umberto, the main street of Rome — a victory parade. This was the March on Rome.

An old Roman stood on the sidewalk watching the long procession of blackshirts. As their banners passed bearing the motto, "I don't give a damn," he smiled. But presently a Fascist jumped from the ranks and ordered him to take his hat off to their standard.

"Young man," said the old Roman, "I take off my hat. But remember, we old Romans for two thousand years have seen processions such as this passing down this very street, and taking my hat off to your banner, I say with you, 'We don't give a damn.'"

Spontaneous acclaim welcomed the new regime. The nation was tired of the constant trouble between Red and blackshirt and hoped for the best. Il Duce had won much of the nation — the royal house, many of the clergy, the landed aristocracy, the powerful industrialists, many small merchants and professional men. He had not, however, won the labor unions. These were his uncompromising enemies. They wielded great political power and were identical in policy, personnel and leadership with the Italian Socialist party which had elected one hundred and fifty-six deputies to parliament.

To change his political fortunes he had turned a somersault that night. From violent anti-monarchist, he was bowing to the king. A confessed atheist, he was flirting with the church. A wild revolutionary, he was kissing the hands of aristocratic ladies. A rampant ex-Socialist, he was the flaming glamor boy of Italian industrialists. Since he had risen to power on a wave of reaction and was applauded by such strange newly-won admirers, it was natural that the labor organizations regarded him as a capitalistic tool, a traitor to his professed beliefs and an enemy of the working class.

No Italian statesman in history had ever desecrated

the monarchy as Mussolini had previously done. No one, on the contrary, lived to use the House of Savoy so flagrantly as a stepping-stone to absolute power. At this time, though, he embraced and eulogized the dynasty in a manner more royalist than the king.

Now as a courtier of the king, he ordered full ceremonial honors to the crown on every occasion. Decrees were issued declaring the person of the sovereign inviolable. Any word derogatory to the dynasty, whether published or spoken, meant jail. The royal house was very satisfied, happy in the thought that, at last, it had found its man.

At first, he faced a stern opposition in the Catholic party led by a talented Sicilian priest, Luigi Don Sturzo. This party was the strongest in Italy next to the Socialist party. It was essential to neutralize its power. He found a way.

Hitherto, successive Italian governments had been more or less cold to the Holy See because warmth meant an adverse vote in parliament. In fact, the Bonomi government of just a few months previous had been dismissed for the seemingly innocent act of having ordered the flags from official buildings displayed at half-mast on the death of Pope Benedict XV.

Now, to gain his political ends, Mussolini began a definite policy of appeasement with the new Pope, Pius XI. The crucifix was ordered placed on public school buildings. Religious education was restored in the class-rooms. He erected a huge cross in the center of the Coliseum as a commemoration to the Christian martyrs. The popular celebration of religious festivals was encouraged. Ecclesiastics, hitherto, had discontinued outdoor processions because of fear of disorder and desecration from anti-clerical organizations. Mussolini energetically ordered the police to protect all religious manifestations with the maximum severity and to exact the most respectful reverence for the sacred emblems.

This display of outward devotion to the church marked him as worthy of Vatican patronage. He went further. He chose several leaders of the Catholic party for cabinet positions. Vital support was thus taken away from Don Sturzo. Catholic party members went by hundreds into the Fascist party. Disintegration of Don Sturzo's organization set in. In time, the ecclesiastical authorities frowned upon the Catholic leader as a political priest.

And the landed gentry hailed the new man of action as a savior. He had at times lashed them with a vitriolic vehemence. Now he came to discipline the unruly peasant who had been enjoying the luxury of revolt under landlord oppression. He had sent his punitive expeditions to break up the peasant co-operative societies. In many rural centers, the handiwork of the blackshirts stalked in death and mutilated bodies. The landed gentry paid their share in this work of rigid extra-legal authority by contributions to the men as well as to the organization of the Fascist party.

These owners of vast acreages rejoiced that they also had found their man. In power, he would keep the peasant in his place. The police and soldiery were now at his command. He could make the peasant work instead of complain. The lords of the land reveled not alone in this new order but also in the blissful thought that it was the return of those *happy* days when the landlords were absolute masters of their fiefs.

As if to show his gratitude for their contributions or respect for their birth, the man of destiny ordered the publication of a heraldic directory of the noble families, the better to establish the bluebloodedness of his aristocratic patrons. To those who had only the semblance of nobility or no nobility at all he was ready to concede something for their good gifts and organizational favors. Some were made senators and others received ostentatious decorations permitting them to wear a wide red and white ribbon over their bosoms when on parade. He often took a million and gave a sash.

But it was for the industrialists that he had conserved what seemed at first the greatest bounty. Certainly, he had risen to power through them. They had most generously financed his punitive expeditions and kept his newspaper alive. They had regarded him as the one force capable of putting unruly workers in their places. He would insure the right of the owners to run their businesses as they saw fit.

He made speeches about the glory of capitalism, as though he had just discovered it. He eulogized private enterprise, private ownership and private control. Capitalism's future was even greater than its past. It was illegal to meet in groups of more than five without a permit. Workmen were intimidated into silence. He ruthlessly abolished all workingmen's co-operatives either by wanton destruction carried out by the marauding

blackshirts or through strangulation of their business.
And this was just what the great industrialists wanted.
They had made common cause with him, thinking they
had struck a good bargain — to keep him in office as
long as he favored their interests.   He was given power
to rule; they were insured freedom to reduce wages,
increase hours and pile up dividends.

All this cheering and even glamorous support was
conceived as on a pay-you-back basis, with labor and the
peasantry as the pawns.   The supporters, however, had
reckoned with the wrong man.   He desired to rule but
not at the nod of the royal house, the church, the landlords, or the industrialists.   They had counted on his
being an amenable man of low estate lifted by them to
great grandeur and glory.   They had counted on his
being thankful to them for all this.   They did not
realize that his political astuteness bordered on genius.
He had been a revolutionary.   They thought that revolution was behind him.   On his part, their friendliness
was a means to an end, a strategic move.

He had only started.

CHAPTER V

BAYONETS AND BUTTER

But the opposition!

When Il Duce put aside his shoddy black serge suit for the morning coat, he did not put aside his shoddy black serge personality. He was dynamite in a fancy soap wrapper. He was tough, still tough, and had to meet many toughs, the leaders of the Reds. Unlike his royal patron, his newly found aristocratic friends, the industrialists and landlords, he knew what handling tough men meant. He was one against many but he had the government, the army and the police now.

"One can do anything with a bayonet except sit on it," wrote Girardin in the middle nineteenth century.

Mussolini had learned it and now he had the bayonets. As if the army and police were not enough — or perhaps, he did not trust them — he instituted his own police besides. It served a double purpose. This was giving jobs to the boys who had so willingly paraded in Rome and got their medals. He took their clubs and castor oil away and gave them muskets.

Girardin was right in his day. Today he is only half right. Your workman does not have to sit on a bayonet if he does not like things; he sits in on a strike. The sit-down had not been invented in Girardin's day. It had come in time for Mussolini. He mixed bayonets with butter.

Opposition from a wild and threatening organization

of 3,000,000 workers took handling. Their wills were
as strong as their arms. He had no pattern to go by as
did Hitler ten years later when he copied Il Duce. Rebellion, permanently pent-up, was not a solution. He
could talk very loud against their policies. Invective,
no matter how strong, will not kill a fly much less a
rhinoceros.

It was one thing to condemn; another, to rule. They
could always sit down and strike. That weapon had
already defeated the Kapp putsch in Germany in 1920.
A successful general strike would have sent him back
to his Cinderella suit. But he mingled sweetness with
severity in convenient doses and particular places. In
that way the trains ran on time, as has so often been
said. He favored those docile souls amenable to his
will by giving them better jobs. On these he used the
velvet glove; on the others, the mailed fist. He divided
them and ruled. The disgruntled reluctantly obeyed,
but obey they did. They could not risk losing their
jobs in a country where men spring up like mushrooms
after a rain whenever a job goes vacant.

We must not get the idea that on his assumption of
office that he became a dictator immediately. He first
ruled against this strong opposition. In parliament, as
well, it was the same opposition — labor, the unions and
the Socialist party. Many of the leaders conveniently
held positions in both unions and party and lived on a
scale commensurate with this duplicity.

He did not mind parliamentary opposition so long as
it was puny and he was big enough to scold and spank
it. Showman that he was, he theatrically used it as a

whipping boy to magnify his own governmental perfection and to ridicule their deficiencies. The opposition leaders were hamstrung anyway by the laws he had passed. What *they* said in parliament never appeared in the newspapers. What *he* said was displayed in large and heavy type on the front pages. It took more courage than eloquence to harangue against him. Such fortitude was rewarded by "well-merited" clubbings and torture, a sacred party means of rebutting the adversary and winning the parliamentary vote as well as the debate.

But the terror politics blew out its fuse when Giacomo Matteotti, a Socialist deputy, was kidnaped, gagged and murdered with thorough gangster technique the day before he was scheduled to make an uncomplimentary anti-Fascist speech in the Chamber of Deputies. Retributively, this liquidation has remained the greatest stain on Mussolini's career. The whole country turned. The brave ones squirted red ink on Il Duce's pictures on billboards and placards, a token that the victim's blood was on his head. Fascism was shaken and thousands surrendered their membership cards.

No opposition leader, however, stepped forward with sufficient personal rallying power to crystallize the public abhorrence into a general anti-Fascist movement. Had such a leader marched forth, Mussolini, like Sulla of old, might have fled the frontier — also without his toga. He was doing a Coriolanus, it is true, but not in the open, not in the open in these rabid days. His regime was thrown on the defensive.

For seven months he just held his ground. Punitive

expeditions became a lost art and no one boasted of wearing a Fascist button. Only the regular police was assigned to maintain order. Il Duce was unable to enforce a censorship. The newspapers said what they thought and abundantly feasted thereon. Many former adherents came out to tell of dark Fascist machinations and secret wickedness.

He feared that any violent Fascist repression might stir the whole country against him. He could take on anything but it must be a little at a time. He just held on because the mass did not erupt all at once. He kept a majority of Fascist deputies in parliament and this furnished him with the constitutional right to remain in power. The opposition refused to sit in parliament and demanded that he resign. But he held on, waiting, watching and ready to smother or even eliminate the opposition from circulation if they moved en masse against him.

On January 3, 1925, he chose his moment. The temper of the public over Matteotti had cooled. He was strong enough now to enforce censorship. Opposition attacks were stifled. He tightened the police regulations. In a month, he had consolidated his position. Strategically, he was back in his place before the crime. He had resumed the offensive. He was talking big again.

His progress in winning the suspecting and skeptical labor elements was to be slow. He called Edmondo Rossoni, crony of his Socialist days and one who, like himself, had been disowned by the Socialists, to assist him. Rossoni, in fact, had lived many years in the

United States. He had worked as a steelworker in various towns in Pennsylvania. Leaders of the old I. W. W. had chosen him as an excellent organizer for the Italian workmen especially in the factories near New York. He had found it too hot. He returned to Italy.

When Mussolini called him, he was living in dire and unsufferable straits for an ex-leader. He was eager, therefore, to undertake the ostentatious though not yet lucrative organizing of the Fascist labor movement. This movement was designed to run parallel to and separate from the existing unions massed in one powerful body, the General Confederation of Labor. At first, Rossoni resorted to the tactics of the company union with which we are more or less familiar in the United States since the passage of the Wagner Act. To distinguish his organization from the old unions, he called them labor syndicates.

Rossoni with the help of the Fascist industrialists and the blessing of Mussolini began recruiting but met with scant success because of the strength of the Confederation and the hatred of labor in general for Mussolini. But it was to be a long process. Mussolini was patient. He knew that if his regime was to be safe he must win the working-class or keep the country in a state of perpetual unrest.

It took time. He offered the union leaders an olive branch. They refused it. Certainly they refused. He was trying to wreck the great workingman's structure which they had built up. But he could make laws. He could give the workingman more than they could by the issuance of a decree. He was not yet strong enough to challenge the great and powerful industrialists by giving labor too much but he was good at fixing. To the industrialists, he played on patriotism; to the workers, on social well-being.

In four years he had made such headway that the members of the old unions were forced by law to join the syndicates for protection. He gave them more. This was the butter. The syndicates by law became the sole bargaining authority. At least, on paper, the workers were promised care of their interests under legal supervision.

By this stroke, Mussolini had rendered the old unions inoperative and their leaders immobile. He had undermined them. He had tried even then to induce a few picked leaders to join. They were too proud to accept the offer from a man who had planned and was succeeding in their downfall. Their unions which were once strong and controlled in some measure the political direction of Italy were being slowly neutralized by law and the favored syndicates.

The relations established between the employer groups and the syndicates laid the foundation for the corporative state. The complete structure had not yet been fully conceived. It was slowly developing. On April 21, 1927, the Fascist Grand Council issued the Labor Charter, another basic law and regarded by Fascism as a labor Bill of Rights, written by Mussolini himself. Since it provided for many more working-class privileges than the General Confederation of Labor had ever obtained, it administered the coup-de-grace to the dying remnant of Italian trade unionism. The syndicates were now the sole voice of labor in fact as well as form, the accepted instrument of labor authority.

"Work in all its forms," proclaimed the charter, "organizational, executive, intellectual, technical and manual is a social duty. On this basis, and solely on this basis, it is protected by the state."

"Syndical or professional organization is free," it decreed. "But only the syndicate legally recognized and placed under the control of the state has the right to represent lawfully the whole category of employers or workers for which it is constituted."

All other organizations not in the Fascist orbit were squarely outlawed. Much more, legal authority was stamped upon every syndical agreement. Collective bargaining and the check-off on syndical dues were obligatory. It was illegal to strike. All disputes must be brought before the labor Magistracy, "the organ by which the state intervened" to settle trouble.

For the first time in Fascist legislation, the word "corporazione" or guild was introduced. This was a larger unit of labor organization than the syndicate. It was a group of syndicates in a particular industry. The unions of the bus drivers, taxi-drivers, trolleymen, conductors, enginemen, etc., made the transportation guild, for instance. "The guilds constitute the unitary organization of the productive forces and represent their interests.

"The Corporative State," said Article VII, "considers private initiative in the field of production as most efficacious and most useful in the interest of the nation." Collaboration was a duty. The employer must bear the legal and moral responsibility of management.

Professional men and artists must achieve higher perfection in their respective branches. The state would intervene where private initiative failed. Night work must be paid more than day work. One day rest in seven was compulsory. After a year's service, the employe was entitled to a paid vacation. Every employe discharged for reasons beyond his control must receive an indemnity according to the years of service employed. Fines may be imposed for infraction of rules.

The final nine articles were like little tit-bits for good measure. They gave employment agencies under governmental control, accident insurance, maternity insurance, sick benefits, unemployment relief, recreational and educational activities. It was all butter, full-cream and generous.

The modern industrial state is a most complicated mechanism. Perfection in organization with its craft unions, industrial units, agricultural trades and professional classes was to take years. It was not until 1928 that a complete blue-print of the new state in action was possible. It was composed of 1589 different crafts, trades, professions and jobs, each requiring a separate collective labor contract. More than ten million persons were to be assigned to their exact places. It required time to adjust each one. It required patience to get each small unit co-ordinated in the vast and intricate scheme.

Mussolini undoubtedly knew that the transition from free organization to statal incorporation was not just a pleasant day off in the country. No one could have foreseen its extent and complexity. Italy possesses both a varied, highly developed agriculture and a diversified industrial installation, from pins to battleships. Each productive instrument whether in men or means must be registered, brigaded and allocated. The whole must form a smoothly working machine similar to the military establishments but far more complicated and certainly much more extensive than any army which had ever been mobilized.

Under the system which has prevailed in all industrial countries, the proprietors command their own properties, managing their affairs so as to make the greatest return on their investments. This kind of control could be adapted to his dictatorial nature. He could be boss without much tinkering with the gearing. He could wave his flag at the top of the pyramid. Besides, it would safeguard the right of private property and protect individual enterprise, which he had called "the cement binding the great granite blocks of production." The employers were the administrators, the managers, and necessarily occupied places near the top layers of the pyramid. They were the ruling elite.

But, he had previously waved a red flag in the revolutionary school of Socialism, had sung the *Internationale* and from a soapbox had aroused the rabble. Now, while he rejected Socialism by recognizing the right of private property, he also rejected capitalism by disallowing the employers the complete control of their industries. They could only be bosses under him. To harmonize this double contradiction, he included workers as well as owners through all the layers of the pyramid from top to bottom. The say of the workers was equal to that of the owners. It was a dual command. Above it all, however, stood the authority of the head man, the final arbiter. When disagreement obstructed, the state decided, was his Louisan formula.

Perhaps someone should apologize for the composition of this state. It is like the drawing up of reorganization plans for the army. Its make-up reads like a military manual. It is abundant in grades and ranks. Blocks of individuals are squared off to stand in straight lines and to remain standing so as not to disturb the symmetry of the whole. That is, everyone must keep in his place. One always belongs to some federation, association, union or syndicate. If you grasp the enormity of the organization of the millions of men in the military establishment with its corps, its divisions, its brigades, its regiments, its battalions and its companies, you have an inkling, one might say, of how the corporative state is blocked out for the millions in the economic and social structure.

As it has worked out, Mussolini, as prime minister, or president of the council of ministers as the Italians call him, is the operating executive. Some Fascists laboriously though unsuccessfully maintain that they have a representative system. Perhaps we should not quarrel very much about it except to observe that the representatives are picked from the top all the way down through the planes of the hierarchy until we reach the workers. The Fascist maintains vehemently that though appointed they are expertly representative. Perhaps it is right. They undoubtedly know what they are supposed to represent. They undoubtedly know on which side their bread is buttered. Every one of us is representative of something.

Specifically, Mussolini at the top appoints his cabinet ministers. This is the second layer coming down the pyramid. One of the cabinet members is Minister of Guilds. Under him, the productive structure operates. Descending from the ministry, there are nine great confederations, the heads of which are recommended by the Minister of Guilds and then approved by Mussolini. Four confederations are composed of capitalists and four of labor. They represent industry, agriculture, commerce and finance. The ninth confederation is allocated to the professions and the arts. These great bodies encompass the whole of Italian productive power.

Below the nine confederations, we come upon the next subdivision, the national federations. A confederation can only be a grand grouping. For purposes of close control, it must be split up into its various industrial, agricultural, business or financial categories. The industrial confederation, for example, is divided into forty-five national federations of employers and into twenty such organizations for employes. Each federation represents a distinct industry — steel, glass, chemicals, mining, shipbuilding, transport, paper, textiles or whatever it may be.

Here is truly rugged regimentation.

It is interesting to note that while the confederation of industrial employers has forty-five national federations that of the industrial workers only has twenty. This is because much of the work in very different industries is the same and requires the same skill. Such

labor is classified in one group. Crane drivers, furnace-
men, mechanics or enginemen work in many different
industries but belong to but one labor grouping. It is
a pointed example of vertical unions operating within
horizontal unions.

The agricultural confederation is divided into four
national federations for employers and four for employes. The businessmen are classified into thirty-seven
national federations but the corresponding organizations
for business employes number only five. This is another case where the types of work are less varied than
the types of business. Store clerks, for instance, constitute one group but in that group may be represented
any number of different businesses.

The broad base of the pyramid is the syndicate. In
America, this corresponds to the trade unions, pure and
simple, without, naturally, any statal entity.

The syndicate, whether of employer or employe, is
the principal operating unit. It initiates, organizes and
administers. It is closer to the workingman than any
of the other directing units. It negotiates and makes
rules. It signs the labor contract. More than the association, it is mobile and more responsive. The secretary
occupies a position which has become a career profession in the Italian civil service.

In Italy, the feud between craft unions and industrial
unions is solved by admitting both into the syndical
structure. The factors of the quarrel between C. I. O.
and A. F. of L. in the United States therefore do not exist
there. Craft unions are given their vertical locations in
the productive set-up. Industrial unions occupy their

horizontal locations. In a mine, for instance, the workers engaged in the actual extracting from the ground belong to their particular labor syndicate of that branch of the mining industry, or horizontal union, while the carpenters, blacksmiths, the plumbers and other crafts are members of their regular craft union, the vertical body, which spreads through every industry.

To do a complete job, Mussolini also scrapped the old Chamber of Deputies, the members of which were formerly elected on a geographical allotment exactly like the United States House of Representatives. Italy was then familiar with political fence-building, platform-making and back slapping, at least, at election time. Now there are none of these beloved democratic excesses. And here, too, Fascists still say there are elections. There are. The new deputies chosen first from the top are afterwards voted and elected by large majorities since no one else steps forth as a candidate.

And since there is now no geographical defining of electoral districts, the deputies come from organizations representing labor, industry, agriculture, the professions, old soldier groups, cultural associations and the various entities chosen by Il Duce as responding to "the modern needs of a dynamic nation." And, while it is of small consequence that the deputies cannot make laws, they serve the otherwise useful purpose of creating the atmosphere in the Chamber itself for the Chief to glorify himself magnificently and to castigate his enemies unmercifully.

He officially calls the new body the Chamber of Bundles and Guilds.

Your reporter should tell you whether it has all been for the best. It is a mixture. It depends upon what one values most. It would have nothing to recommend it had it done all harm and no good. In this system, one is badly imposed upon if to chatter is important. Others more expert than you are appointed from on high to order you to work, to choose your play, to pick your reading and to watch over your loyalty. You are the more appreciated if you accept the good things provided without complaint. A smile enhances your position.

Of course, workmen do get higher wages and shorter hours and better living conditions. There are all those insurance schemes to protect in sickness and in health. There are plenty of very well-equipped hospitals built since all this was put into action. The children go places, — to the sea or the mountains when vacation comes. Reductions on the railroads, at the theaters and for concerts, are always coming your way if you show your syndical card. You can belong to athletic clubs and swim, row, play football or even ski. There are more playgrounds, stadia and recreation centers to take care of all this now. Besides, the standard of living is higher.

For all these boons, the workman must be duly thankful. If he says that everything is fine, then he obtains the bounty of a just and generous dictator. But, if he does not like his work, his boss, his food or his play and says so, he descends to the low estate of an ingrate, a traitor and a fool. He may get along but it will be difficult. He may talk, but only one way — everything is fine in Italy under Il Duce.

CHAPTER VI

WHEN MUSSOLINI APED THE ENGLISH

He did not know a pair of spats. A morning coat, a riding crop, breeches, tails, pumps were all new to him when he became prime minister. He had never worn a top hat. He had never owned more than two suits, always twelve-dollar suits, black, shoddy and looking as if he slept in them. He did wear very high stiff collars, so high that U. S. Consul Wilbur Keblinger, watching him make a speech at Trieste was inspired to ask why he did not let the advertising space around his neck.

But as prime minister he threw off the role of dapper apache and became a dapper gentleman. He dressed. He over-dressed. On the day he assumed power, the tailor was called to the Chigi palace and told to outfit him — quick, a trousseau — prince albert, striped pants, tuxedo, full dress, shirts, ties, collars, gloves, spats, everything. He ordered, too, a green suit with not too unobtrusive red stripes, lengthwise and cross-wise, a sort of subdued Scotch plaid, for street wear. It was a change from black, he thought. When Baron Russo, his chief adviser saw it, he was mortified at such a suit for the prime minister. He was asked what he thought of it. Valor was mingled with discretion, when he ventured,

"Excellency, a beautiful suit for a visit to Scotland! You are not going there now?"

Excellency was piqued for the day but he never wore

the suit again.   He was Italianissimo.   He was Benito
Mussolini, Il Duce of Fascism.

Jumping from rouser to ruler, many things were new.
Many ways, many words, many habits had to be
changed.   It is a job to be debt-dodger today and dictator tomorrow.   But he was lucky.   The big luck was
to be prime minister but he was lucky also in finding
Baron Russo, a ready-made factotum, a left-over from
the past administration who came to work that morning
to get fired because he did belong to the past administration.   Baron Russo, aquiline of face but squatty of
stature, knew the ways of being a grand seigneur for he
had generations of them behind him and had been a
professional diplomat all his life.

Besides being able to tell Il Duce what to say and
how to say it, he could tell him what to eat and how to
eat it.   Besides being able to tell him what to write and
how to write it, he could tell him what to wear and how
to wear it.   These things became so important.   Il Duce
wanted to show the world that he could be a gentleman
as well as dictator.

Official receptions, royal audiences and diplomatic
dinners were a blank to him.   He had never attended a
single one.   He wanted to do them right.   Baron Russo
knew all.   Baron Russo stayed.

And the first big affair was the dinner at the British
Embassy.   Sir Ronald Graham, His Britannic Majesty's
Ambassador, had asked Il Duce to be the guest of honor.
He was tempted to accept.   He accepted.   But though
he ruled millions, he was scared at the dinner.   It was
an uncharted and mysterious journey for him.   A mis-

take at a diplomatic dinner would lose the glamor he was successfully building. Baron Russo was the solution. He asked this encyclopedic diplomat what to do.

"It is very simple, Excellency," replied the baron in his suave and sympathetic manner. "You will sit next to the British Ambassadress. Watch every move she makes. Use the same spoon, the same knife, the same fork that she does. Everything she does, you do."

It was advice simple enough. Baron Russo saw to it on the night of the dinner that the dictator was meticulously correct. It was Il Duce's first full-dress suit. He gloated over being a grand seigneur. He liked the bejeweled studs, cuff links and the immaculate white vest, white shirt, white tie, the satin collar and tails. Baron Russo persisted, too, in making him especially soigné in his person — especially shaved, manicured, hairtrimmed, massaged and bedewed. Every hair of the few he possessed was in place. Il Duce had never known the existence of such intimate personal service.

Thus, tonsorially and sartorially caparisoned, he barged into the grand reception hall of the British Embassy, the center of the gaze of diplomats and aristocrats.

It was natural that he should be the lion of the party. All the attention was paid to him. He did not know, however, how to act the official big man. He used his face too much. He scowled. He grimaced. He thought perhaps that by bulging his bovine eyes, he resembled Alexander the Great. But while a scowl, a grimace, a glare might make him look like Napoleon to the masses, it had the opposite effect on hardened connoisseurs of facial calisthenics like the diplomats.

They had learned to solve subtler moves like twitches, lifted brows, dropped eyelids and drooped lips. A poker face would have fooled them completely. Il Duce wore no poker face on this first adventure.

But they lionized him just the same. They would have been foolish to do otherwise. And while he was falling down as the strong man, he was also betraying barely little better than small town urbanity in his social flourishes. He received their adulation like a small town mayor, for that was about the highest he knew in mundane dignity. He had not yet had a chance to acquire the superior aloofness of ambassadors and princes.

When your reporter was presented to him, we shook hands.

"This is indeed a great honor," your reporter said deferentially.

"The honor is mine," he replied just as the small town mayor would have done to a prospective voter. As prime minister, he should have said "It's a pleasure," affable but curt, courteous but superior.

He offered Lady Sybil, the ambassadress, his arm and led her into the great dining room. The baron had told him he should do it. I watched him. In fact, everyone watched him. Though no one knew of what Baron Russo had told him, it was plain that he took every cue from the ambassadress. At table, she sensed that he was copying every move. Then as a perfect hostess she emphasized each little act. She picked up her knife or fork or spoon in such a way that he could not miss the cue. It worked perfectly.

Soup was served in cups. He followed her with the correct spoon, a bouillon spoon which must have appeared very diminutive to him since Italians really use a ladle of somewhat generous dimension for their succulent *minestrone*. Then her ladyship lifted her cup and took a sip. Again he followed but drank. This aping was his major concern especially since he was very unskilled in small talk. There she did not help, for she too, lacked talent in the art.

It was a long ordeal through the eight courses. But, he took it as a part of his new vocation. The whole company then left the dining room to return to the great reception room. He and Lady Sybil led the way. He stayed well on to midnight, for so many of the diplomats wished a word. He was anxious to make a hit with all of them.

Finally, he thought it time to go and bowing before Lady Sybil, he kissed her hand as Baron Russo had told him to do. He thanked her for the great occasion and said that he owed it to her to have come through what was first an ordeal.

"I noticed how you tried to put me straight on everything," he said. "Only once was I confused."

"And when was that?" inquired the lady to the manor born.

"I did not know the English drank their soup like beer," he retorted smiling.

But, he got along with the British. He had great admiration for the British Empire in those days. It was what he hoped Italy could be.

When Austen Chamberlain came to power as For

eign Minister a lively friendship began. The Tories liked Fascism in those days. It had stamped out Bolshevism in Italy, they said. Even Winston Churchill told your reporter that had the scourge of Communism threatened England he would have considered it a duty to do the same thing as Mussolini had done to maintain the rights of all classes of the people. There were many visits from British statesmen to Italy. It was always a pleasant place to go to from England.

After Locarno, Sir Austen sent down his private yacht to cruise around the Mediterranean and especially to call at the Italian resorts. Perhaps prevented by the press of official business from making the long trip around Spain through Gibraltar, His Britannic Majesty's Foreign Secretary cut across France to join his luxury boat on the Riviera. As if combining business with pleasure in the manner of American movie magnates touring Europe in search of talent, he mingled rest with statesmanship in search of a soothing powder for the now threatening and restless Mussolini. Reaching Rapallo, he invited Il Duce to breakfast, to lunch, to tea, to dinner and any other prandial diversions customary on yachts.

Mussolini accepted.

By this time, Il Duce had had some four years' practice in trimming himself in diplomatic high life. He had gone a long way since the British Embassy affair. By this time, he had acquired the social graces of the most sophisticated marquis, and there was little more to be learned about white ties, black ties, spats and top-hats.

However, this thing of the visit to the yacht of a British aristocrat and statesman was a new social adventure. Quick! Quick! The correct thing! Baron Russo was again consulted. He had won a perfect percentage in royal audiences, diplomatic dinners and aristocratic receptions. Nevertheless a yacht trip, even to him, was out of his landlubbing capabilities. He, in turn, had to consult someone else. The day came and with it the result of his consultations.

He outfitted the Duce in a sort of seafaring blue serge coat buttoned with large and conspicuous black bone disks like the winter tunic of a New York ferryboat pilot but without the gay red chevrons, the gold stars or the silver eagles. He gave him a seafaring cap of miserly visor, slouchy top and all too sober black braid about the brim like Tugboat Tim's. His shoes were black more from accident than from choice. Masqueraded more than attired, the Prime Minister of Italy was sent forth to meet His Britannic Majesty's Foreign Secretary on *that* royalist's elaborate craft.

It was a bright and sunny Mediterranean day and Sir Austen was waiting on the quarter deck. Tall, slim, sleek and monocled, here was the aristocrat. He wore white trousers and white shoes. His navy blue coat had the yachtman's cut while in jaunty fashion upon his head was a white yachting cap with generous visor, its top stretched like the surface of a drum. His straight lines all converged to make him lordly.

Il Duce was ferried from shore on a motor launch. Reaching the yacht, he grabbed the ladder and climbed briskly up the side. He saw Sir Austen. *Corpo di*

Bacco! A cold sweat froze him. His carefully collected outfit was like the morning after the cook's night off. He thought he was dressed all wrong. And this before an English aristocrat. He should have worn white shoes and white pants. What had Baron Russo picked for him? The cap! His slouchy black tugboat biretta made him a stevedore. His sea-faring suit was only a disguise for a tanker's cook. His black shoes made him a deck hand. And all this before the tall, slim, sleek and monocled figure of Sir Austen Chamberlain.

It did not seem to bother Sir Austen at all as he stretched out his hand to welcome the dictator of Italy. He was anxious, most anxious indeed, to make him feel at home. There was a difference in stature. The Duce could not reach up so Sir Austen had to bend down. And that little move did not help either. A photographer had sneaked along and had sent up word through a steward that he would like to take their pictures. It was supposed to be a good omen for the peace of Europe to have the pictures taken and the two, yachtsman and tug-boat skipper, posed. Il Duce knew it would not come out happily. He was right. When it was published, people laughed. What was he doing on a yacht with an "aristocratico britannico"?

But they had their conference on the peace of Europe. It was long and, as the official communique said, "they found themselves in perfect agreement on the policy to be pursued to assure the continued good relations between Italy and Great Britain."

Now, when the Duce returned to shore, he called for

Baron Russo and wanted to know what right he had to think that he could prescribe the correct yachting attire. He raved. He was to see Sir Austen the next day, too. He paced the floor and told the baron to go out and find at all costs the proper clothes so that he could measure up with that English aristocrat. It was said that his eyes spit fire. Some reported that they rolled in opposite directions as he declaimed that a black biretta was all right for a ship chandler but not for the Prime Minister of Italy. Others said his cheeks vibrated like the string of a bass violin. Foaming, he proclaimed that black pants were for stevedores but not for the Duce of Fascism.

"Get me white pants, white shoes and a white yachting biretta," he was quoted to have growled. "Make the biretta a wide brim and a gold border. Do it right, this time."

Baron Russo moved and moved quickly. He sent and searched throughout the whole of Rapallo for white pants, white shoes and that white biretta. He telegraphed to Genoa and had the best hatter bring all the best white caps. By night they had got somewhere. They fitted the Duce in shoes and in pants. Finally the great white biretta arrived, wide brim, large visor and better than Chamberlain's. He was ready now to match the Englishman as a yachtsman, too.

Now, he was himself again. Next day, dressed in the new outfit, he set out to match his newly acquired lordliness with generations-long self-sanctified English superiority. I watched him board the launch at the wharf. He was a little boy dressed for confirmation, so decorated, so unused to the new clothes, so conscious that the clothes somehow did not belong to him. But, bravely he went forth.

Chamberlain was pacing the quarterdeck. His steward rushed to tell him Mussolini had come. He walked to the ladder. Again he wanted Mussolini to feel at home. In deference he was dressed in a navy blue suit — coat and pants, black shoes and to top it all, a black cap, a get-up as much like the one Il Duce had worn the day before as it was possible to assemble. But he was still tall, slim, sleek and monocled.

At first sight of him, Il Duce was startled but he did not get fussed this time. Gaining the quarterdeck, he stretched his hand to Sir Austen and as they shook, they both laughed, each trying to pass the laughter off as if it had something to do with the fair and balmy weather.

"Ha! Ha! Fine day. Fine day. Fine day," they said.

The greetings were bounteous. No one spoke about white pants, white coats or white caps. They went to their conference for the peace of Europe. The Duce got over his confirmation clothes and gave blow for blow in discussing Europe's ills and what England and Italy were to get out of it. Pictures were taken again and it made no difference whether it was a white biretta or a black cap, it was still the aristocrat and Tugboat Tim.

He was not dejected that night. He was glad to see the baron.

"There's one thing about me and the English," he said in a musing mood. "They can never accuse me of wearing the same thing twice."

Il Duce got into another slight snarl about the game of golf. It was not about something he should wear or about the fine points of the game. It was about how the game should be managed.

Englishmen had built the Rome golf course back in the 1880's. For many decades, it was the only course in Italy. The Italians were glad that the course was built for it served to attract tourists. Britishers had always managed and financed it. A Scotch professional, Robert Doig, had taken care of it for over thirty years. The executive committee was composed of Britishers and Americans. The British and American ambassadors were always honorary presidents. Of its hundreds of members from time to time, not more than five were Italians.

Fascism came. It undertook a great drive in sport for it was axiomatic that the good Fascist with or without a good tailor must at least look a good physical specimen. The great mass games like football, rowing, tennis, field and track were placed under the direction of the Fascist party. No one knew that this order was to affect the unostentatious though stately game of golf because the Italians outside the five members of the Rome Golf Club did not play golf.

What happened? Just as the club was doing nicely and paying all its debts in walked Giuseppe Cicotti, one of the unskilled Italian players. With almost pontifical pomp, he notified all the club employes that from that moment on, he was assuming direction of the club by the authority of the Fascist party. This word went through the place like a scared deer and it was just as erratic for no one even amongst the Italian employes conceived it possible that an Italian would want the job of directing this ancient and honorable game of Scotland.

It was soon to come out, however, that Cicotti *had* been appointed chief Fascist commissar for golf with the title of president. He naturally superseded the leisurely and dignified persons of the British and American ambassadors, who though their elections had become a matter of form had preserved the democratic principle by being chosen for office by the free votes of their colleagues, the members of the Rome Golf Club.

But it was the law and all the "old guard" with any executive positions stepped down. The club passed under the supreme direction of Commissar Cicotti. Of course, the members were sore. They had always considered the golf club as a sort of extra-territorial reservation for Britishers and Americans exiled in Rome either from choice or duty. Cicotti filled up the other offices with the remaining Italian members and there were barely enough to go around, since two vice-presidents, a secretary and a treasurer were the absolute minimum.

It was quite natural for the oppressed constituents to talk about this invasion of the democratic principle to the British correspondents. It was a fine news story especially as an antidote for the very injured feelings of the outraged members. The newsmen did their very best.

Their dispatches told of the British beginnings of the club, how Britishers and Americans had built it and supported it and that were it not for them, there never would have been a Rome Golf Club. They said that either Sir Ronald Graham or the Hon. Henry Prather Fletcher, the American ambassador, had always presided at the meetings and had been elected by the free and direct vote of the golf constituents. Now by an exercise of arbitrary power, a new president had been chosen by Mussolini. No one had been consulted and no vote had been taken.

And to make the situation even blacker, hereafter no elections would ever be held again. The club had passed like so many other things under the very heel of the dictator. The democratic way of life had been outraged, they cabled.

The British newspapers played up the story evidently in response to what was considered the justifiable indignation of their countrymen at home as well as abroad. Indeed, it did not stop there. Letters were written to editors and to members of parliament from an outraged golf democracy. Threats were made that no British or Americans should ever play on the Rome golf course. Cries of boycott were raised and tourist traffic to Italy diminished.

It was this latter feature which made the affair serious — for the Italians. Tourist traffic in Italy is a major industry. Tourists must be encouraged to come. Now, various attempts were made to explain away the arbitrary rule of the golf club. Membership of British and Americans on the executive committee was offered. The government was going to build a club house to show its good will. The Fascist party meant no oppression. It was just a means to make golf more efficient.

Disgruntlement continued. A mild boycott set in.

Someone spoke to Mussolini. The golfers staged a sit-down strike. The Italian tourist bureau tore its press agent's hair. The press agent tried to bribe the newspapermen with wine, women and song. The bureau said they did not want to mix tourism with politics. The newsmen countered that the golf commissar had killed the democratic principle.

Mussolini caught sight of your reporter in the official party on an excavation visit to the Roman Forum.

"Come here," he ordered threateningly. "What are you trying to do? You are ruining the country."

Albeit I was an American newsman working then for the United Press, my dispatches were also published in Great Britain. He thought me one of the crusaders though I had not touched the story. It was not big enough for heavy tolls to the United States.

"What have I done wrong now?" I bleated.

"This attack on Fascism about golf," he thundered. "It's without foundation."

"The British are enraged because there are no elections," I pleaded.

"There *are* elections," he barked with dictatorial finality. "Of course, we do not elect in the English way from the bottom up but in *our* way, from the top down."

CHAPTER VII

'MID PLEASURES AND PALACES

Whatever it was about your reporter, neither the present generation nor posterity will ever know. Some quirk or irk, some wart or wen tickled a sympathetic nerve in the dictatorial psyche. We struck it off. His face lit up whenever he saw my artless and non-committal frame — neither fat nor thin, tall nor short, blank nor loaded. It was nothing to attract anybody's attention. My face lit, too, whenever I received this signal of platonic gratification.

It all helped me much to become a good correspondent, at least, as long as I could hold this trinket of captivation before his eyes. We were so thick that we did pieces together — newspaper pieces. It was when I had transferred to the United Press and had become the Rome manager of that agency. They wanted his life, his philosophy, his political ambitions, the world solution or anything, written by himself. I asked him.

"Yes," he said. "We will do it. My life, no. Everybody knows now that I am the son of a blacksmith. My politics, no. It comes out day by day. Let it be an account of how I spend my time."

We agreed. Every day I called and got material from him. I did the actual writing. Every day I brought an article covering the material he had given me the day before. He examined it and approved it. It was not ghost-writing since his literary gifts were the equal of his political skill. He could write his day much better than I. It was only a means of lessening the burden and getting the articles out.

Twelve articles were written in the first person. We covered everything from rising to sleeping. Much in them has been repeated, but it was all new then. He told of his predilection for fish, milk and grapes. He ate no meat. It was his physical culture life, he said, though a previous attack of ulcers of the stomach probably had more to do with it. He drank no wine — ever. This was another steering away from rude indigestion, disagreeable to ulcers. He boxed, he fenced, he walked and rode a horse. The articles told of his stables, his riding-master and his equine thrills though he had only learned to mount on the day after he became prime minister. He shaved with a safety razor. His favorite composer was Vivaldi, a sixteenth-century Italian, though he ungrudgingly gave credit to Beethoven, Wagner, Brahms and Bach. He only took five hours' sleep but what he lacked in length he made up in depth. Napoleon had said the same thing.

The articles created a stir. American newspapers praised his Spartan self-denial. He was popular in these States then. I was credited with "a historic journalistic achievement." All, however, was forgotten and nothing was forgiven when I missed the grain forecasts for Yugoslavia the following month. The New York office wanted to know where I was when those figures were given out by the International Institute of Agriculture in Rome. I countered by saying Yugoslavian grain was not important to America. They slapped back by in-

sisting that Argentina, where they sold a million dollars'
worth of news a year, must have grain figures to calcu-
late how much they would make on their own stock. I
took the rap. *Sic transit.*

Our literary collaboration took place in the Chigi
palace where he then presided as Minister of Foreign
Affairs. It was shop. But to be invited to the house
was really getting the brass ring on the merry-go-round.
I was invited. It was unique. At least, I did not know
of any other newsman who went tramping in and out
of Mussolini's house. Even the females of the profession were never invited to the house, that is, still limit-
ing them to the profession.

It was my social duty as well as my reportorial aim to
make myself a most desirable companion. It was virtually mixing business with pleasure because the nicer
I was and the greater hit I made, the more favors I
would obtain in the exercise of my chosen field of en-
deavor. Seldom it was that I trespassed on the bounty
of my host by introducing any shop because I had already perceived that he was quick to detect any effort to
pump him. And well he might, for a long career of
newspaper work was already behind him. It would
take a smart journalist, indeed, to outsmart him in the
profession which was his stepping stone to greatness.

It was fatefully pathetic that after arriving at such
power he was unskilled in drawing-room conversation.
He wanted to put on the drawing-room manner which
perhaps was the most pathetic of all. His small talk
was not fitted for the manner. He had gibes, wise-
cracks, retorts and epithets gleaned and used amongst

the peasants, the plumbers, the plasterers and other sturdy folk. Only when the old cronies were around would he dare use them. A famous obstetrician had offered his services free to Rachele, his wife, when she was in expectancy. Replying, he reverted to his peasant ruggedness of language.

"Tell him," he said to Alessandro Chiavolini, his private secretary, with a proud gesture of the head, haughty in its proletarian virility, "that my wife is capable of delivering our kids in a stairway on the way to work."

But he could get along somehow by groping on quite intellectual subjects. He knew French literature as well as Italian. He liked Balzac, Maupassant, Sorel and Zola. He could quote them. He had what was more than sufficient for a parlor command of philosophy. He was wont to repeat, perhaps too often for the sake of variety, that Aristotle far outshone all those before or after in his analysis of the wisdom of the ages. Besides, he was grounded in the modern philosophies — Nietzsche, Schopenhauer, Hegel and Goethe. In the economic and social fields, his knowledge, though saturated with revolutionary doctrine, was wide and varied.

But in all these, he was awkward because he was choosing subjects which were professorial by nature while he by nature was a man of action. He had outbursts in this highly intellectual realm but could never properly develop his theme. It was as if he did not belong there and was uneasy. It was quite all right with me for neither did I. In that way it passed as supremely successful. Both of us were pleased.

But where he fell down was in the frivolities of the times. He acted as though his high station did not permit him to talk about the weather, coffee, dancing, bridge, tennis, floods, trains, ink or hunting. He knew, too, that when he talked to aristocratic ladies or the wives of diplomats that he was outclassed in such thrills as yachting, fox-hunting, horse-racing or thoroughbred dogs. It was not that the aristocrats did not try to meet him on common ground. Oh no, they were anxious to make a hit with him. Power and position were his to give as well as to withhold whenever he desired. The aristocratic ladies he met were looking out, too, for their husbands. They tried very hard to say the right thing.

There was never any way for me to return his largesse. I was, however, constantly on the lookout for entertainment which, though it might not amuse him would, at least, interest him. A quartet of Fisk University students toured Italy. They had made a tremendous impression. I suggested to him that he would like them. He asked me to bring them to the house.

There were three men and one woman. The fact that they were colored did not deter him from putting on his official manner. He showed no trace of condescension for when I appeared with my troupe in the large living-room of his house at Via Rasella, where he lived then; he came to greet us dressed impeccably in a full dress suit. I wore a dinner jacket and so did the three male performers while the lady was begowned in her high-tone concert attire. It was all very elegant.

Rising to the importance of the unusual event, Cesira, a vivacious woman-of-all-work and then his only maid, had adorned herself as if for her patron saint. She stood there with a second welcome. Her hereditary finest rather than her Sunday best was fitted over her wiry and slender form to combine in a striking contradiction. I had never before seen her in this historic frock. While the costume was intended for the rugged stature of a peasant woman, here it caressed what could have easily been the graceful figure of a finely delineated aristocrat. Her unspoiled sincerity, her wit, vivacity and ready response conspired to create the heresy that this servant should have been a duchess.

She had not been in the habit of receiving guests in the strange and unquestionably rich raiment of *signori* and *signore*. For that reason it was hard to distinguish just where her function as hostess began and her task as maid terminated. She was countrylike in her greetings and repeatedly hoped it was not too cold for March. She made much fuss over everyone. She incessantly told everyone of us to feel at home. She assigned each to a place.

And it was assuredly a new role. I had hitherto seen her show what was perhaps ignorance rather than disdain for the little niceties of service. She never used a tray but brought plates and cups and saucers one at a time to the table. On one occasion, I saw her serve Il Duce a cup of coffee for breakfast with a bunch of grapes perilously clinging to the side of the saucer. The grapes seemed to beg for room at least sufficient space to be considered a part of the morning repast. It was Il Duce's usual breakfast.

She never bothered with courses. When it is said that her cooking was plain, plain is meant. Il Duce could not indulge in the piquant Italian sauces. Whether Cesira could cook a highly seasoned Italian meal well, I never knew. She said she could but Il Duce had no need for it. If she possessed the art, it was lost on him.

I sat upon a sofa with Il Duce while the quartet was arranged at the opposite end. There was a pianoforte but they sang without accompaniment. One could see and even feel a powerful earnestness to make a penetrating hit. It meant certain success in Italy and favorable acclaim at home. They showed that effort of trying to reach out with their hands and even with their lips to create the drama of deep emotion. Hands and lips often won the battle. They sang all the old favorites about the River Jordan, Elijah and the Chariot and God's Big Wheel. After each number, he was lavish in his applause. They were doing well. He praised the music itself, much of which, he said, possessed a deeply liturgical quality comparable to Palestrina. The quartet bowed and bowed its recognition but spoke little in the presence of so powerful and highly placed authority.

A sort of intermission broke the concert into two parts, first undoubtedly to give the singers a rest, and secondly so that Cesira could come forth in all her grandeur and serve elaborate Italian pastries. She also passed the glasses for champagne. We have already said that Il Duce touched nothing alcoholic. On this occasion he raised his glass to drink to the quartet who

had so overwhelmingly triumphed. He just touched
the sparkling nectar to his lips and considered the deed
done. I drank mine.

More from artistry than sympathy, our colored singers
shrank, too, from the ordeal of drinking such expensive-
looking libations, suspicious also that cost meant po-
tency. Cesira was overcome with the refusal to take
champagne, albeit that it was Italian champagne. She
orated to them on the fact that it would do them good
and that it was indeed already cooled and from the original bottle. But they barely lifted up their hands so
as not to make the gesture of refusal too pronounced.
They wanted to be so elegant even about their refusals.

Il Duce watched the proceeding. When refusal was
made final, he assumed the pose of a very injured host.
How could they refuse the best that money could buy
even though domestic?

"You do not drink?" he launched at them almost as
if they had committed an act of sedition.

Meekly, the head man said no.

Then it was discovered that Cesira was taking the pastries away from them, too. They were left untouched.
Now, it was lèse-majesté. They had refused everything.

"What! Neither do you eat my cakes?" scowled Il
Duce at them, believing that a potentate should consider it an affront.

"We does not eat while we sings, suh," said the head
man.

"Oh! Oh! I see. All right."

Now, he reversed his tone as if he understood the

tribulations of the finest artists — they must not eat while singing.

"Put them away, Cesira," he said. "Bring them back when the singing is over."

Presently the concert was resumed and they again delighted him with more of the type "liturgico." By the last number, he was truly captivated. Again he ordered the cakes and champagne. Now he took command.

"Eat! Drink!" he decreed peremptorily.

This time the negroes drank. They were hungry and ate but not fast enough. The sparkling giggly-water went to their heads. I privately predicted what might well be called over-familiarity. I was not wrong. Il Duce promised them his autographed photograph. They returned the compliment in kind.

"And sure enough suh," said the head man, "when you-all comes to Nashville, we suttunly 'll do de same fo you."

In contrast to the Fisk singers was the concert given in the Villa Torlonia where he afterwards moved. Now it was the Morgan sisters of Boston who performed. This was a female trio of violin, harp and pianoforte. This, too, was a grand occasion, given in the grand salon amidst paintings and tapestries. The girls were accustomed to appear in concert in colonial attire with hoop skirts and elaborate headgear. They put it all on and were ravishingly diversified in coloring. It was presidential. The Duce wore a full dress suit. I wore one, too.

But while the affair was ponderously ceremonious on

the one hand, it was fresh and ingenuous on the other. Rachele, his wife, had at last emerged from a period of splendid isolation and had resumed a limited though evidently satisfactory conjugal familiarity. She was present. Romano, the latest Mussolini offspring — he who was to be born in the stairway — made known his identity with a squawk while being fondly caressed in the arms of a nurse. Arnaldo, only brother of Il Duce, also was there, having dropped in as he was making one of his periodic trips from Milan, where he ran their newspaper. The Morgan girls were accompanied by their mother.

While the hoop skirts and the full dress suits complied with presidential dignity, the attire of Rachele, Mrs. Morgan, Romano and Arnaldo harmonized instead with the family character of the evening. Donna Rachele wore a blouse of some checkered material and a black skirt. A toque was perched on Mrs. Morgan's head. She kept a jacket on though the place was comfortably heated. Arnaldo came in a black serge suit. Seeing his brother and myself in gala dress, he apologized for his "suit for promenading" as he called it.

The meeting of brother and Duce revealed an unpublicized trait of his. Here was the stern dictator of iron discipline melting before the only man in the world for whom he held any affection. They spoke in low caressing tones. They inquired of personal things. Outside, he forged men to his will by bayonet and bludgeon; here, the bonds of blood were stronger than the bonds of iron.

"I have a deep affection for my brother," he murmured later to me. "To be sure, he is too fat but that is not his fault. He is, of all men, the one to whom I turn first when I think of unstinted devotion and unfetterable attachment."

It was after the first number had been rendered that Il Duce enthused in the trio and especially in the oldest girl, the violinist. But, just as he was pouring out his praises, Romano bawled. No one, no matter how much he wished, could laugh his caprice off. Just what his protest was, I could not decipher, but that it was a protest there was no mistaking. All the pettings of the nurse resulted in abject failure. Rachele sat unconcerned. For her, crying children seemed a rule rather than an exception.

But the head of the Italian government had been used to making decisions in trying times and here was an occasion demanding more decision than tact. He was ready. Just when Romano had reached the very apex of his spearhead on the concert, the Duce brought out his frown, fixed his stare upon the nurse and with one brisk and unmistakable nod of the head motioned nurse and offspring into the kitchen. The exit was as unceremonious as the nod.

The concert then proceeded and pleased him. In between one of the numbers, he wished to pay a compliment to Boston.

"Boston is the atheneum of America," he offered to Mrs. Morgan as an act designed to show his skill as a host and man of the world.

It was quite evident that Mrs. Morgan, though a native of the place, had heard it called many names, but never before had she heard it seemingly slandered. She would have understood him better had he called it "The Hub," "The Bean City" or "The Home of the Braves" but atheneum was distinctly new.

"We like it," she replied somewhat shyly and not a little uncertain of herself.

Then he turned to me for confirmation of his worldly knowledge. More honest than tactful, I disagreed with him and tried to explain that now there were so many centers of culture in the United States that it was hard to assign to any one of them the honor of being "the atheneum of America."

He was irked with me. I knew immediately that he had not been looking for information on Boston but for a setting to show off his genteel and polished finesse as a host. If I had used a little savoir faire instead of matter-of-fact bluntness, I would have come out of the atheneum with triumphal colors and so would he. I would have been happy, he would have been happy and Mrs. Morgan would have been duly impressed even though she did not know what it was all about.

He turned directly to the girls and began complimenting them individually. It was the eldest who came in for the greatest praise.

"I have heard all the great violinists of the world," he said impressively as she listened with anxious emotion. "I have heard Kreisler, Elman, Menuhin — Germans, Hungarians, Italians, all. I am telling you that you are the equal of any of them. Certainly, you are the greatest woman violinist in the world."

We were all impressed. We were silent for a moment. Then he turned to his brother and told him to write a piece for the newspapers about what he had said. He turned to me and asked me to send a dispatch on the concert. I did.

The Morgan trio were great radio favorites at that time. We have heard little of them in these later days. It may be marriage. If beauty means something, it is marriage.

The girls asked him to give a little selection on the violin. He waved his hand and said that he never played for anybody. They pleaded but he would not budge from his place on the sofa.

Finally, it was time to go and we all filed out of the salon into the hall. We were just getting on the girls' wraps when there was a burst of a Vivaldi concerto coming through the corridor. He was not a virtuoso. He had been like a shy child who really wanted to perform but shied at it before an audience. It was so paradoxical in a man who could thrill thousands in a hall or in a public square but could not play his violin before even a handful of modest people. He could do the one well; the other, well, fair.

There was gaiety about Rachele though she had known that poverty of despair with which the peasants and working-class of Italy struggle. Her girlhood was spent barely above the subsistence level. Near the town of Forli in the Romagna region, she worked with her mother, a widow, in the Mussolini tavern, operated by Il Duce's father. It served as a rough rendezvous for a rough internationalism. It supplemented the small pickings of a village blacksmith. She worked there but was gay with the revels of that Romagna peasantry.

She was passing from teens to twenties. Mussolini in his late twenties had been away in exile. He had had his escapades in Trent, in Lausanne and in Geneva. He had already sowed bushels of wild oats before he found this luscious blond girl as if by appointment in his father's tavern. There could be but one result. They lived together.

His father had warned the widow and the girl that they must both be wary of him. There could still be but one result.

"Leave him alone," admonished the father. "He will be of no account to you and probably will leave you for another trip to some foreign country."

They begot children. Marriage as a legal bond was not important to Mussolini in those days for he was saturated with the recklessness of free love. It was an arrangement. Formal marriage did not take place until he became prime minister fifteen years later. This gave legal status to the children born.

Mussolini took the little mistress with him to Milan in 1912 when he was chosen editor of the Socialist newspaper *l'Avanti*. They lived in a modest five-room apartment in the manner of a very poor editor. For Rachele, however, it was a considerable lift toward the higher rank of society. She had never known the luxury of more than one room where the cooking, sewing, knitting, everything was done. The chickens, the pig and the lesser live-stock might indeed have inhabited the same room.

I could not but admire the latent strength and placid courage that emanated from her. Her complacent satisfaction with home and family when company came was one side of her nature. She possessed, too, the fiery combative spirit of the peasant girl ready to defend home, children and lover. When another blond woman was said to have shared the attention of Benito in the newspaper office in Milan, she invaded that office armed with a butcher knife. She was there to get that girl. Editors and reporters rushed to disarm. It was not without a fight. They succeeded but one of them still carries the scar of her challenging defiance in a deep gash across the face.

The beauty parlors of Rome have never succeeded in catching her as a client. Her nails are still unpainted, her eyebrows unplucked. She has had her hair done. Neither rouge nor lipstick glut her impoverished vanity case. Her clothes have never got beyond the sort of Sunday best of the lower middle class. Here, too, the great couturières of Rome were left cogitating, for she shunned them as far too comprehensive for her simple tastes. She has a seamstress come in and together they pick out an occasional new dress from the fashion magazines. These unprofessional creations are cut and made up right there in Villa Torlonia. In winter she alternates a short sealskin coat with a silver fox, the highest she has ventured in feminine extravagance.

When she came to preside over Villa Torlonia, Cesira was there but was immediately retired for a complete new staff. Under Il Duce, the maid-of-all-work had had entirely too much of her own way, it was charged.

Cesira contended it was not true but that it was just as well since the signora and herself were two types which never could get along together. Cesira had only taken care of Il Duce. When Rachele moved in, she brought the four children, later increased to five. She recruited a man servant, a maid and a cook. These were deemed quite sufficient to attend to the big man's needs, the cooking, the washing and mending for the children and the ordering of the fourteen rooms. But, try as much as she would to be the lady of the house, Rachele could never divorce herself from many of the kitchen and household chores. She still washed the dishes and gave a hand in the cooking.

To be sure, the part Rachele plays is often turned to political advantage. With wife and children, Il Duce must show himself a family man. Since it is a government policy to raise large families, he must exhibit his own contribution to Italian demographic strength. Pictures are taken showing him in the act of fondling the younger offspring and of admiring the older with Rachele benignly looking on. The newspapers know enough to give these pictures the lavish space commensurate with this patriotic example.

It is a strange though convenient anachronism but Rachele has never appeared at any of the formal functions where her exemplary husband is scheduled to be the chief figure. She is never invited to diplomatic dinners nor flashy aristocratic receptions. At the opening of the opera every year, the élite of Fascist society occupied the boxes. Never once has Rachele sat beside Il Duce. He occupies a box to which he invites the intimates of

his office.   Flanking him is the box of the Governor of
Rome, who officially is the host since the opera is a municipal enterprise.   Upon the latter's wife falls the dazzling honor of playing hostess to the big man.   The talk
between them is the main act between the acts.

When there are big functions of state, the absence of
Rachele is given the fade-out.   No one should notice
it.   At the wedding of Crown Prince Humbert to Princess Marie José of Belgium, Il Duce was paired with
Princess Françoise of France.   In the marriage procession of King Boris to Princess Giovanna, he took the arm
of the Duchess of Bourbon-Parma.   When a dinner or
reception is given to a visiting prime minister, Mussolini
accompanies the visitor's wife while some high ranking
Fascist's wife joins the guest of honor.   It never looks
too bad.

When the two elder boys, Vittorio and Bruno, were
brought to Rome in their teens, they were a problem.
They were placed under the care of a Fascist militia
major but they wanted to do the town.   They became
reckless with cars.   Fights resulted between father and
sons.   They called *him* a speedster.   Why did *he* not
slow up?   Rachele more often than not took the boys'
part.

"You can run the government but you can't run this
family," she told him.

CHAPTER VIII

APPLE OF THE DICTATORIAL OPTIC

Along with the pleasure of power came many a head-ache. Mal-à-têtes multiplied in the dizzy heights of grandeur and glory. There were too many Italians, too many disgruntled ones, too many out to get him and occasionally some foreign country refused him his own way. But he had one continual headache which, though it seemed inconsequential compared with the cares of state, dogged and worried him because it stuck like a feather tipped with molasses and was difficult to flick off. Paradoxically, it was his greatest treasure in the world. It was Edda, his eldest daughter.

Her birth and origin are lost in one of those delightful romances of youth which we picturesquely describe as having taken place under the rose. The locality was Forli in the year 1910. We know that she came into the world wearing the auspicious halo of a *liebeskind* or love child. This happy omen heralded a secure depth and perpetuity of affection which was transformed from the connubial to the paternal. Her mother, unsung and unrecorded, passed into oblivion in one of those tragedies emerging either from the caprice or stubbornness of nature. The child was raised in the Mussolini home and later brought up by Rachele, who, as we have seen, assumed the responsibilities of wife, an arrangement on which even our own common law would have bestowed a benign sanction.

It was quite plain when the other children came along that Edda was different.   Not alone was she different from the Rachele boys but she was distinct as a personality.   She possessed a drive and force impressive when contrasted with the adenoidal lethargy of Vittorio and Bruno.   She was assertive, dynamic.   Just as cubs emit an occasional evidence of their leonine will, she showed a leonine determination in matching her demands with all.

In 1912, Mussolini was appointed editor of *l'Avanti*, then the great Socialist daily newspaper of Milan.   He left Forli taking Edda and Rachele with him.   Edda was cooped up in a working-class apartment of five rooms with no activities outside the school and this cloistered though not quite sheltered life.   Her playmates were the sons and daughters of workmen.   Poverty had ticketed her either for work or a good husband.   She had never had more than two dresses or never more than two or three of anything.   Social amenities, permanent waves, polished nails, or a party dress were in another world.

She became the prime minister's daughter when she was twelve.   Rachele still kept the five-room apartment.   She was fifteen when Fascists began to use her for flag-raisings, openings of social centers and awardings of cups to winning swimmers.   Your reporter saw her initial appearance.   She presented a banner to a new bundle of combat.   Mussolini was there.   The event coincided with a visit to Milan he was making.

The ceremony occurred in a hall no bigger than an ordinary class room.   The new banner was tied with a blue ribbon in such a way that a slight tug at the ribbon would unfurl the flag. The officials and Mussolini stood about the banner. Edda was at his side dressed in a green jacket and skirt and a red hat. Adding to this gay though unsubdued elegance, she wore a pair of mannish, brown kid gloves with the wrists turned back. The officials spoke telling of the greatness of the occasion. Mussolini responded confirming the greatness. Then it was Edda's turn to pull the ribbon.

Grabbing it with her gloved right hand as a telephone lineman would grab a cable, she gave it an unmistakable yank as if she was supposed to tear the whole thing down. The yank was bound to have ill consequences even though the main staff was strong enough to withstand the blow. The ribbon jammed in one knot. The banner remained more tightly tied. She hurled back her head, gave her bag to her father and then with both hands again seized the ribbon. Determinedly she gave it a snap that would have done credit to a sailor severing a small hawser. The flag unfolded.

"I knew I would make it work," she said.

Il Duce smiled. Laughter was in order all around.

She grew into a lithe athletic figure and later became a good horsewoman and a swimmer. Her face was chiseled in the type of Garbo. Her eyes protruded exactly as her father's. In physique, she was a contrast to her brothers whose chubby features marked them unmistakably as the sons of Rachele.

Mussolini had been in power three years and Edda became a greater problem for him than the Reds, the Greeks or the French. He had picked a school for her, the finishing school of the Most Holy Annunciation near Florence.   It was where many great princesses of Europe had been educated including the present crown-princess of Italy.   But this school was not for her.   She attended but refused the discipline imposed by the nuns. Punishment had no effect upon her.   One morning a sister went to call her and found her bed empty.   It caused a stir.   She had escaped during the night and had taken a train back to Milan alone.

This was now worse than if she had attended no school at all.   Il Duce tightened his lips at the forebodings of her untamed nature.   She had got beyond the control of Rachele.   She challenged any adverse will. This only daughter picking her life in the gay and worldly city of Milan was a worry.   She went to cafés, attended sports events and frequented the dance halls. Bunions grew on the eyebrows of the dowagers of Milan.   A climax was bound to come.   She fell in love with a prize-fighter.

In Rome, as Il Duce plodded hour after hour with reports on Italian finance, on education, on unemployment or foreign affairs, it was Edda who increased the thump at his greying temples.   He consulted few and those whom he consulted gave him consolation rather than solution.   They recommended schools.   But he knew she was beyond all that since she fled the Most Holy Annunciation.   He searched for his own solution. She had fallen in love with a prize-fighter.

He told her on the telephone that he wanted her to spend her seventeenth summer at Courmayeur, a little mountain retreat at the foot of Mont Blanc on the

Italian side. He thought that if she climbed a real mountain, it would keep her out of mischief. She told him that she wanted to spend the summer at Riccione, a popular seaside resort on the Adriatic. She preferred the sea, she said.

But it was at Riccione that the prize-fighter had a summer job as a life-guard. It kept him in trim as well as pocket money while awaiting the opening of the squared-ring arenas in winter. It was a job, too, which permitted him his evenings off where he could frequent the varied and multitudinous dancehalls, gay with youthful Italian flesh of both sexes and gaudy with striking colors and lights, low or high depending on the class of trade. He was a lion to all.

Poles separated the vacation plans of father and daughter. They were extremes which permitted no bridge. Geography was minor. Mountain climbing offered no compromise with dance halls, beach parties, boiling crustaceans and the prize-fighter.

Mussolini stumbled upon a new approach. At that time, he was taking English lessons from Lillian Gibson, an English intellectual who was correspondent for the Paris edition of the *New York Herald*. Miss Gibson called in the palace every day but not always would he take a lesson. Her culture extended to the arts, philosophy, literature and languages. She had previously been assistant principal of a very aristocratic girls' finishing school at Dresden. She spoke four languages well. He knew all this. He thought he had a solution. It might be a solution.

It was in the Hall of Victory of Palazzo Chigi, where he then had his office, that he revealed to Miss Gibson the new inspiration. His own English lessons could be temporarily abandoned. He picked up enough anyway from English and American visitors. To her he unfolded as a sort of dream his hope that she could domesticate Edda, teach her some fundamentals and even the most elementary readings in literature. The little wild girl could speak only Italian and without any academic purity. She could learn English and French. She could acquire something about the niceties of manner. She could, perhaps, be polished up.

He told Miss Gibson that he had suggested the stay at Courmayeur and also that Edda had disagreed. He told her also about the prize-fighter. It was not necessary for him to say much on this. He did not say much. He knew that the neat and hopeful companion would understand why it was necessary to keep the prime minister's daughter on the highroad of propriety. Miss Gibson did know all about it, too — I said that she had been assistant principal in a finishing school. She accepted the responsibility proud of its lofty position, heavy in heart on its uncharted possibilities. He paid her two thousand lire a month, a very high salary in Italy and nearly twice what she received as correspondent of the Paris edition of the *New York Herald*.

He telephoned to Edda to show her the new world. It had been foreign to her thoughts — to travel with an English woman. Edda promised to give it a try. Since it was something new, she agreed also that she would at least start out by staying at Courmayeur. He was pleased. He told Miss Gibson. It was all arranged. The English woman would start from Rome and meet Edda in Milan and from there they would both go to Courmayeur to begin this new life. It was the first of May when it began.

Courmayeur is beautiful if you like the mountains. The towering grandeur of Mont Blanc is there all day for you. Courmayeur, however, is shut in on three sides. On the north side the climbers begin their ascent of Europe's highest mountain. And here it was that the restless Edda must spend the summer. It was only May and the village had not yet thrown off its drowsy winter blanket of melting snow and ice. The place was dead.

Miss Gibson made a hit. The little girl liked her gentle manner and her talk. Day after day, they took walks, and the talks on travel and people which Miss Gibson infiltrated into the conversation seemed to keep the girl sufficiently buoyed for her volatile nature. Then they began taking drives up into the Alps. Edda was glad to go to France and then Switzerland. They took drives over the whole of Piedmont. It was interesting. It was succeeding.

As June wasted its lazy Alpine days, the explosive soul began to show an impetuous discomfort. Edda voiced complaint. She hated the sight of the plain-clothes men around to protect her. She could not stand this locked-in mountain village. She could not bear the towering mountains. They were only rocks and snow. Miss Gibson tried her soothing ways. They failed to work now.

One morning the wild girl arose and declared for the future.

"I'll not stand it any longer," she told Miss Gibson, gesticulating with her hands, gently biting her lips and throwing back her head. "Order the car. I'm going."

Protest and suavity were unavailing. Risk of paternal rage was of no consequence to her. The car must be there. Miss Gibson, too, must obey. Miss Gibson obeyed. When they had had breakfast and had packed, they piled their baggage into the car.

"Drive to Riccione," she said.

Mussolini owned a ten-room house in Riccione. They naturally went there and found that Rachele had already moved in for the summer. It was easy. Miss Gibson was assigned a bedroom and Edda took her regular cubicle. Then the days on the seashore began. Edda saw her boy that evening. They called at a couple of the gay places. Miss Gibson accompanied them ostensibly on the grounds that she had not seen Riccione yet.

Now, teaching a vagabond temperament the manners of a princess became increasingly difficult. Her companions it seemed had swarmed in from Milan. They ranged from a butcher's daughter to a lawyer's son. The prize-fighter was easy because it was quite consonant with duty for him to talk to the Prime Minister's daughter while watching the wayward swimmers since it was not quite certain that anyone could drown in Riccione. You walked a mile in the sea before getting beyond your depth.

The days were now lingering along pleasantly though

perilously. The girl who was to be finessed was getting no finesse. Miss Gibson felt her mission failing. Irksomeness set in between governess and pupil. She appealed to Rachele for some relief from the constant companionship of prizefighters, butchers' daughters and tailors' sons but that only complicated matters. Rachele was resenting the presence of this Rome-sent woman in her house. She consulted with her own confidential friends. They naturally agreed and added that he, meaning Mussolini, could have only sent Miss Gibson to Riccione, not to take care of Edda, who was now seventeen, but to disrupt the household. They averred they would have none of such a thing themselves and would drive her out of the house.

Miss Gibson with all her instinctive tact and gentility was now as much at home as a boilermaker at a faculty meeting. Glared at by the Rachele intimates and even by Rachele herself, she was subjected to a barely tolerant endurance. This suggested to Edda, too, that she could be unburdened of the cultured chaperonage. She did not openly join the anti-Gibson campaign. In her independence, she saw the prizefighter, the butcher's daughter, the tailor's son and the otherwise unlettered accumulation without limit to time or space, cafés or cabarets, beaches or bars.

The intrigue became so intense that Miss Gibson now felt it clearly decisive. Her presence was both undesirable and useless. She immediately requested the prefect to provide her with a car. With it, she rushed to Rome. At ten, one evening, she arrived and asked for admission to Villa Torlonia. The guards recognized her

as the English teacher.   She was admitted immediately
and forthwith was received by Il Duce in his private
study where he listened to the story of backyard intrigue, youthful exploration of youth and his daughter's
erratic and erotic urge.

He only answered that he had hoped for too much.
He was disappointed.   He risked Edda and her prize-
fighter for the rest of the summer.   In the fall, he
ordered her to come to Rome and stay with him.

She welcomed this chance to get to Rome.   She was
taught to ride.   He took her with him on his morning
gallops.   She liked it.   He brought in friends for her.
He had private movies in the villa.   That winter, she
also made a trip to India chaperoned by the wife of a
Milan industrialist.   A reception was given in her honor
at the vice-regal palace in Delhi.   Ready hands of Italian consular officials put her correctly forward before
vice-regal stuffiness and stiffness.

It was the winter following when she attended a reception at the Italian embassy to the Holy See that she
met the young secretary, Count Galeazzo Ciano.   Then
he was twenty-six and she was nineteen.   He was tall,
good-looking and had travelled the world.   She was
Il Duce's daughter.   There was a flash.   He mentioned
it to his father who had been one of the closest lieutenants to Il Duce.   The old man could see that for his
son it meant career.   The father mentioned it to Mussolini.   For him, it solved a problem.

With such far-reaching ramifications of state and
family the wedding was made a great occasion.   What
a royal wedding is to the crown, this was to Fascism.

The Cianos were aristocrats and knew how to act. The Mussolinis had had no weddings. To them, they were principally functions where you ate more than you ever ate in all your life. Nevertheless, announcements were made that the marriage would take place on April 24, 1930. It had to be an affair.

Il Duce regulated the size to conform to the simplicity of Rachele, for certainly Rachele must be there. A reception was given in the Villa Torlonia the day before the wedding. This was held down to a minimum of aristocracy with a maximum of Fascism. Your reporter was invited. All the editors of Fascist newspapers were there. The members of the cabinet attended and the heads of the diplomatic corps. Ambassador and Mrs. John W. Garrett were present to speak for the United States if words were necessary.

Il Duce and Edda received the guests in the great salon. Mussolini was dressed in a morning coat and Edda quite gay in an afternoon dress. Since Il Duce knew every one of the guests while neither Rachele, Edda nor young Ciano had hardly seen any of them, it was on Il Duce that most of the work fell. As he greeted me, he turned me over to Edda and said:

"I am not used to weddings. We must have them sometimes."

"It's your politics," I returned. "Many weddings! Big families."

The guests were all ushered into the garden. The newspaper editors, Fascist chiefs and the diplomats were standing under trees or sitting at tables. Rachele presided at a table where Countess Ciano, mother of the groom and Count Ciano, the father, sat. Rachele did not move about the tables. She wore a simple black satin blouse. Besides the sitting, a smile constituted the sum total of her social effort. When all the receiving seemed over, Il Duce and Edda joined them. Caterers served the refreshments, and the reception, unlike most dictatorial assemblages, proceeded quietly and without ostentation.

Someone remarked that it was wonderful how a woman of such simplicity as Rachele could hold such an elaborate affair.

"She stays put," remarked a facetious Italian editor. "Common sense is more desired than social grace here."

Just as the reception was held between a minimum and a maximum, so the wedding itself was maintained to the least common denominator. Instead of one of the big basilicas, the local parish church was used. Instead of some important cardinal of the Catholic Church, the little parish priest officiated. There were no soldiers, no uniformed diplomats. In the midst of this simplicity Edda was formally married to Galeazzo Ciano. One problem was solved, a headache eased.

We can hardly call it a wedding present but the groom was immediately promoted to consul-general, a job for which one must usually wait until fifty. He was appointed to the important post of Shanghai. There Edda began learning English principally from American naval officers. She was captivated with American slang and still uses such expressions as "boloney," "oki-doke," "eye-wash" with spirited amusement and even avidity. Their first babe was born there and was given the name of Fabrizio, though Edda playfully called him "my little chink."

They had only been in Shanghai a year when the groom was recalled to become Mussolini's chief of press bureau. In accordance with Fascist doctrine, promotion kept pace with expanding family responsibility. Another boy was born. On this new bambino they imposed the fateful name of Marzio, a synonym for Mars. That was 1933. Edda has had no children since.

In four years, the groom became Italian minister of foreign affairs. This all had its influence in fashioning the *savoir faire* of Edda. At twenty-three, she undoubtedly was the youngest wife of foreign affairs in the world. She had by this time, too, learned as much as was necessary about beauty parlors, tea gowns, evening gowns or any gowns, shoes, hats, coats or permanent waves. She was thrilled but she was still restive, dynamic and leonine.

It was quite logical that her circle of friends in Rome should grow to almost unmanageable proportions. She made them and discarded them with equal dispatch. She easily threw off any ties of officialdom which held down her eruptive spirit. She went about a lot but the receptions in embassies and aristocratic palaces were not to her liking. She quarreled with Crown Princess Marie José in an official reception over the materials of a dress. It was a tough argument. Society staggered. Royal anger rose. Father was told about it and counseled her that she should not offend the royal blood. To her, blood which was not red was white.

The Count went to the Ethiopian war as an aviation

squadron leader. Their pictures were taken at his departure and were spread over the front pages as an example of patriotism in connubial self-denial. During his absence, Il Duce accompanied her to an occasional concert. It was good politics to appear in public that way. She began to brood. The Count was quite safe as an aviator since the Ethiopians fought only on the ground. She continued to brood, — over her loneliness. She did not wholly solve it but remedied it. She was seen with former Milan beaux. The war only lasted six months and the Count returned. She had burned a candle but not in the window to light his way. At least, he returned as hero and cabinet minister.

After the war, she thought it would be nice in England. She went there and hoped to find a place for her husband as ambassador to the Court of St. James. She was received but coldly. England's blue bloods did not like the way Mussolini had calumnied the English in the Italian press. She could see that England was not the place though she had set her heart on it. She had asked Il Duce to fill the embassy with rare old Italian paintings for her eventual residence. The paintings were sent but the English refused to approve Count Ciano. He had made nasty remarks about Britain in the newspapers.

In June, 1936, she rose for a girl of her limited accomplishments but unlimited aspirations to what must have been the height of ecstasy. Alone, she made a triumphal entry into Berlin. Naziism had been in power but three years and the bonds between Naziism and Fascism, intermittently torn asunder, were now being welded again. This was a chance for Hitler, Goering and Goebbels to make a hit with Il Duce and, at that time, they needed a friend. The staff of the Italian embassy with their wives and high Nazi officials welcomed her with flowers in beflagged waiting rooms and carpeted station platforms. It was the beginning of a queen's sojourn.

And did the Germans know Edda? Blond masculinity in rigorous Nazi uniforms sprang to attention with a click of the heel, a deep bow and a kiss of the hand. Hitler himself was host at an elaborate state soirée in her exclusive honor. The dazzling outlay in Nazi sumptuosity and virility caught the breath and wobbled the head of the little girl from the five-room apartment in Milan. Goering, Von Ribbentrop, Goebbels and youth of the élite guard in full regalia attended a state dinner in the Italian embassy where she ruled in her own as well as her father's right. The newspapers were filled with articles, pictures and praise of the sweetness from across the Alps. She was queen here.

What was described as a flame flickered between Edda and Rudolph Hess, chief party secretary and Hitler favorite. Those who saw them together averred that Hess looked so attentive as a friendly escort. Whether Hess had been assigned to insure Edda's safety in the Reich was never officially announced. There were many handsome secretaries in the Italian Embassy. Edda eventually returned to Rome but symptomatic of her German triumph was the increased warmth in Italo-German relations. The Rome-Berlin Axis was eventually consummated. This led to the undoubtedly jealous diplomatic observation that Hess was its father and Edda its mother.

Edda generally rang the bell.   She accompanied the Count on an official visit to Budapest.   The historic Hungarian custom of a hunting party was a major event in the program.   Repeating historic precedent, she showed a marked partiality for one of Horthy's sons, for it always happens to sons on hunting parties in Hungary.   She later made a trip to Poland without the Count and without a conspicuous success.   We should not wonder at this since she had been assigned the impossible task of inducing the Poles to surrender to Germany.

Her conquering prowess led her on a most important mission to South America and especially to Brazil.   Here she had the uncommon task of inducing the government to exchange their coffee for Italian silks, textiles and an occasional warship.   She succeeded magnificently.   And more, she had a bigger mission.   It seemed beyond the reaches of a little girl in green jacket and red hat.   She deposited several million Italian lire in the banks of Rio de Janeiro at a good rate of exchange. There it remains to await events.   If the Mussolinis have to go anywhere, why should it not be Brazil?

CHAPTER IX

A THING APART

Il Duce has loved women but, off and on, has treated them roughly. A lot was pose, flippant aping of Schopenhauer, a subtle self-praise for his many more or less ardent affairs. What he said of them contradicted his life, influenced decisively by two great women.

His conquests were irregularly spaced. He lived sometimes for years loyal to one woman and then, at other times, he changed lovers with the agility of a trick cyclist.

Most of the early tales of his amorous accomplishments are laid in the rugged regions of the Trentino bordering the South Tyrol. While he lived there it was ruled by the old Austrian Empire. Since the last World War, it has belonged to Italy. His field of operations was in the ancient city of Trent where high cliffs rise on either side to give the scene a frowning austerity.

Not that the landscape had anything whatever to do with his erotic conquests for he had done quite well in the plain. But it was in Trent that perhaps we can say he went out for love as a youthful Don Juan exploring a new scene, acquiring a certain mastery and certain finesse very sorely needed because of his reckless youth and his impetuous nature. His stay in Trent lasted only three years. He was expelled by the Austrians for political incompatibility and not for any illicit incompetence in the realm of Eros.

His one outstanding romance there concerned that of the local schoolmistress. He had obtained the position of schoolmaster and in the fateful maneuvering of destiny lived in the same boarding house as his female colleague. The school year was long enough to permit of much social exchange but the combining of circumstances hastened more than anything else a forward step. Place, youth, beauty and impulse united to usher in a grand and rampant passion.

While the school year lasted, this convenience of adjusting the exactions of teaching the young with the exigencies of great love made life indeed very much of an endurable existence. We are told by the old inhabitants of Trent that the schoolmistress was a brilliant and talented educator buoyed with such vivacity that she might have come from either Naples or Sicily. She was dark and olive skinned and possessed the winning trait of always seeming to smile. This intrigued many, they said, because it was difficult to discern whether she was smiling in warmth or snarling in disdain.

But to the colleague and companion, she evidently smiled in warmth for education and love lasted with undiminished ardor for the whole of the school year. Finally for the pupils, examinations took place and marks were given; for the lovers, it was one sad break, he to look for a summer job in his home town of Forli and she to return to her parents. No one knows whether this temporary suspension of ardor was welcomed or not, but what we can say is that both longed for the resumption of school in the following September.

Out of the blue, he received a notice from the Board

of Education of Trent that his services would no longer be required as molder of the lives of their youth. He could not understand this scornful depreciation. He inquired. The school sages had decided that he was too *fulminous,* which though it might not be sufficient reason for the rejection of a talented and promising young educator was accompanied with the unsolicited smack that he had flogged the boys a little too much even for the otherwise Spartan sensibilities of the virile town of Trent. He was terrible.

And the schoolmistress? She was retained.

Accordingly, the august body appointed a successor to the flogger, who they trusted was imbued with a somewhat gentler Christian instinct. They were not disappointed. They found him a sympathetic soul. He was a contrast and gave the arbiters of learning a complacent satisfaction in that their boys were not now being flagellated along the road to knowledge. The successor took the flagellant's place at the boarding-house, too. The successor succeeded him with the girl.

When this tragic news reached the fallen educator, he flew into one of his impetuous rages. He immediately started for Trent equipped with a sharp weapon. Changing trains at Verona, he met some revolutionary pals and unburdened on them the sad story of both his economic and romantic plight. He confessed, too, that he was on the way to get the man who had broken up his happy romance and ruined his promising career in the educational field. The pals laughed at his wild scheme of risking an Austrian scaffold to satisfy what they called a passing lust especially since there were many

more available schoolmistresses, if it were necessary that
she should be a schoolmistress.

He was taken by their arguments especially since the
joy of revenge would be so brutally treated by an un-
sympathetic Austrian court with further unwelcome
complications in an Austrian jail if not with an Austrian
hangman. The warm ardor of love gave way to the
cold expediency of life, for besides righting a romantic
wrong, he had to make a living. He surrendered the
lover and with it the career of educator. He got a job
on the Italian newspaper of Cesare Battisti, an Italian
patriot, in Trent. He wrote well. His style was alive
and fiery. Its very fire was bound to arouse the Austrian authorities. In his articles, he said that the Austrians had no business in Trent. They replied with a
police order. It was he who had no business in Trent.
They had the police, too. He was taken to the frontier.
He went to Switzerland.

Life in Switzerland was hard but he found his milieu.
It did not take long for him to survey the expanding
revolutionary horizon. And just as much, if not more
than the pamphlets he read or the lectures to which he
listened, it was the young women then enlisting in the
beginnings of world revolution who set his course in
radical action. Amongst them were French, Belgian,
German, Italian, Hungarian and Russian women.
Lenin was there. Zinovieff lived amongst them. Van-
dervelde often spoke to them. But the one who fash-
ioned this wild youth's life in revolutionary doctrine
was Angelica Balabanoff.

She was a little woman and belonged to that Russian

upper middle class which had done all the work in the interest of Russian emancipation. Her family was wealthy. She could have stayed in the Czarist regime in complete luxury but she chose the active life of a revolutionary in the aim of Russian freedom as did Prince Kropotkin and even Lenin. She was five years older than Mussolini but she discovered in him the spirit of an untamed colt and she admired it. In his dire poverty, she helped him to get little jobs such as writing short articles and translating. The pay was poor but subsistence was necessary. He admired her. She had what he so much lacked, culture. Certainly, he admired her. No wonder his viewpoint on love had changed from the affair with the schoolmistress! Angelica showed him a panorama. He saw new and greater horizons. It was a spiritual and purposeful existence. Poverty, poetry, and philosophy and world revolution served as a binding tie in two reciprocal natures.

By her, he was guided to learn about Marx, Engels, Proudhon, Bakunin and Sorel. Socialism became a religion to him. Together they dreamed of the common ideal of an emancipated proletariat. Years of such blissful and yet culturally fruitful devotion had connected his life inseparably with Angelica Balabanoff. But again, he was hounded by the political police for revolutionary writings. Again, he must flee. This time it was back to Italy.

The final break with Angelica came when he attempted to lead the Italian Socialist party into the last World War. This was when he had assumed that very lofty post of editor of the *Avanti*, which by the growth of the party eventually reached a circulation of more than a million. The conviction was slowly dawning upon her that he was obsessed with a military ambition. Dejectedly, she detected his insatiable ego which tolerated no opposing opinion and even rejected the direction for the newspaper which the leaders of the party had determined.

Balabanoff remained in Switzerland during the last World War. She was one of those who accompanied Lenin and Trotsky from Switzerland through Germany and Sweden back to Russia after the signing of the Brest-Litovsk treaty. She participated in the October revolution. The Communist International selected her as its first secretary. After three years of sacrificial devotion to her chosen cause, she again met a major disappointment. She was convinced that the direction set by Lenin in subordinating the Communist International to his own foreign policy was out of harmony with the ideological course of the revolution. In 1921, she left Russia and came to the United States, disheartened and disillusioned with the turns of the working-class movement.

She is now in her early sixties living quietly in a modest hotel off Central Park in New York. She is still vivacious and vital. The Socialist cause is her great ideal. Bitterness pervades her when she thinks of the betrayals of the working masses. She told me that the one consuming trait in Mussolini's life was destruction. Reminiscing on the days in exile in Switzerland, she said that Mussolini's one outstanding aim was to destroy the Roman Catholic Church and the Italian Monarchy.

She believes that to gain his political ends, he has played as a friend of the church and of the dynasty but the hate for religion and royalty still remains.

When Balabanoff passed out of his life, it was Rachele, who then attracted him. We cannot attribute to her any share in the fashioning of his intellectual and spiritual personality. She gave him nevertheless a family which, as we have seen, became a political necessity in the turn which his destiny took.

The Socialist party in Milan organized numerous after-work activities and one of them was the People's Theater where tickets were sold for cost. Productions were usually limited to "uplifting plays" which reflected the dire lot of the poor contrasted with the wasteful extravagance of the rich. Cecile Sorel was playing for it one evening. A box was placed at the disposal of the *Avanti* and tickets distributed to the staff according to the necessities of the service to the newspaper. One place went to the editor and another to the dramatic critic.

The editor was able to spare the time and entered the *Avanti* box at the beginning of the second act. All the occupants naturally did some sort of obeisance to the youthful though authoritative executive. But of three women present, he fixed his attentions on a genuine Titian blonde. The chatter between them during the rest of the performance was vivacious and, no doubt, exploratory also. He liked it. The blonde was very equal to it. She was the dramatic critic. She was Margherita G. Sarfatti, wife of a distinguished lawyer and Social Councilman in Milan, who died in 1921.

Here was a woman of wide intellectual pursuits whose field while being revolutionary extended to many branches. Your reporter knows Margherita as an intimate friend and knows also of her culture. She speaks and writes in five languages. She has written books on art and politics. She has written novels. There was a difference between her and Angelica. Angelica was an uncompromising revolutionist saturated completely in revolutionary theory. Margherita had much revolutionary doctrine but she had also acquired the classical philosophies of economy and politics. She had studied Goethe, Hegel, Schopenhauer, Nietzsche, Dante and Shakespeare. She was erudite in history, the arts and literature. She once had a contest with Colonel Theodore Roosevelt on who could quote more Kipling. She won.

But here was Mussolini getting out the *Avanti* which must necessarily be filled with revolution. What he had gleaned through the guidance of Angelica was a fitting equipment for the task. No better training for such a position could have been provided. Another expulsion was, however, soon inflicted upon him. This time, it was the expulsion from Socialism. Without a party, he had to found his own. We have seen how he did it. Now it was that Sorel mixed with Nietzsche had set the course of his political star. Now he could only become a superman. Now he must "live dangerously." Margherita had set him upon the new course.

She mapped out his classical education. He began his study of history, philosophy and sociology. His courses were just about backwards from the way youth ordinarily skims or, if he is studious, absorbs such knowledge.   In our preparatory and college courses, the students first learn the classic leaders in historical and economic thought.   It is only after they get to their junior and senior years that they are supposed to learn about Marx, Engels, Kropotkin, Proudhon and Bakunin. But what boy could hope for the happy combination of private tutor where abstruse philosophic systems were made more sublime and much easier by companionate collaboration.

Margherita made a classicist out of him.   It was not until his thirties that he discovered Machiavelli and began to shape his political fortunes on that Florentine's model.   He passed from revolutionist to imperialist. Since he also discovered the rise and fall of the Roman empire, he made a vow to reconstruct that empire leaving the great world revolution to Trotsky and Lenin. He became very proud of his adventures into philosophy and just after becoming prime minister addressed a meeting of Italian philosophers in which he lamented that there were no more Aristotles.   The great scientists could go so far but must all stop where the word "God" is written, he said.   He learned of Adam Smith, John Stuart Mill, Malthus, Quesnay, Mendel and many others.   In his speeches he often condemned the economists of "the Manchester School," the more to impress his hearers, whether erudite or not, with the breadth and profundity of his own knowledge.

It would not be right to say that what Mussolini achieved he owed to Margherita.   He commenced with his own native equipment, which was considerable.   She did much. He had qualities approximating genius in the realm of leadership. She often turned his head in a new direction and opened up to him avenues which he had not known existed. The inspirational companionship with all the emotion of a *grande passion* lasted from the modest offices of the *Avanti* through the expulsion from Socialism, the growth of Fascism and finally to power and then great power.

There was an unavoidable suspension when he was called to Rome to head the government but the enormity of the new vista opening before him created such stupendous joy that the forced separation was a minor inconvenience. Both were joyous. He gloried in his power. She, recognized by his lieutenants as *l'ispiratrice*, basked in his reflected glory, satisfied to meditate that she had been a stimulation to a superman and inwardly thinking that he was partly her own creation.

Separation was made bearable by the glamor which came upon both of them. And as if to fill the little void which living apart had brought on, Margherita made periodic trips to Rome where she was received by the high personages of the party with the honors appropriate to the spiritual though unofficial consort. This was never the chief purpose of her visits. Besides, she delivered lectures, consulted government chiefs on the promotion of the arts and gathered material for her magazine *Gerarchia,* of which she was the editor. Most important of all, however, she saw him.

But in time the thrill of official attention began to wear off. They both agreed, as otherwise it could not have been, that she should take a house in Rome. She leased a spacious apartment with long and flowing salons in the aristocratic Via Nomentana. It was diagonally across the street from the Villa Torlonia. When she was finally installed, she made this place the rendezvous of artists, men of letters and politicians after the manner of so many Parisian women of influence. Every Friday afternoon Signora Sarfatti was at home and it was a "must" if one was a struggling artist, hard-working writer or aspiring statesman and wished to obtain the sanction of the *ispiratrice*.

This did not mean that she had no time for Il Duce. Not at all. He always had the green light. The house when he came must be without visitors of any kind. If you happened to be there when he telephoned that he would take a run over, Margherita got a headache for you, a heartache for him. You were put out somewhat unceremoniously and down the stairs. The servants would look to make sure that you had cleared the hall before his car arrived. He came unseen by anyone. Of course, he never telephoned on Friday afternoon. This gave the artists, writers and politicians the illusion of a favor.

It happened that I was often caught by his visits. Every time, too, I was ushered unceremoniously out of the house and the stairway made clear for him. His car did not stop at the front entrance but drove into a courtyard from the side. In this way it was not necessary for him to enter through the front door. The car waited in the courtyard until he was ready to return. Actually, I only saw him once and that because I did not have sufficient time to make my getaway. I cer-

tainly did not want it to appear to him as if I were
snooping around his amatory explorations.

But had I been suspected of too much attention to
Margherita, our position could have been very easily
explained and a secret of many years and conjectures of
many newspapermen solved. The secret answers the
conjectures. It is this. Margherita and myself prepared
all the articles signed by Mussolini for the Hearst newspapers. I did the actual writing. Margherita combed
the articles for any barbed arrows which in her judgment he ought not to disperse. All he had to do was to
read the article and approve it.

It often happened that he would not approve the
article. Then it was necessary to write another article.
On one occasion, I prepared three distinct articles for
him before finally getting his approval. It was a lucrative undertaking for me. The articles appeared once a
month. He never took a cent. Of the income, the
Hearst newspapers took the first forty per cent of the
gross. The rest was divided between Margherita and
myself. I received a twenty percent share and Margherita took the rest. The most I ever made was $500
per article. This naturally gave Margherita a thousand.
He allowed her this luxury so that she could keep up a
good appearance in the capital amidst any sneering
aristocrats.

When present for the evening's fun, he was certainly
the man of the house. A maid and cook waited on him
with the deference due some pagan divinity. The cook
had been with Margherita for thirty years and had seen
the beginning of the union. The maid was German

but while her length of service was not as great as the cook's, it was compensated in the expression of her devotion to her mistress and her master. She adored Il Duce.

In 1932, Margherita moved to Via dei Villini. This apartment was much bigger. While it was more convenient for the weekly at-homes, it was not so convenient for Il Duce. It was near enough to Villa Torlonia but it had no courtyard. He had to enter through the front door. Since there were many more other tenants in this building than at Via Nomentana, Margherita had jumped at a disadvantage. He was often seen. We cannot say that it was just as well because after years of this surreptitious bliss by the side entrance, the ardor of Il Duce's affection began to wane coincidentally with having to use the front door. He stopped coming. She visited him in Venice palace.

When he had come to power, he announced that he was going to do much for women. He was going to give them the vote. He never did. He had changed. He had forgotten how strong women had shaped his career. Now that he was a superman, he began to practise as well as to preach depreciation of women.

"It is his own life and work which dominates the thought of the man," he told me once in Chigi palace. "His life may be momentarily shaken by a great love affair, but he will soon regain his equilibrium. He makes the conquest and the woman is his. When that is settled he returns to his career. The woman if she loves him becomes his slave. I have never believed in the inherent greatness of women. They have never produced a single great artist, philosopher or scientist. Woman is merely man's plaything."

While the ardor for Margherita was turning into embers, he was receiving younger adventuresses. It became a social achievement to boast of being in Il Duce's favor. Most of those who received the supreme thrill were reaching the higher rungs on some professional ladder in the arts. Through their fame they crashed the palace doors. Young widows and even married women sought and succumbed to the dictatorial conquest. One married woman on whom he was casting a pleased eye, let it be known, albeit in subtle terms, that he was the father of a newly arrived daughter.

A young though persistently aspiring Italian woman writer succeeded in the call. He afterwards discovered that her mentality and vivacity were not synchronized with his and decided summarily to prohibit her the freedom of the palace. When a guard obeying his new orders stopped her as she was boldly and imperiously marching in, an act which had become the usual thing, she could only believe that a mistake had been made. She protested. The guard insisted. She was not allowed to pass. She could not see Il Duce. She wrote. She got no answer to her notes. She connived to attend public gatherings at which he was present. She had to get near him. She worked and worked. I was there when it happened. She sat down beside him at a newspapermen's reception. He tried to show his annoyance by ignoring her. He snubbed her.

"Don't you remember, Duce," she pleaded appealingly.

"Away," he snapped, rose and walked measuredly into another room.

Immediately he called one of the presidential detectives and ordered him to have her removed. The next day, he issued instructions to the presidential police that under no circumstances were they to allow her to be present at any function he should attend.

He had cut her off like a dead branch. It happened to others.

Today we cannot but ponder on what pervades his mind now nearing his three score years as he contemplates the desertion of the two women who had the greatest share in advancing him toward his destiny. We cannot say that Mussolini never would have achieved dominion had not Balabanoff first opened the horizons on which he chose to direct his upward movement. Her help and inspiration did speed the course. She was a Jewess. Today such companionship could not be possible as in Switzerland thirty years ago. His blood has changed.

Just as sad is the fate of Sarfatti, who is also a Jewess though converted to the Catholic faith. Exiled ignominiously from her native Italy when the anti-racial laws in answer to Nazi pressure were enacted, she found refuge in France. But France was invaded and again she had to flee. She went to far-off Montevideo. In Italy her name has been expunged from all the great institutions and enterprises over which she formerly presided. The command is to forget her contribution and to liquidate her influence as if she had never existed.

One place, however, still must preserve the name of Sarfatti. It is carved in marble. At the Jewish synagogue in Venice, a plaque to her son stands against the wall. At the age of seventeen, he was a volunteer in the last World War and was killed in action. He had won the gold medal for military valor, the highest decoration in the Italian army. There the name of Sarfatti still stays.

"Man's love is of man's life, a thing apart . . ."

CHAPTER X

AND DELIVER US FROM FAME

What of the king?

Your reporter met King Victor Emmanuel often. Often I conversed with him. Royal etiquette prescribes that the king lead the talk. You may ask no questions. He asks the questions if you have anything he wants to know. He can, however, tell much more than he can be told. Whether he talks or you talk or whether anybody talks at all, the field is his. I knew it but often forgot it. I asked questions, too.

This king is a human encyclopedia. He would break the bank of "Information Please." Fadiman would crown him a season's find. He is Kieran, F. P. A. and John Gunther in one. Architecture, mechanics, chemistry, agriculture, philosophy, history, animal husbandry, government and the military sciences are at his fingers' ends. He can tell you the cost of operating a powerhouse, the page on which he read of a German spy in America, the mileage to all the cities of Europe, the budgets of nations, the dates and strategy of battles, the best breeds of cattle for the Alps or for the plains, the author of any book in any language referring to Italy, the winner of the Derby in any year, or — what do you want to know?

I called on him on one occasion in the summer lodge at San Rossore, near Pisa. Most formal for me, it was informal for him. I wore a morning coat, striped trou-

sers and high collar — like a king.   He donned a tan
sack suit and sport shirt — like a reporter.   He sat in an
arm-chair.   I was supposed to get the chair and he a
divan, a royal custom.   Erroneously, perhaps, he had
given me my choice.   I took the divan.

He crossed one leg over the other and discoursed
pleasantly and not in the manner of orators.   As always,
I forgot his unhappy handicap of only being five feet
two.   But what he lacked in bodily height he more
than compensated in mental depth.   He is a big man
in everything save stature.

We explored such wide-apart subjects as the annual
increase in the lean of the Tower of Pisa, the natives of
Rhodes, Italian dentists and the reinforcing power of
cement in old buildings.   Circuitously, we came to the
kind of news Americans liked.   The reporter was supposed to know something about that and tried to show
off his knowledge.   But the king read American newspapers, too.   He noted that we cover "practically every
human activity" — gelatin to securities, double-breasted
coats to riots, "your star" to "Fair Enough," used cars to
Toscanini, besides the medley of movies, Japan, crime,
legislation, train wrecks, wars and the World Series.

At that time, too, he discovered that much attention
was being given to Mussolini's attempt to raise two
water-logged Roman galleys sunk for 1800 years in the
Lake of Nemi, not far from Rome.   Archaeologists had
expected to find rich works of art in the submerged
craft.   Your reporter with others of his trade had told
the American public what the archaeologists had said.
The king smiled.

"Sir," I interrupted, somewhat uneasy about the royal smile. "Don't you expect to find anything?"

He stretched and lazily lifted his eyebrows.

"Nothing," he said pleasantly as he looked at me. "There's nothing there. A nice nothing."

It was a blow to our reportorial rectitude but who could know better than the king?

"Treasures are never left alone — long," he continued apparently amused. "If there was anything there, someone would have picked it up centuries ago. A treasure only sixteen feet in water would not remain loose when an ordinary diver could seize it. Too many fingers would itch. Certainly, the treasure hunters have stripped everything especially since they had 1800 years to do it. You can depend on it."

The king tossed it off as a great joke that anybody paid any attention to the hydrated barges. He was surprised to find Americans so eagerly reading about the expected archaeological gold mine. He marveled how we were engrossed in the tomb of the Egyptian pharaoh and had facetiously baptized the mummy, "King Tut."

Returning to the galleys he insisted that it was easy enough for a diver without a breathing apparatus to descend, grope for anything valuable and then return for air.

His naval officers in the Libyan war of 1911 had hired a Greek to go down some eighty feet to explore a sunken Italian warship, he said. This diver's only equipment was a heavy stone roped about his waist. He used a rubber hose for air. When he tired under water, he cut the rope and rose to the surface.

"You will find an account of it in the *military ga-zette*," the monarch said suavely and then offhand cited the page, the month and the year.

Your reporter, whom protocol and good manners had forbidden the use of a notebook forgot the reference in as many minutes as Victor Emmanuel had retained it in years. The king, however, had successfully proved his point. And more than that, the galleys were finally raised and beached yielding one lone copper wolf's head, which apparently had escaped the itching fingers of treasure-hunters during the centuries. It was the sole token of the "great archaeological riches."

We do not hear much about Victor Emmanuel III because he shuns publicity. Each New Year the director of the official Italian press agency, silk hat, white gloves, morning coat and spats, asks audience. He is accompanied by his secretary, also in silk hat, white gloves, morning coat and spats. The secretary carries a large, handsomely bound volume. It contains the press clippings for the past year of all stories referring to the royal family.

The two are admitted into the ante-chamber of the throne room in the Quirinal palace. When their turn comes, the king's aide ushers them into his presence. His Majesty wears the uniform of a field-marshal. Head agency man, secretary and volume bow to the king. He smiles and greets them. He knows them from last year, the year before last, and the year before that.

The director makes his set speech:

"Majesty, I have the honor to present to you the press clippings of the past year referring to the royal family."

The king continues to smile. He makes what also has become a set speech, for it is the same, year after year.

"We thank you for this volume of clippings," he says. "It will, however, please us most that you and your subordinates say as little as possible about us and our house in the newspapers. We do not like being in the press. Keep this in mind."

The agency head, the secretary and volume bow obedience. The volume is left on a table. The king watches and the two agency men back toward the door, their annual ceremony completed. It is the only press conference that King Victor grants.

It is lack of publicity that hides him. No monarch of today, however, attends to the job of being king with such Spartan severity. He rises at six — every day, summer and winter. Bath, toilet, breakfast and a scan of the morning newspapers are over by seven, when he receives his secretary with the night's despatches. This latter routine is finished by nine. He begins his conferences. These continue until one o'clock. He then lunches with the family. Work begins again at three — inspections, reports, ceremonies — and lasts until eight. Dinner comes and then voracious reading. The King of Italy never goes out at night, except on what is a king's business — the opera opening, a patriotic function, some academic inauguration.

The rigid regularity which rules his life was instilled into him from his boyhood, when he carried the title of Prince of Naples. King Humbert, his father, decided that his playing days were over at twelve. Undersized and delicate, he had been in charge of nurses. The stern parent decreed that he must prepare for the profession of king. He called a known disciplinarian, Colonel Egidio Osio, who had served in the Ethiopian campaign of 1868 with the British under General Napier. He appointed him the lad's head tutor.

Osio made out the daily schedule. He was to rise at six o'clock, summer and winter, and be ready for instruction at seven. Lessons lasted until noon, except for one hour when the boy was drilled in horsemanship, shooting and fencing, regarded as sufficient for his physical training. Study continued in the afternoon.

At fourteen, he entered the military academy. Following the custom for royal sons, he was soon made a lieutenant, then a captain and later a major. When he reached twenty-five, he was promoted to the rank of lieutenant general. He protested. He told his father that he had not yet learned how to be a colonel. King Humbert explained that should Italy be at war, it would not be his job to lead a battalion or a regiment but to watch for the success of the whole army.

"You have got to be promoted," said the king gruffly. "On you will rest the responsibility of the nation. It is more important that you know how to handle generals than colonels."

As sovereign, he has been at times the object of a fanatic admiration by his people. This wild enthusiasm for him prevailed immediately following the victory of the first World War. It has both sagged and soared since then. At that time, he was popularly credited with playing a great part ordering the strategy, stiffening the civilian morale and organizing the final offensive. Generals received their share of glory but the vital turn in crises was universally believed to have originated in the will and intellect of the king. Three momentous decisions earned him the title of "The Wise" from his more zealous subjects.

His first great decision came after the disaster of Caporetto in 1917. He summoned his ministers and staff and ordered a general reorganization of the armed forces. Italian morale was low, shaken. Defeatism had set in. It was a blow for the allies. The whole of the allied high command suddenly rushed to Italy to consult.

Victor Emmanuel met the allied staff. Lloyd George and Field-Marshal Sir William Robertson for Britain, M. Painlevé and General Foch for France convened with the sovereign and his generals at Peschiera, eighty-five miles west of Venice and one hundred and twenty-five miles from the Italian front.

The king personally spoke for Italy. He was no puppet commander but the active general of his generals as his father in his boyhood had told him he was destined to become.

The king was master in the crisis. The monarch gave the allied command a complete analysis of the cause of defeat. A fog had enveloped his northern flank which prevented artillery operations. Thirty thousand regular officers were lost in the fighting up to that time. The army was led by hastily trained subalterns who were not skilled in keeping their men in hand during a difficult movement of retreat.

"I was greatly impressed by the calm and power he showed on such an occasion," wrote Lloyd George. "His country and throne were in danger. He did not betray a single sign of fear or defeat. His most anxious concern seemed to be to cancel from our minds the impression that his army had been routed."

The allied generals in the meeting then proposed that the Italian army withdraw its forces and take up a position on the Brenta one hundred miles from Caporetto. There was a hush. Victor Emmanuel spoke. Clear in his own military plan, decisive in mind and firm in will, he rejected the allies' proposals. His military erudition and skill staggered the generals. He told them that he had no intention of retiring so far back as it would lengthen his line and endanger his right flank. It would mean giving up two whole regions including Venice. He then outlined his own plan to retire to the Piave, fifty miles from Caporetto.

"Gentlemen," concluded the king with strained determination, "the Italian army will make its stand upon the Piave."

There was no further argument. The allies accepted his decision. His judgment was vindicated.

His second great decision was made when he personally called on his chief of staff, General Cadorna, to tell him that he was relieved of command. He could discharge as well as decorate generals. Then he motored to the headquarters of General Armando Diaz and appointed him to replace Cadorna.

His third great decision was in choosing the correct moment to start the Piave offensive. It was late Oc-

tober, 1918. The action extended over a week, result-
ing in the complete rout of the Austrians and the signing of the armistice with Austria on November 4. Germany was left to fight alone. One week later, the
Germans signed the final armistice of the war.

But even more momentous than the three decisions
in the World War was his choice of Mussolini to head
the government. This as we now can judge was momentous not alone for Italy but for the whole world.
Many of the twisting paths which international affairs
have taken were determined by the devious and confus-
ing directions pointed by Mussolini. He opened the
way for Hitler. Then came Ethiopia, Spain, German
rearmament and what we have today.

King and dictator, however, pulled together. The
sovereign did not mind being used. He was well aware
that it suited Il Duce's aims to strengthen the monarchy.
The king was pleased that his prime minister had turned
a movement from clamoring republicanism to loud
cheers for the dynasty. Before Fascism, the king was
often the subject of indignities in parliament, in the
press and on the public platform. His runtish stature
was a delightful eccentricity for the caricaturist. But
now with Mussolini to face the growing power of
Socialism for him, it was a miracle.

But lifting Mussolini to command has not always
meant the best relations. There have been violent disagreements. When Mussolini wished to establish a
medal bestowed by him personally, the stocky though
erudite monarch stepped in and promptly told Il Duce

that the bestowal of decorations was solely the prerogative of the crown. Mussolini went further. He had had a plan to organize one single ministry of the armed forces. His choice for appointment to that post fell on Costanzo Ciano, who then was a lieutenant commander. To it all, King Victor replied that he favored the merging of the defense ministries into one organization but he could not accept his choice for minister.

"Why should we appoint a man who has never advanced beyond the grade of lieutenant commander when we have so many field-marshals with wide experience?" he told Il Duce.

The proposal was set aside a long time but was finally incorporated when Mussolini took personal charge of the three ministries. This was not all, however. The armed forces were placed under one Chief of Staff. The king's choice for that important position was Marshal Badoglio. He was pro-monarch and anti-Fascist. He was the king's man. He was the watch-dog for the royal house.

I was often present with King Victor at the annual army maneuvers. It was impressive to note how deferent all the generals were to him. Whenever he followed a movement through the binoculars, the staff was always beside him making the first explanations whether Mussolini were present or not. The king could always depend on the fidelity of the army. This fact was evident. It was evident also that Mussolini was always trying to further the training and experience of the Fascist militia. He was watched in this both by the general staff and the king himself. Sometimes the king acceded; more often he refused to sanction preference for the militia command.

And now Italy's entrance into the present conflict has all been the doing of Mussolini. He had convinced the monarch that most was to be gained from the German tie-up. Victor Emmanuel, however, from the time when he was a student in the military academy had been taught the prudence of Italy's remaining on friendly terms with England. His whole life had been lived under that policy. His culture was made more basically English than German.

As a young man, he visited London and was invited to Windsor Castle and Buckingham Palace. It was his first contact with the English royal family. Queen Victoria reigned. Speaking perfect English and showing such a precocious knowledge in all things from Shakespeare to submarines, the Prince of Naples became a favorite in her Britannic Majesty's court. During his visit, he was called back again and again. When he finally left to return home, she told him that he was the kind of prince a nation is blessed to possess.

"Victor Emmanuel," she later announced suggestively to her many daughters, "is the most talented and most intelligent prince in Europe."

This contact with the British royal house never was broken. A personal friendship was built up with many of the sons and daughters of Queen Victoria, who frequently visited the Quirinal Palace.

This is in contrast with the king's attitude when his own daughter, Princess Mafalda fell in love with Prince

Philip of Hesse.   He abhorred the idea of his children
marrying into the German royal houses.   But the plead-
ings of Mafalda and the promises of Hesse were so in-
sistent that he finally approved the match.   It did not
end there, however.   He refused permission for the
marriage to take place in Rome.   Instead it occurred at
the summer retreat of Racconigi in the Piedmont Alps.
Hesse wore a German uniform at the wedding.   This
inflamed the royal displeasure.   The new son-in-law
was always an outsider.

Friends of mine at court have confirmed to me that
King Victor was violently opposed to the Axis.   He was
drawn into it.   He did not think that Mussolini was
going to adopt it as a basic Italian policy.   He thought
the Axis was just a temporary maneuver.   He had often
seen Mussolini turn from one side and then to another
in his diplomatic jockeying.   He thought it just another international juggle.   But when Italy was carried
so far and the strength of the German war machine was
so evident he had to resign himself to the inevitable
alliance with Hitler.

We cannot, however, condone it all.

As I look back at it, I can discern a certain lack
of royal self-assertion.   It is perfectly correct in international affairs to be friends with everybody.   Mussolini certainly explained it that way to him.   But when
measures like the anti-Semitic laws came up for the royal
assent, he should have refused to follow.   These laws
were too symptomatic of being in Hitler's power.
When the anti-racial campaign started, the king had
said privately that no such laws would ever be approved

while he was king.   Mussolini contended that discrimination against but 40,000 Jews was of little consequence in comparison to the greater welfare of 45,000,-
000 Italians.

"Sometimes it is necessary to destroy a whole generation in order to save a race," Mussolini once remarked
to me during his period of consolidation of power.
With such a concept of race purity what did persecution
of the almost negligent and unobtrusive Jewish population of Italy matter.   They could perish in order to
insure the booty expected from the Axis victory.

But the step was decisive.   Italy was getting more
involved in the Nazi net.

Certainly many Italians are asking why the king did
not come boldly forward and establish a firm policy of
Italian neutrality.   This would have endeared him in
the hearts of his countrymen for generations.   He could
have insisted on the liberal principles which his own
royal house had granted for centuries, a strict observance of religious and racial toleration.   His wide knowledge of men and things certainly put him in a position
to know that Italy would be drawn into a suicidal struggle.   His own marshals like Badoglio, Caviglia and
others had advised him against any Italo-German military combination.   The strength of Mussolini as a military strategist was not established in actual combat.   The
king should have remained firm, unshaken, faithful to
his throne and his people.

Triangular quarrels developed frequently between
the marshals, Mussolini and the king.   Theoretically,
the sovereign must be above such misunderstandings

even though they are in such high places.   But he was
by his position the only authority who could decide the
issues.   Quarrels occurred over the use of the Fascist
militia in the army maneuvers, over the excessive pay
allotted militiamen in comparison with army men, the
system of promotion, the corresponding rank of a militia-
man compared with a regular army officer and other
controversial points of military procedure.   Since it was
Mussolini's purpose in most of these moves to increase
the power and prestige of the militia for his own personal ends, it was inevitable for the marshals to favor
the king and for the king to favor them.

Now coming into the scene on army, navy and air-
force organization is Crown Prince Humbert, his only
son.   He has been trained in that military tradition
where the army in its historic and chivalrous glory must
be the first consideration of the royal house.   He is now
thirty-four, but even when Fascism came to power in
1922 he had already been steeped in the unassailable
role of the king's armed forces.

As a boy of eighteen, he kept a strict distinction between the soldiers in the royal tradition and those of
the "new ruling class" coming into existence.   Following the custom of promoting the sons of the monarch,
he was quickly advanced through the grades.   He was
made a lieutenant at eighteen, a captain at twenty, a
major at twenty-four, a colonel at twenty-six and a year
ago was placed in command of Italy's army of the Alps,
with the rank of a full general.

His personality seems too pleasing for a strict disciplinarian.   But this does not correspond to his quali-

ties in the field. He demands the strictest obedience to every army regulation. I once saw him keep two militia officers at salute for a half-hour. They had not sprung to attention and saluted him until he had forced them to it by an unmistakable glower. When given, he did not answer their salute until he was satisfied he had administered a lesson.

I attended his wedding to Princess Marie Jose of Belgium. It was the greatest royal function I ever witnessed. The celebrations lasted four days and were filled with levees, court receptions, diplomatic soirées, parades, reviews, gala performances at the opera and the richness of religious pomp. In the public manifestations every region in Italy was represented. Thousands of boys and girls in native costumes created such a riot of color and variety of display that few scenes of that nature have ever equaled it. This single expression, however, showed the reverence in which the royal family is held.

Humbert speaks most of the languages. His English has a marked Dublin accent as one of his early nurses was a woman from the Irish capital. He went through the various stages of the education of a prince by learning all the military arts and sciences and finally passing through the Royal Military Academy in Turin. He is a natural athlete. He can ride, ski, play tennis and swim. He is what may be called handsome. He is six feet two in height, which is naturally a part of his maternal heritage. He resembles Robert Young, the movie actor, in features and coloring. He told me that he had a great admiration for American girls. In fact, he was having an affair at the time with a Hollywood actress.

Disagreement with Mussolini heralded his entrance into official life.   Since the Fascists salute with outstretched arm, the young prince thought this all right for political organizations but somewhat ungainly for military units.   It created much confusion at first because all Fascists used it.   When the militia saluted a regular army officer, they did not know whether to return it with the military salute or the Fascist salute. This confusion lasted for months.

"Why do they not all salute like the army?" asked the prince of Mussolini at a review.

"Highness," replied Mussolini, "the Fascist salute is as ancient as Rome itself."

"So is a chariot," returned the prince, "but I would hate to fight a tank with one."

In the maneuvers of 1939, which showed the deplorable state of the Italian army, the Crown Prince was disheartened by the inefficiency of his various organizations.   He called his staff officers together.   They had a private meeting and all decided that if the army was to be brought to a full state of effective operation the influence of political officers must be eliminated.   The army must proceed along a strictly military policy, he said.   This was a blow at interference from Fascist hierarchs.

Mussolini and the royal house have got along.   Each needed the other.   While mutual dependence continues they will continue to get along.   Had Mussolini been self-sufficient, anything could have happened.

CHAPTER XI

BASS HORNS AND A DUMMY

Proud we are! We, we will not let Mussolini run this country. Strange as it may seem, the Congress of the United States has passed laws giving Il Duce exactly what he wanted. He asked for oil in 1935. Congress gave it to him. He advised an embargo on arms to Spain. Congress gave him the embargo, too. Congressmen listened to his bass horns and read what he told them they should know. Sometimes they did not know he was doing it. They believed they thought it all out themselves.

Long before the Nazis started their powerful propaganda machine, Il Duce was operating at full speed. He had always been working in the trade. He used every kind of artifice — loud talk, soft talk, balcony talk, radio talk, newspapers, lecturers, tourists and even our own editors. His propaganda ministry was divided into three great sections — radio, press and "tourism."

He built powerful short-wave radio stations the better to get his advice to distant parts. He was using radio for propaganda long before our broadcasting facilities ever touched an international message of "goodwill." We had far more powerful stations. We were too exalted to spread "goodwill" then. We were not to blame for thinking that the best propaganda was no propaganda. We had no need of telling anyone we were something which we were not.

Besides, Mussolini bought out numerous newspapers in many countries. He started a good many in others. In New York, he dictated the policy of several foreign language publications even in our own domestic affairs. He built up several good dailies in Buenos Aires, Rio de Janeiro, Sao Paolo and other South American cities. In Egypt, Palestine, Spain and Turkey, several big newspapers were told what they could say and what they could not say in local and international affairs. He bought up the Rome correspondents of foreign newspapers. They sent rosy reports of Italy in exchange for a monthly check from the propaganda ministry. This was a very cheap way. The most notorious case was that of a French journalist who had been violently anti-Italian. He turned overnight to wild pro-Italian reporting. Simultaneously, he moved into a luxurious apartment and rode in a luxurious automobile.

Il Duce has sent lecturers to tell us the virtues of his plans. Many of them have been believed. He invited American lecturers to Italy and paid their expenses in de luxe suites on steamers and royal apartments in the hotels. He generously and seemingly with no ulterior motives invited several groups of American editors to see Italy and to tell the story of what they saw to their American readers. He made it easy for tourists by granting reductions of seventy per cent on the railroads.

Many nations practise these forms of publicizing their lands. We can take all these things with our eyes open. We can accept or reject what we hear on the radio. Our editors who visit Italy can publish what they please. These methods may turn some of our people, but not many. The motive is too apparent. It is not the system by which our congressmen are influenced. Mussolini and his propaganda ministry have invented a far more subtle institution than steamer tickets, radio programs and dinners for editors. It is masterful in its accomplishments. It is still operating. It is still influencing the opinions of millions of citizens of foreign countries all over the world.

This is the Charlie McCarthy on Mussolini's knee.

Il Duce has discovered that people listen to a Charlie McCarthy but hardly know that the Edgar Bergen exists. Besides, when something nitric must be said, well — it is better through a dummy. If someone objects, it can always be blamed on Charlie.

Every time you have seen the name of Virginio Gayda in the newspapers, you have met the little man on the dictatorial knee. He has snapped at all the big nations in a big way. He has flattered them, too. It all depends on what is in it for Italy. He has spanked Uncle Sam, set fire to France, wiped out the British Empire and, at one time, crushed the Germans.

With war on, he is more important than ever before. People want to know what Mussolini is going to do next. Gayda is expected to tell them in advance. He is the world's most quoted man.

Getting across through Charlie what Mussolini is supposed to be thinking makes it furtively confidential. The dictator is telling things to his little man privately and the little man is letting it all out publicly. It seems exclusive, yet with no obligation to keep it a secret. The newspapers print it.

Gayda is editor of the *Giornale d'Italia,* a prosperous Rome newspaper. Writing his daily article gets his Charlie McCarthy role to all of Rome's correspondents. Sometimes the suavity of Il Duce sweetens the two to four columns a day. More often, dictatorial rage fires the page. Newsmen prefer these ventriloquized blasts to the stilted reserve of the official propaganda office.

Today, Gayda prepares the international public for every Italian peace or war move. Mussolini decides the objective. Galeazzo Ciano is brought in on the strategy board. Duce, dummy and diplomat work like a backfield and the newspapers of the world run the interference for them. Everyone recalls now how they feigned a line plunge on Tunis, then on a double reverse, took Albania instead. Such football strategy is important in war, too. They made a dash for Greece expecting to take Egypt. That play was smothered.

The world knows the faces of Mussolini and Ciano almost as well as Gable and Garbo. The world has never seen the shy and diminutive Gayda even though his ravings are read in every civilized country. He has never been shown on the screen and rarely indeed has anyone ever looked at his photograph. He occupies no official position on the governmental rolls though that of being the unofficial Charlie McCarthy surpasses in importance the function of the most pompous cabinet minister.

Newsmen learned long ago that Gayda was on the inside. Daily they rush for the *Giornale d'Italia.* It is a "must" coverage like city hall at home. Some of them have won the little editor's goodwill and he gives them the galley proofs. This means a scoop.

Correspondents would like to have personal access to Mussolini. Of course, it would expose Il Duce to direct questions. Often he would not want to answer. With the interposed dummy, the talk is all one way — no questions. Enveloped in an effective smoke screen of dictatorial red tape, it typifies an oracle. The voice is that of Gayda, the newsmen are told, but the words are Mussolini's. They cable those words.

Gayda protects both dictator and government. Officially, Mussolini does not talk at all. But he says things through the little editor that he could not possibly say directly. He can attack foreign statesmen and mention them by name. It is a new technique and stumps the diplomats. When the matter comes to a showdown through the complaint of an ambassador or other envoy, Il Duce simply says that it was the voice of Gayda.

Since he has been in power, the dictator has changed international loves a great many times. Gayda changes with the whims.

During the Ethiopian disputes, the British Home Fleet was sent to the Mediterranean to crush the Italian navy. Gayda saved his country's battleships from partial if not total annihilation. How? Prompted by Il Duce, he kept writing articles. The British correspondents in Rome kept lifting them and feeding them to the British public.

Italy was Britain's best neighbor in Africa, the articles said. A confidential report by a special commission of the British cabinet came into Mussolini's hands and he gave it to Gayda. This report told the British ministers that strategically and economically, Britain had nothing to fear from an Italian occupation of Ethiopia. Gayda published it. The newsmen cabled it. He also warned that Italy had a fleet, too. The army could muster 8,000,000 bayonets, his articles said.

A complacent British public did not want to be disturbed. They liked the sound of the confidential cabinet report but disliked the threat of naval action and of 8,000,000 bayonets. The ordinary taxpayer could not investigate how strong Italy's navy was or whether Il Duce really had 8,000,000 bayonets. His military experts could have told him quite, quite another story but he did not want to be bothered. He did not want any showdown. He preferred to believe Gayda. The Home Fleet was ordered home. Gayda had done it.

Meanwhile the Ethiopian war brought Fuehrer and Duce together after a quarrel over Austria. It was when Hitler offered goods to Italy just as the League of Nations imposed an economic boycott. From scoff, Gayda turned to praise. Every day, he poured honey for the Germans. They were cultured now. He has continued to cuddle them ever since. When they signed the military alliance with Italy on May 22, 1939, he wrote:

"This alliance is the culmination of the common social, economic, political and ethical developments of the two allies. One can add to these the perfect homogeneity of the two countries, non-existent in any other powers in the world."

But despite the "perfect homogeneity" and the military alliance, when England and France went to war with Germany in September, Italy did not move a sol-

dier except away from the fight. No black-out was ordered. Instead, Italian workmen began tearing down
the air-raid shelters built in anxious August days. The
big ships *Rex* and *Conte di Savoia* were sent out to sail
the oceans. The whole Italian navy put out to sea to
capture not French destroyers but to protect world trade
for the Italian merchant marine. German citizens were
refused passage on Italian ships. Italy made a commercial agreement with England for millions of tons of coal
in exchange for thousands of airplane engines. It was
convenient for Il Duce to make it appear that he was
not going in and was profiteering on staying out.

Simultaneously, Il Duce was telling Gayda to say
what great soldiers the Germans were. The little man
also had to take the Poles to task for resisting anyway.
He talked so loud he seemed to be running his own war.

"Italy did everything to show the Poles the seriousness of their situation," scolded Gayda. "Why further
war? Poland had no reason for being."

Then he turned to bellow at England and France.

"There is no menace to your legitimate interests," he
counseled. "Why great massacres of men and irrepa-
rable devastation? Wars are fought in defense of national interests and yours are not affected."

He said these things to please the Germans. This
made them feel that Il Duce was still behind them.
The blasts had a sincere ring. Again it was strategy.
The Germans were to believe that they were the words
of Mussolini. The French and British were to feel that
they were the voice and words of Gayda — why, a German could not travel on an Italian ship, Mussolini was

going to make motors for the French and British. But Il Duce was watching events. He must know first who was going to win the war before finally picking his friends. He waited until the knockout of France was imminent. The rest seemed sure and easy.

When Italy declared war on prostrate France and beleaguered Britain, Gayda's loves and hates were effectively readjusted. Though he must continue to punish England and praise Germany, there was still much to be done in placating Russia, flattering Japan and obstructing the United States. It was essential though not difficult to change his contempt for Bolshevism to warm regard. His previous alarm of the "Yellow Peril" was transformed to faith in Japanese destiny without apology. What once was admiration for "the young, virile and dynamic drive of the star-spangled republic" became scorn for its "lethargy, irresponsibility and decadence."

The real aim of the Gayda technique regarding the United States was to influence legislation in Congress and to create a divided public opinion. This may seem fantastic but the frequent Gayda quotations prove it conclusively enough. He succeeded in doing it in Britain. And he did win early skirmishes here.

His articles are designed to produce disruption. They are deliberate plants for our correspondents in Italy to send to America. What is ironic is that he uses our own press to confuse our own people and their legislators. Our newspapers maintain their offices and correspondents in Italy to gather his blasts. They pay for cabling these dispatches and then allot him columns often on the front page. It is not necessary for him to swing our entire public opinion in favor of Il Duce. It is enough to win a small balance which by its weight can threaten, obstruct, retard and negate the movements in our body politic.

At the time our neutrality legislation was being discussed, he released a full charge intended to quicken and increase the isolationist trend and even to threaten us if any other course were taken. It was another case of the 8,000,000 bayonets on the British taxpayer.

"Some advice must be given to the United States," he reproached. "Let them pay attention to their own affairs which are not altogether happy and brilliant. Let them leave Italy in peace."

"Many mental and political conflicts," he continued in the same sarcastic vein, "as well as many economic disorders of Europe have been created already by the undue intervention of the Americans. Protected by distance, shielded by their irresponsible carelessness and by their opaque ignorance, the United States talk, arouse, menace and delude. They foment intrigues in Europe, provoke inadvisable movements and quarrels without noticing the effects, satisfied to withdraw at the last moment without burning their fingers or compromising their affairs."

"It is time that all this come to an end," commanded the assertive Italian Charlie McCarthy. "Let the United States remain in America. Let them be content with attending to their many and complex internal problems not yet solved. Let them not be sorry for themselves, if, after refusing this timely advice, the European states chosen as the target of their blows decide finally in their own defense to intervene with the same spirit in North American affairs."

This was published in most of our newspapers.

During the changing surges of the war, he was given our front pages to show us how incessantly wrong we are. We should stay out of Europe, he said. We get into trouble in Asia. South America resents us. Our gold standard is an outworn concept of national finance. Conscription was a mistake for a peace-loving people. Britain cannot win so why does the United States help the illusion of victory in British hearts. Hemisphere hegemony is imperialism. Our pan-American policy is destined to failure.

The most audacious display of Gayda strategy aimed at defeat of President Roosevelt for re-election. Whether any of us desired Mussolini's advice made little difference. The little editor gave it to us anyway and was allotted the front pages to do it.

The *New York Herald Tribune* gave the story a place of honor on page one right next to a photograph of Wendell L. Willkie. The story called the President a war-monger and warned that arms and men were being sent by Mr. Roosevelt to Britain. Gayda even charged that the responsibility for the war could be leveled against the Democratic party. This party, he said, was in conflict with the ideological and political aspirations of the Axis powers. He also characterized the committee of William Allen White, staunch Republican, as "a strange creation of Rooseveltian policy largely financed by Wall Street bankers."

Gayda told us all about our own intimate affairs as if our own press were either not skillful enough or not sufficiently courageous to inform their public. He doubtless did not know that Mr. Willkie was a relentless campaigner and uncommonly dexterous in persuading the electorate of the President's shortcomings.

It may well have been, too, that the New York dailies wished in good faith to inform the large Italian population of Il Duce's position. Gayda was craftily capitalizing on that good faith. Three hundred thousand votes could have defeated Mr. Roosevelt in New York State. A half million Italians were registered. Similar conditions existed in other close states. Mussolini knew it. He had planned for another Gayda coup like the Home Fleet.

Il Duce chooses his men well. No man is more admirably fitted to be Italy's fresh kid than Virginio Gayda. He has worked in every European country and possesses the richest experience of any newspaperman living. After his graduation in the economic sciences from the University of Turin, he was chosen by the liberal organ, *La Stampa*, to travel through Eastern and Central Europe. He trekked through Austria, Serbia, Turkey, and the Balkans and witnessed the rising tide of Slav hate against the Central Empires culminating in the assassination at Sarajevo.

His dispatches were greatly admired throughout Italy so that at the outbreak of the first World War he was appointed by Italy's most powerful newspaper, *Il Corriere della Sera*, of Milan, to represent it in Russia. When Italy entered the war in 1915, his government made him intelligence officer in the embassy at Petrograd, now Leningrad.

He saw the complete collapse of the Russian Empire and was a witness to the Revolution of February, 1917. Terrifying scenes came before his eyes in October of that year. He saw hundreds of thousands of soldiers without discipline and in revolt. They sold their arms and their uniforms for bread or vodka. Thousands of young Russian women became their prey often at the point of the bayonet. Gayda followed the chaos which culminated in the seizure of Petrograd by the Soviets and saw the birth of the Soviet regime.

When the World War ended, he was transferred to London, resuming his newspaper work as the correspondent of *Il Corriere della Sera*. His brilliance in international affairs recommended him to *Il Messaggero* of Rome. He was offered the management of the paper. He accepted. When Mussolini assumed power in 1922, *Il Messaggero* was a mild supporter but when Fascist interests acquired *Il Giornale d'Italia*, Gayda became the editor and has occupied that post ever since.

His first-hand experience in every European country and his thorough knowledge of international affairs make him ideal for a living Charlie McCarthy for Il Duce. From his daily columns, the world's correspondents glean the news that Italy wants to give. It is a big man's job though he must act as the little man. Besides, he writes magazine articles and broadcasts. It would seem that his true profession is only his hobby, for in the odd moments he turns to his bread and butter job which is that of managing *Il Giornale d'Italia*. For this and many other things, he is personally responsible to the Fascist regime.

His sports are limited. He climbs the Alps and Apennines. Neither golf nor tennis have ever attracted him. He plays a smart bridge hand. His presence is always sought at diplomatic dinners as the most desirable and most interesting man in the whole of Rome. He is invited everywhere, accepts wherever his whim dictates. His five languages — English, Italian, French, German and Russian — enable him to get around to everybody. He can read the press comment of the world in its original form and from the original newspapers. He needs no translators.

His mildness of manner contrasts sharply with his clarion blasts in the newspapers of the world. In conversation, he talks with a suave intonation. Never does he burst out in cataclysmic emphasis. His gestures are few. He is accustomed to sit in one chair for an entire evening and narrate for hours at a time. Telling things is his great art.

His articles are all well organized and bolstered with facts, both historical and statistical. From two to four columns a day is a test for any man especially since his themes demand so much background, such thorough research and mathematical precision. From his long and flowing phrases, the correspondents pick out the most pointed. When these are cabled to the four corners of the earth, they give even a greater impression of his directness and pungency.

He is a greying blond and his physical movements are neither vivacious nor slow. They are just normally timed. Though he is fifty-four, he looks forty-four. Physically, his medium stature has maintained a meager and unchanging girth—thirty-two. The skinny frame gives him the aspect of an ascetic. His face is brightened by a natural geniality. He would adorn with consummate perfection a professorial chair in any university.

His mental processes have been accelerated by years of mental toil. His mind springs like that of a young and brilliant lawyer leaping to instant rebuttal against the retorts of an adversary.

There is little wonder that Mussolini chose him as his Charlie McCarthy. When statesman and journalist sit across the desk from one another, the dictator is enthralled with the masses of information at his puppet's command. Il Duce tells him with what nations he desires friendship. For this, the little man turns on the warmth. He possesses the feel of the susceptibilities of peoples. When he is told to hate, he likewise serves his master well. He can play upon all those historical and racial animosities which poison the air to bitterness. Mussolini has but to name the nation. Gayda knows all the answers—why it should be loved, why it should be hated. He can love the United States, England, Germany, France or Russia with the same fervor that he can hate them. To him, it makes little difference which is scheduled for odium or embrace.

His success as the stentorian dummy of Il Duce is proved by the world-wide authority of his words. Singlehanded he fooled the British taxpayers and sent the Home Fleet from the Mediterranean. He saved the

Italian navy. He helped win the Ethiopian war. There are few newspapers in civilization which have not quoted Gayda. Our own press pays the cable tolls and gives him the front page. He tells us whom to elect as President, what laws to pass, who our friends must be, where we may go and why we should not arm. He needs only a few to believe him and his work is done. We pay to be confused, and democratic confusion is perhaps the dictator's greatest weapon.

CHAPTER XII

ONE GRAND MOMENT

There were four billion lire in gold in the Bank of
Italy on January 1, 1935. Mussolini could have got a
quarter billion of gold dollars for them if he wished.
In strict propriety, the gold was there as a guarantee of
Italian paper money. It was the right way to guarantee
paper money. But Germany had learned to do without
gold and had printed money on faith. Italy, too, could
print money on faith and use the gold to buy oil, steel,
trucks, munitions from countries who would not take
paper. With men and arms Italy could seize lands and
become an empire.

This was an old Mussolini dream. He talked of empire from the time he got to power. Others held the
lands and an Italian empire seemed like reaching for
the moon. He thought of Anatolia in Turkey. He
might be able to beat the Turks. He thought of Tunisia. He could not beat the French. Finally, he
thought of Ethiopia. He could beat the Ethiopians.

It made little difference that he had signed a treaty
with France and England guaranteeing the independence of Ethiopia. It made little difference either that
as early as 1924, he had personally welcomed swarthy
Haile Selassie, then crown prince of the dusky land,
to Rome. King Victor, too, greeted this tawny heir-
apparent in the royal waiting room at the station, carpeted, beflagged and gay with cuirassed guards of

honor. In the palace, the tapestries, the gold plate and the golden liveries were all brought out to make his highness feel a sovereign.

Mussolini, too, sponsored the entrance of Ethiopia into the League of Nations against the protest of Great Britain, which then maintained that its dark and savage population was not ready for international jousting. When Haile Selassie was finally crowned Emperor of Ethiopia, Lion of Judah and King of Kings, on October 7, 1928, Il Duce sent the Duke of Abruzzi, uncle of Victor, to Addis Ababa to attend the coronation and to present as a mark of Italian admiration a brand new modern tank, which the crowned one naively accepted as a token of Mussolini sincerity. On August 2, 1928, Il Duce, as a promotion scheme for Italo-Ethiopic love, signed a treaty of "friendship, arbitration and conciliation" with the ebon King of Kings. To celebrate this final act of eternal betrothal, he dispatched to His Ethiopic Majesty the highest decoration within the prerogative of the Italian crown, the Collar of the Most Holy Annunciation. This supreme mark of affection automatically raised the Lion of Judah to the rank of cousin to King Victor. They were pals.

But in 1935 with four billion lire in gold in the bank, the lands of Cousin Haile Selassie sprawled invitingly at Italy's feet. Il Duce scanned to see if anyone was looking. It was three times the size of Italy. The idea burned in him. Empire was there. He kept repeating it to himself. He dragged out the old argument — Italy was overcrowded and must have living space. He did not say that he was doing all he could to increase Italy's population and thus make his problem the more acute. The real worry was what England and France would say. He had signed that treaty, yes. Now he wanted to possess the land he had declared independent. He had sworn friendship with Haile Selassie and now lust to crush the chief filled his mind and body. He laughed it off. World opinion is a rag doll, he said. Treaties are not eternal, he proclaimed.

Stealthily, he approached France. Conveniently, it was Pierre Laval who was French foreign minister. Those there were who knew that Laval was "slippery as an eel, wily as a fox and shifty as a broody hen." Frenchmen had said that his name read the same backwards as well as forwards and, for that reason, you could never tell in what direction he was looking, much less where he was going. He was perhaps the right man for Il Duce in this shady deal. They met in Rome in January, 1935. Closeted in Venice palace, they agreed. No one knew it then. We know it now. France would close an eye to Il Duce's grab of Ethiopia. Il Duce would forget Tunis. Laval was quick to seize the advantage. Mussolini would be placated without any cost to France. He would regard France a friend for helping him. They did not tell their secret to the British. With French support, Il Duce could defy England.

He could not ask directly for Ethiopia because the British would promptly say there was a treaty. He popped the question first by requesting a discussion of African affairs. The British were perplexed. He met with Ramsay MacDonald, who was then British prime minister, and Sir John Simon, British foreign minister, in Stresa, on picturesque Lake Maggiore. Etienne Flandin, prime minister of France, was there and so was Laval. The meeting aimed primarily and indeed urgently to unite them all in what they called the Stresa front against the threat in evidence by the ominous signs of German rearmament. Il Duce said he would unite but wanted to talk about Africa, too. The British replied that they all must be sure of Europe — Africa could take its turn. Telepathy recorded a wink between Laval and Il Duce.

He took the British evasion as a refusal. He expected it for he had already been making plans. Laval's silent approval put France against England. He enjoyed it. Two months previously, he had sent out General Emilio De Bono, "Little Beard," to organize the campaign against his friend whom he had made a cousin of King Victor. He had already begun to call the black monarch a barbarian and slave dealer. Craftily, any signs of too much military activity he tried to conceal. He gave "Little Beard" a civilian title of high commissioner of Italian East Africa. "Little Beard" was to organize their own colony. The troops he began sending were only a garrison, he said.

He had begun to stir up a warlike spirit at home. This was no easy task. The Italians did not want war. Everyone said so openly at the risk of being clapped into jail. The Italian general staff did not want war. The officers also talked openly even though they faced a summary court-martial. He was keeping the idea of invasion of Ethiopia a cagy and vague project. Marshal Badoglio, chief of the general staff, did not actually know what was intended by the movements of troops until one of his officers told him that the Ministry of Colonies had requested these reinforcements. The staff officer then added that Il Duce was going to invade Ethiopia. Badoglio was enraged.

"As long as I am chief of the general staff," he thundered, "I shall condemn this mad scheme."

For this expedition, De Bono was Il Duce's confidant. He always said yes.

But the preparations became so formidable that Great Britain was finally suspicious. So many Italian soldiers and so many cannon were passing through the Suez Canal that they knew it was not just an ordinary exercise. They began to try to win Mussolini over. They offered him a piece of their own East African colonies. Anthony Eden, who was then British foreign secretary, made a trip to Rome to persuade Mussolini not to go to war.

"We must have living room," replied Mussolini as he sat across the desk from Eden in Venice palace. "You offer me a piece of Somaliland. Thank you. I am not a collector of deserts."

"But this will be a costly campaign in money and blood," said Eden.

"Italy is a nation on the march," replied Mussolini, coming out from diplomatic calm to sword-rattling bluster. He pounded his fist upon the desk. He threw back his head and stiffened his jaw.

"Italy is prepared," he continued, glaring straight at Eden.

He reached for the electric buttons on his desk.

"Look here," he declared. "I press this button and eight million bayonets are ready for attack. I press this button and five thousand airplanes take the sky. I press this one and the whole of the Italian navy of three hundred warships steams for battle."

Eden was amused at the blustering though naive boast.

"And excellency," replied the British foreign secretary calmly, "which one do you press when you want a glass of lemonade?"

There was a dead silence. Eden burst into laughter.

You cannot laugh at Il Duce. The interview was rudely over. He pouted and refused to attend a dinner that evening to which he himself had invited Eden.

But he had to get Ethiopia, and on the cheap. Of course soldiers are plentiful enough in Italy but it was equipment which was going to cost, and even though he had a quarter of a billion dollars in the bank it was not much as military things go. Some told him it would take a billion dollars cold. He recruited a number of explorers, veterans of African campaigns and former African colonial administrators. These were to go into Ethiopia with presents and money. He coined for this purpose hundreds of thousands of Abyssinian talers, a silver piece worth about fifty cents and used as money there. The recruits should pick out the powerful chiefs, buy them off and, if possible, get them to fight on the Italian side.

This could not be done in a day, since such genteel and slippery work succeeds best with a fine and velvety hand. If too precipitous it often meets a scornful though perhaps reluctant refusal. One must drink a cup of Turkish coffee before talking about money. One must drink two or three or many more before even hinting at disloyalty to the Emperor.

It was, however, much cheaper to have patience and to induce a chief to accept even fifty thousand dollars to get his defection and his warriors. It would save four or five times that amount in military stores and munitions. Oftentimes a thousand did the trick. The biggest bag was Ras Gugsa, a cousin of Haile Selassie, and his twenty thousand mad and terrible nomads. He was purchased for a few thousand dollars, an Italian general's uniform and a red and white Italian sash across his breast.

At home, Il Duce was beginning to change stealth to open enthusiasm. He worked it artificially though with skillful mob technique. He created reasons why the British should be hated. They ate five meals a day. Their troops travelled in passenger coaches. They were fat and decadent. They had no military prowess and could not fight like the Italians. He told his people in the press and over the radio that Ethiopia was a rich, rich land. Gold was there. It had oil, coal, timber, cattle, wheat, coffee and cotton — all the things which Italy needed. The newspapers announced thousands of volunteers but these were recruited from the prisons where freedom was purchased by enlistment. It looked as if everyone was going. What a chance for Italy!

For five months troops and materials were shipped to

"Little Beard" in a steady stream. By August, an army of 200,000 with a thousand airplanes, three thousand trucks, four hundred tanks and two thousand cannon had reached the colony which was to be the jumping-off place for the invasion. With such a powerful force, the morale of the troops was the highest. It was naturally high when they had the odds on their side. They knew the Ethiopians had neither airplanes, tanks nor cannons. This force was going to pay back the Ethiopians for the beating they gave an Italian army at Adowa in 1896.

The whole campaign became a gay enterprise in a promised land. In fact, Vittorio Mussolini, as an aviator, said that it was great fun to drop bombs on defenceless Ethiopians, a statement which he has found very hard to live down. With this great force, fatly fed and strongly armed, "Little Beard" kept the gaiety going. If he could not give orders with a smile he did not give orders at all. He was everybody's friend. One would have thought him more of a politician seeking votes rather than a commander ordering men into battle. An officer he addressed as "My dear," and a soldier as "Little Boy." The corps and division commanders did practically as they pleased, pretty sure to get "Little Beard's" kind word that everything was all right in Italian East Africa as long as the four billion lasted and the King of Kings had no cannon, airplanes or tanks.

The campaign could only move between October and June because during the rest of the year Ethiopia is a mud swamp from the torrential rains. To start the shooting, some reason had to be trumped up. It would not be to the honor of an officer and a gentleman to give battle without being worked up.

King Victor's dusky cousin was finally charged with committing outrage. This outrage — of which he knew nothing — was a planted border raid at Wal-Wal where several Italian black troops were killed. The Ethiopians were accused before the whole world as flagrantly and willfully threatening the security of the Italian colony. At home, a lot of righteous indignation followed. All Italians, however, understood that the first bloody deed done, the best way was to possess Ethiopia as quickly and cheaply as possible. Everybody was happily worked up now.

Mussolini gave the word on October 2, and "Little Beard" ordered his magnificent army across the border into the new empire. But things did not go as well as was figured. The giant forces were stymied by an unexpected resistance and by many slips in the organization. "Little Beard's" left flank was disconnected.

While this was going on, the British sent their Home Fleet into the Mediterranean. It was intended as a shake of the British fist. It would have been quite possible for the British Navy to have stopped the war at any moment. It was only necessary for them to close the Suez Canal. Italian lines of communication would have been broken.

It was an anxious moment for Mussolini. Outwardly he kept up a very gay personal front. He was gayer than on any of the best days of his regime. He desired above all to act confident. Your reporter saw him very frequently. The dictator's head might have been buried in his hands.   Instead, he was daily out riding, swimming and making personal appearances, playing the theatricals of sure success.

"How can you do it?" I asked in some wonderment.

"This is my strength," he boasted, gesticulating with his arms to show even the outward evidences of physical health.   He smiled as if there truly was nothing on his mind.

But while he was undoubtedly worrying about what the British fleet was going to do, he received word through the Italian intelligence service that this great armada had only carried enough supplies for a two-week cruise and that the ships were practically unarmed, equipped with little or nothing in firing power.   This was news.   There was nothing to fear now.   Supplies and men continued to go to Ethiopia for he knew then that Britain would not fire a shot.   Now, the gay and carefree humor was more than a mask.   It was real delight.

But "Little Beard" continued to make a bad job of it. It was critical.   The only man Mussolini could call upon with any hope of changing defeat into victory was he who had stigmatized the whole thing mad and had been ignored.   Preferring success to pride, Mussolini asked Badoglio to straighten out the muddle.   As a true soldier, the chief of staff smothered his own convictions and obeyed.   More troops and supplies were sent to reinforce the beaten armies.   "Little Beard" was relieved but to hide defeat, Mussolini promoted him to the rank of field-marshal as a token "of his having completed" the first phase of the expedition.

Badoglio reorganized the forces and changed the whole plan of the campaign. His tactics and strategy are studied today as a great military achievement. Luck played its part, too, for Haile Selassie instead of fighting a guerilla war chose to fight in the European fashion, a method with which he and his sooty and nude savages were disastrously unfamiliar. The Italians, in contrast to their boast of culture, used gas on the valiant though hopelessly unprotected blacks. In the debacle which was impending, Haile Selassie fled the country and sought refuge in Palestine. Then the way was easy for Italian empire.

While all this was happening, the League of Nations faced the painful dilemma of ignoring the war or having a showdown. One member of the league had attacked another member of the league and this was not league sportsmanship by Rule 16. What could the members do? The regulations only provided one method and that prescribed that all the members should band together to boycott the commerce of a bully. It was called sanctions. Mussolini kept telling the league that the clause was obsolete and again that "treaties were not eternal." But it took more than an argument to convince anyone. By this time, he had massed four hundred thousand troops in Eritrea.

The League therefore decided on a showdown. It voted the boycott. Fifty-two nations ceased all trading with Italy — more or less. By this method, they thought they would be able to prevent continuance of the war. Nothing came from England, France, Belgium, Norway, Sweden and supposedly all the members of the

League. It seemed to be a big blow. But appearances deceived. Mussolini exploited this event to stir all Italians to the cruelty of an unjust, unforgiving and misunderstanding world.

And despite this economic ostracism, no one suffered in Italy. Some specialty articles were missing like English woolens, French perfumes and Dutch cheese but they were all things which the grand mass could easily get along without. Where the pinch came was in the heavier goods, in raw materials and munitions. These Italy needed and these too she obtained. Germany came showing samples of steel, guns, machinery and chemicals — anything. What she did not get from Germany she easily obtained from the United States — oil, trucks, foodstuffs.

And did he not capitalize on the sanctions? November 18 was placed on the calendar as a black day. Sanctified as a "Lest We Forget," it was posted up on placard and billboard as the day when Italy fought the whole world. Just as our merchants invite customers to shop early by posting up the days before Christmas so his propagandists posted up each day the number of days that Italy had lived against the "tyranny of the League of Nations." It was a proud boast since they were beating the boycott. Nothing was said of the great American and German leak. The gold in the bank, however, was going.

American operators had a chance to sell oil. They would never willfully jilt the goddess of opportunity, our national heroine. Italy was filled with all kinds of these petroleum vendors, including the much publicized

William Rhodes Davis, who gained the front pages in January, 1941, by being reputed to have brought a peace treaty to America from Germany. Davis tried to sell a process of converting pitch into gasoline. There are great pitch beds in Sicily. The Italian military men were ready to listen to him, but there was always a question of finances which the Italians found difficult to concede. Besides, we sold Italy three or four thousand trucks and quantities of raw materials all paid for in the gold which was taken from the bank.

The Germans came with whatever else Italy wanted. They were paid partly in gold, but they would accept fruits, olive oil, silks and sulphur as well. It was a great lift to Mussolini. In fact, it was this great German and American help which completely nullified any effect the sanctions of the other fifty-two nations were inflicting on Il Duce's war effort.

What happened? From that moment on, the great friendship of Italy for Germany began. Hitler forgot that Mussolini had called him names. They now began to appreciate one another as if their mutual affection had been lying dormant and unknown. This was official. The inherent antipathy of the Italian for the German and the deep-seated mistrust of Teuton for Latin were smothered in "common aims, common culture and common systems." Officially, they were friends. Officially, that friendship grew. Officially, it led to the Rome-Berlin axis.

But the glorious day when victory smiled upon Italian arms approached. Badoglio at the head of his vast army entered Addis Ababa on May 5. For Il Duce, the anxious hour when he could reach for the empire about which he had dreamed but thought that only by colossal luck would he ever achieve had truly arrived. Whether Ethiopia was worth anything or not made little difference. Italy had seized a country ruled by an emperor. Empire at last was an Italian reality.

The nation's entire radio chain was ordered hooked-up. Newspapers and broadcasters announced that Il Duce would speak to the people of Italy from the dictatorial balcony of Venice palace at seven o'clock sharp on the evening of May 9, 1936. Every citizen of true Italian faith must listen. To insure that no one would miss the visual manufacture of history, the church bells would ring summoning every man, woman and child into the public squares where loud speakers would blare the birth of empire.

On that buoyant May evening, multi-multitudes of Romans massed into Venice square. It was filled an hour before history was expected. Hundreds of thousands crammed the approaches. Even *they* were buoyed with fervor because the loud speakers would bring them the epochal event. Cheering and band playing blasted the heavens. Cheering and band playing were blasting the heavens in all the cities, towns and villages of Italy. Everyone knew and burned with pride that imperial nativity was at hand.

With what superb hauteur Il Duce walked his spacious office, the Mappa Mondo (Map of the World) salon, that evening, awaiting the stroke of seven, we can only surmise. He looked at the huge mosaic of this planet along the entire west wall. It is the masterpiece after which the salon was named. We can be permitted to think without much risk of contradiction that he expanded both chest and head. He had conquered an empire. And more, if one empire can be conquered, why not two or three? Why not? The world was before him. Again, he looked at the map of the world. He could not help it.

The hour of seven struck. The moment! He marched out on the balcony which opened from the salon. The cheering was tumultuous. He stood with a haughty stance akimbo. He raised his hand for silence. They cheered. He raised his hand again. They still cheered. The thrill was electric. He knew a greater thrill was to come. He began to speak. They still cheered. He could not continue. He beckoned for silence. It was coming. Finally, an anxious hush cleared the way for the grand moment.

Filling his lungs, he shouted out the ecstatic news.

"Officers, non-commissioned officers and men of all the armed forces of the State in Africa and in Italy, Blackshirts of the Revolution, Italians both men and women at home and in the whole world, Listen!" he said.

There was a breathless silence. He paused.

"By decisions which later on you will learn and which were approved by the Grand Council of Fascism," he cried out, "a great event is fulfilled. The destiny of Ethiopia has just been sealed, today, May 9, fourteenth year of the Fascist Era.

"All knots were cut by our shining sword and the African victory will remain in the history of the Father-

land, united and pure as the glorious soldiers, dead and
living, dreamed and wished it."

Now he made a long pause. One could see by the
raising of his diaphragm that something was coming.

"Italy finally has her empire," he thundered, loud
and emphatic.

It was the grand moment. The thousands exploded.
He waved. It was his supreme hour. It was his greatest glory. He waved again. Excited hearts awaited
with suspended breath. He had more to say. He motioned for silence again.

"Here are the laws, O Italians," he proclaimed as a
High Priest from an Aztec altar, "which close one period
of our history and open another as an immense passage-
way to all the possibilities of the future :

"The territories and inhabitants belonging to the Empire of Ethiopia are placed under the full and entire
sovereignty of the kingdom of Italy.

"The title of Emperor of Ethiopia is assumed for himself and his successors by the King of Italy."

Wild shouts reverberated through the square. He
had appointed an emperor. But he had not finished.

"The Italian people has created the Empire with its
own blood," he continued. "It will fructify it with its
work and will defend it against any power whatsoever
with its arms. In this supreme certainty, raise on high
your emblems, your arms and your hearts to salute after
fifteen centuries the reappearance of the Empire on the
fateful hills of Rome."

Then he interposed a rhetorical question.

"Will you be worthy of it ?" he cried out.

The great mass responded with a devastating and unanimous "Yes."

"Your cries are like a sacred oath," he concluded, "which binds you before God and before men, for life and death. Salute the King."

He lifted his hand in the Fascist salute and then withdrew into the palace. The crowd broke out into vociferous outbursts which he answered by repeated returns to the balcony and repeated salutes.

The whole of Italy applauded him. Every Italian rejoiced. Italy finally had her empire.

It was the grand moment.

But the four billion lire in gold were all gone now.

Italy was broke.

Italy was an empire

Mussolini head

CHAPTER XIII

ALLAH IN A BLACK SHIRT

The gold was gone but the world was big. The one grand moment had excited Il Duce to bigger empire. If money were needed, use paper. He could print it; many would take it.

He said that he wanted Tunisia, Corsica, Nice and Savoy. Both France and England offered to do something for him. It was not enough, he said. Il Duce desired much more. What he coveted was the vast Moslem empire to the South and East, from Morocco to the Himalayas. The Roman eagle would then spread its wings over 4,000,000 square miles and dominate 300,000,000 souls faithful to the Prophet.

Il Duce had been working on this, another of his extravagant dreams, for fifteen years — boring, intriguing, bribing and flattering. He boasted big armies to everybody and especially to the sons of Islam. He thought them mystified by military might, particularly Fascist might. His own "fifth columns" ballyhooed him as an invincible warrior through Egypt, Arabia, Syria, Palestine, the Sudan, Tunisia, Algeria, Morocco, Iraq, Persia, Afghanistan and even India and Turkey. He aimed to supplant France and England there.

Every international event was exploited by his wily agents to show the "weakness" and even "perfidy" of the French and British as contrasted with the "power" and "magnanimity" of Imperial Italy. Much of it was undercover penetration but by far the greater effort was visible in the press and very audible on the radio. Besides, under Italian direction the organization of Nationalist groups with anti-French and anti-British programs proceeded without interference in practically every Moslem country or protectorate. The Italians swapped Trojan for Arab horses.

In the grand manner, he thought he could stagger the Moslems when he promoted Victor Emmanuel III from *rex* to *imperator*. He counted that the defeat of Ethiopia's Christian ruler — albeit his own was Christian, too — would lift him in the minds of the Moslems to divine honors. Somewhat impetuously, he proclaimed himself "Protector of Islam," and staged an investiture.

Contrasted with the elaborate ceremony of the coronation of the Sultan in old Constantinople, when the shining sword of the Caliph studded with diamonds was unsheathed in the mosque of St. Sophia, the show was drab. Il Duce decided to use a sword, too. He bought it in Florence with government funds. The unromantic public square of Tripoli, capital of his North African provinces, was chosen for the great induction. Local Jewish jewelers incised a few Arabic designs on the sword.

The Protector-elect mounted an Arab charger and awaited the approach of two hundred mounted Lybian chiefs. The first carried the sword, which had only that moment been handed to him by Marshal Italo Balbo, the governor of Lybia, to present to Il Duce. It had no diamonds. One had to economize now. When

the chief got near enough, he passed the weapon to I
Duce much as if it were an umbrella.

Italian carabineers called for silence. A large space
was cleared about the Duce's charger. "Attention
Mussolini speaks," they said.

"Mohammedans," he shouted, rising in the saddle
"You have presented me the most acceptable of all gift
— this sword, symbol of force and justice."

He proclaimed it in Italian as if he were haranguing
his own meek Fascist cronies. Few of the Arabs under
stood, which made little difference anyway since none
of them had given him the sword.

"Fascist Italy," he continued, resting the weapon up
right on the horse's trappings, "wishes to prove its fel
lowship with Islam and its sympathy with the Moslem
of the whole world. Before long, Rome will show you
with her laws how she cares for your increasingly greater
destiny."

This did not go over since every Mohammedan at
tributes all good to Allah and none to "a dog of a Chris
tian." The absence of applause was explained in that
it was not an Islamic custom.

But, unsheathing the sword, he raised it straight
above his head.

"Mohammedans," he cried out with terrifying power
"Spread these my words in all the homes of your cities
and your villages even to the last shepherd's tent. You
know that I am a man sparing in promises but when
promise, I fulfill."

No applause, no congratulations. A band played the
Fascist march, "Youth! Youth! Spring of beauty!"

Ironical as it may seem he offered to become protector
of the Holy Places in Jerusalem as well. He thought
the generous gesture would please the Church. He
never saw any incompatibility with carrying water on
both shoulders providing he could get anyone to believe that the pails were full. The gesture was pleasing
but the protectorship of Islam was not, however, to go
unreproved. The Vatican did not like it.

"A Catholic power," said Pius XI to a group of pilgrims, "should not be the protector of the infidel."

The Mussolini Moslem empire was not unlike the
Kaiser's contemplation of Berlin to Bagdad or the *Drang
Nach Osten*. Germany, too, had a hand in this objec-
tive. The Kaiser used Turkey as his wedge to get to the
Indian Ocean. Turkey is not available for the project
today. In the German hope, Italy took the place of
Turkey. The fact is that both axis powers wanted the
same thing.

German projects paralleled Italian hopes also with
regard to Spain. The Italians placed great confidence
in the strategic value of the Balearic Isles as air bases in
the Western Mediterranean. The German plan included them for annexation to Italy. Franco did not
see it that way.

While the German general staff planned all the
moves, certain definite objectives were given to the Italians. The conquest of the keys and of vital naval and
air bases were assigned to Italy because she alone had
a fleet and was supposed to enjoy a much boasted air
superiority over British aviation in the Mediterranean.

"Italy," said the *Deutsche Wehr*, the German military organ, "is the naval force of *Mitteleuropa* in the Mediterranean. Enormous and even Napoleonic tasks are assigned to her in this conquest."

Italy's own strategic problem was not a simple matter. Sea, land and air power were all necessary in this mastodonic campaign. It was necessary to keep three expeditionary forces in operation. One would operate from the Aegean Islands, another from Lybia and a third from Ethiopia. These would converge for the possession of the Suez Canal and the conquest of Egypt.

The biggest task was to be assigned to Marshal Balbo. He had been in training ever since he was transferred from the air service to the colonies. Two divisions of native troops were a part of his usual garrison with ten divisions of regulars. Balbo had been allowed to conduct his own maneuvers using mechanized units and airplanes of all types for the great blow against Suez. But he quarreled with Il Duce in the summer of 1940 and was tragically, though according to some conveniently, killed in an airplane accident. He was fleeing the dictatorial wrath to Egypt, it was said. Marshal Rodolfo Graziani replaced him.

Even more important than the military organization was the political and diplomatic preparation. It was cheaper. It was precisely where the Italians believed they could outwit the British.

The fifth columns built by Italian agents in the Moslem countries surpassed anything yet attempted even by the Germans. The Trojan horses in Norway, Denmark and Holland were mere hobby horses compared to the Italian contraptions in Egypt, Iraq, Pales-

ine and Arabia. They perpetrated their acts practically in the open. They operated in large numbers
and with extensive means. No barrier was placed
against them as the British naively conceived them as
welfare organizations, hospital associations, schools or
sports societies. They apparently had a perfect right
to exist. Concurrently, in high places, Italian money —
paper money, of course — and honors were doing some
strategic work.

Through native organizations, in the Arab press or on
the radio, the Italian government endeavored to make
common cause with these Moslem millions. Members
of the Duce's diplomatic service, special propaganda
promoters and writers, tried to show how Italy, like the
Arabs, was robbed by the "robber power," England.
This should be a common bond to fight the common
oppressor.

Italian agents contrasted British treatment with the
administration of their own colonies. In Lybia they
said everything was roseate and prosperous. They
flooded the Moslem countries with millions of pamphlets
showing pictures of aqueducts, reservoirs, hospitals,
railroads and schools to prove how much better off they
would be under Italian rule than under the British.
They insisted that relations between Italians and Arabs
were the sweetest. When the Arabs reminded them of
the Senussite massacre in 1927, Italians replied that
Senussi who headed that tribe was a tyrant and oppressor. The native response was that that was exactly
why Senussi had opposed Italian rule — the Italians had
made them slaves.

It was true that while the World War was bein
fought, Italy lost complete control of her African colc
nies principally because her military units were neede
elsewhere. The result was that many tribes defied th
power of the Italian governors in Lybia and Cirenaic;
The colonial ministry succeeded in holding on but the
granted practically every Arab demand. Italy was abl
to hold only the coastline. The interior was under th
domination of the tribal chiefs.

When Mussolini came to power, he decided to sul
due these insurgents. He appointed Graziani, who the:
was a subordinate commander, to rid the colony of th
rebels. The vigor and energy with which this was don
has few parallels in modern colonial history. Whil
villages were burned and sacked, a reign of terror sprea
over all the territory of effective occupation. The popu
lation of Lybia decreased in these four years from a mi
lion to 600,000.

When peace was restored, concessions were made t
the now docile population. The lands confiscated fror
the rebels were parceled out to obedient natives wh
promised to bring it to a full state of cultivation. ,
policy of conciliation which was designed to elevate
Duce as the "Protector of Islam" was followed. Mea
ures were taken against the Jews. Five were flogge
in the public square as a living manifestation that Ital
was the friend of the Arab and the enemy of the Jev
An anti-Semitic policy has prevailed ever since th;
time.

By 1935, conciliation had succeeded so far that Lyb

ent two divisions of native troops to fight in the war in
Ethiopia.

And the maximum respect was ordered paid by officials and the military forces to the Moslem religion.
The mosques were especially guarded. Italians were
warned never to do any act which might be interpreted
as a desecration of the sacred places. They were required to cross the street when they drew near to a
mosque so that they would not contaminate even the
approaches to the edifice. Occasionally, there were
signs in Italian warning any chance strollers that they
had better not soil a holy place with "their Christian
feet."

In his many visits to the Lybian colony, Mussolini
has been meticulous in his observance of Moslem ceremony. He was received in the chief mosque of Tripoli
but was careful to put on a pair of slippers over his shoes
at the door so that as an infidel he would not desecrate
the sacred floor. The local Moslem chiefs were present
to receive him but he was accompanied by no entourage
except the governor. The chiefs were silent, bestowing
that stoic Arab smile which is difficult to believe a smile
at all.

Beyond Lybia lies Egypt. More effort and money
were expended on Egypt than on any other country.
It is a great prize, with its riches in grain and cotton, its
Suez Canal and its position as the gateway between
East and West.

Egypt's precautionary spy hunt and fifth column

purge before the Italian declaration of war was under
way came a little late. Already 60,000 Italians were
resident in Egypt as a well-disciplined, well-organized
and well-equipped contingent of the Trojan horse
Egypt, too, feared a blitzkrieg, since the Lybian armies
of Balbo had been practising marches into Egypt for
seven years — with tanks, airplanes and cooperating sea
force.

Here fifth column activities exploited the cultural
economic and political ties. Italy was able to place
many Fascists in key positions in the government service
because of a long tradition of Italian learning. Besides
there were Italian physical directors, doctors, lawyer
and engineers. Slowly the government of Rome hoped
to supplant all the British civil servants with Italians es
pecially at the expiration of the Anglo-Egyptian treaty
of alliance in 1958.

Italian government funds helped in financing such
Egyptian newspapers as *Al Difaa, Al Makathan, L*
Patrie and *El Ahren*. The latter has the largest circula
tion of any Arabic newspaper in the Near East. It i
owned by Syrian Catholics. *Al Difaa* was able to ac
quire its own presses and an entire publishing plan
through Italian generosity. *Al Makathan* all of a sud
den became wildly anti-French. *La Patrie*, a French
language newspaper owned by Greeks, developed into
an out-and-out Fascist propaganda sheet.

These newspapers also received large display adver
tisements from Italian steamship lines, insurance com
panies and banks, all of which were operated under gov
ernment control. Subsidies direct to the newspaper

themselves passed through the Italo-Egyptian bank. I was told by one of the bank officials that $60,000 monthly was distributed to Egyptian newspapers purely as a gratuity.

The Italians also worked with the Germans. Following Herr Goebbels' visit in the spring of 1939, German agents passed $200,000 to Italian and Egyptian pro-Fascist agents for use in anti-British and anti-French propaganda. The chief Egyptian in these efforts was Ahmen Hussein, leader of the Egyptian green shirts, a native Fascist organization.

Hussein visited Mussolini in Rome. On his return to Egypt he announced to his followers that there was only one path for all Egyptians, the path which Italy had mapped out against England.

"What have these democracies done for their peoples?" asked Hussein at a public meeting. "Hitler and Mussolini have given their citizens order and prosperity."

Every Italian of the 60,000 resident in Egypt was required to become a member of one of the numerous Fascist groups, such as the Action squads, the Balilla, the After-Work Association, the Fascist Youth or the Feminine organizations. Many were born in Egypt so that they know the Egyptian mentality well and how to cope with it. They all attended Italian schools. Nationalism was a religion to them.

These societies were thoroughly disciplined and regimented. They held reviews frequently and were allowed the maximum freedom of action. They were sure that Italy would possess the Mediterranean. They were given maps and booklets showing the bombing distances of Cairo and Alexandria from Italian bases in the Mediterranean. From them, military lessons were learned and imperial objectives studied.

Before the outbreak of war, Balbo visiting Egypt was received in high government circles. He told Premier Mohammed Mahmud that Mussolini desired nothing more than profound friendship with the whole of Islam.

"Yes," returned the Egyptian chief of government cynically. "Just as he did with Mohammedan Albania. Our royal house is descended from a great Albanian family and we felt deeply grieved at what your leader did to that little country."

One of the foreign diplomats later asked the Prime Minister if the Balbo conversation was of any importance.

"Oh!" replied Mahmud with Oriental irony, "we just exchanged hypocrisies."

But the Egyptian government sensed Italian long-range policy. As the world situation was rolling toward its catastrophic destiny and the ties of Italy with Germany were becoming more strongly bound, Egyptian apprehension rose. Suddenly, all Italians were dismissed from the government service. Restrictions were placed upon the practice of the professions by them. Italians, too, were ordered to remain within certain territorial limits, could not move without police permission and were prohibited from visiting the Suez Canal.

There were many reasons for Egyptian hostility. No native attachment resides in an Egyptian's breast for an Italian. The religious issue was indeed strong enough. But worse, Italian small traders, professional men and

farmers constitute a deadly competition to the Egyptian.
When Italy finally went to war, they were all rounded
up and deported even as far as India.

For sheer Machiavellian realism, the strategical diplomacy of Italy in Palestine resembled a glove made of
crocodile and lined with fur, smooth on the inside and
rough on the outside; smooth in dealing with the intricate and labyrinthian ways of the Arab and rough in
challenging the rule of the British.

In such delicate balancing, the greatest finesse was
used. To remain friends with the Arabs while coddling
the Roman Catholic Patriarch of Jerusalem was indeed
a skillful juggling act in which the Italians were to
keep several balls in the air at the same time. They
pleased the Arabs by being extremely antagonistic to
the Jews. They related how they had publicly flogged
Jews in Lybia and would do the same thing in Palestine
were it not for the hated British, who protected the Jews.
Britain was the worst oppressor of the Arab everywhere.

Every means possible was used to impress the Moslem. The Bari radio station in Southern Italy was trans-
mitting daily broadcasts in Arabic. The musical and
cultural programs had been especially designed to meet
the approval of Arab listeners, not alone in Palestine but
also in the whole of the Near East. Italian agents circulated amongst the Arab population recommending the
Italian radio programs for the high quality of music.
They claimed, too, that if the truth were wanted, the
Italian news broadcast was the only one to give it. The
British tried to offset the work of this radio station by
offering programs from England. The Arabs, whether

from choice or from prejudice, still listened to Bari.

During the revolts in Jerusalem from 1936 until Italy entered the war, the Italian consul-general and his staff openly encouraged the Arabs. When the British offered to protect him and the consulate, he pompously refused such protection replying that the Italian flag above the consulate and on his car was a far greater protection than any the whole British army could organize.

High Italian decorations were bestowed upon the editors of Arab newspapers. As in Egypt, lavish display advertising of Italian banks, steamship lines, insurance companies and tourist agencies appeared showing that prosperity was shining upon any of the press which reflected the Italian viewpoint in its news columns and editorials.

The Grand Mufti of Jerusalem, Hamin al Husseini, directed the Arab revolt. He received openly a monthly donation of $15,000 from Italian sources in support of the "Arab cause." In the port of Haifa, a cargo of cement from Italy after close examination proved to be a cargo of rifles, ammunition and other war material for distribution amongst the Arabs. As a token of their solidarity with the "cause," the Italian government appointed Georges Marcos, a native Arab, as consul in Jaffa.

And the fifth column had penetrated Arabia. Here the purpose had not been economic or political as was the case with Egypt and Palestine but strategical. Mussolini occupied one side of the Red Sea by his possession of Eritrea. If he could succeed in possessing the other side, or at least in dominating it, he would be fortified right across the British life-line of Empire. He could harass the southern entrance to the Suez Canal. The importance of Aden as the fortified entrance to the Red Sea now held by Britain would be nullified if a hostile power commanded both banks.

Penetration took the form of sympathizing with the aspirations of Imam Yahya, ruler of the Western slopes of Arabia and sworn enemy of the King of the Hedjaz, ruler of the rest of Arabia. Great Britain recognized Yahya's independence but insisted that he stay away from Aden. Several times he invaded the Aden protectorate and was driven off. In 1926, while one of these campaigns was proceeding, Yahya had been approached by Italian plenipotentiaries. They patted him on the back and agreed that his lot in life as a neighbor of England was a hard one. Italy had much more to offer him than the British. They were a decadent empire, always oppressed their peoples and now possessed what rightfully should belong to him, the Aden protectorate.

A treaty of "eternal friendship" was drawn up and signed by Yahya and Mussolini. The sovereign independence of Yemen was guaranteed. Italy undertook to supply Yemen with technical advisers and munitions, an omen for the further conduct of the campaign against Aden. Marauding of the Aden protectorate continued. Punitive expeditions by tanks and airplanes were still necessary and a part of British policy in protecting the southern entrance to the Red Sea.

In 1937, the treaty of "eternal friendship" was renewed. This time it was done with far more flourish

than accompanied the initial efforts of 1926. Now
Mussolini was conqueror of Ethiopia. No efforts were
spared to show the Imam that he certainly had picked
the right protector. Mussolini was the most powerful
warrior in the world and had taken only six months to
conquer the "Lion of Judah." Two brand new tanks
were transported to the Yahya's capital at Sana and
these were made the token of Il Duce's love for Yahya
as in the case of Haile Selassie. As a further sign of
the depth of the friendship, two anti-aircraft guns and
large quantities of small arms and ammunition were included in the gift. Since only British planes bombed
Yemen, the tokens were not wholly without design and
undoubtedly not entirely free from malice.

Not a single country had been neglected in this whole
Moslem belt. Even in India, the Italian youth organizations had been active amongst Indian students por-
traying how inhuman was British rule over the culture
and intelligence of India. No comparison was made
with Fascist rule over the culture and intelligence of the
Italians. In Afghanistan, Italy had been grooming
former King Amanullah, long time an exile in Rome,
to go back some day to reclaim the throne taken from
him by Habibullah Ghazi. In Syria, Iraq, Persia and
even Turkey, there was Italian penetration but not as
bold as that in Egypt and Palestine. All was within
the dream dominion of the "Protector of Islam."

But the self-proclaimed meant nothing to the Moslem
millions.

"Islam has faith in Allah," declared Mustafa el Ma-
raghi, president of the University of Cairo, the world's

largest Moslem institution of learning. "The real protector of Islam is Allah. Why is it necessary for Allah to desire protection especially from an infidel, who intends to use the devoted sons of Allah for his own purposes?"

It was really difficult for Allah to wear a black shirt with so many Arabs in white robes around.

CHAPTER XIV

SPANISH FORAY

For destitute and debt-ridden Italy to defeat productive Great Britain and France seemed fantastic and foolhardy. With Mussolini, however, it was a realistic program. Morally, he conceived them already defeated by the conquest of Ethiopia. The mighty policing power of the British fleet was a myth. France was ready prey with her vacillating governments. It was easy to outmaneuver France.

He could always annoy and wring concessions. He could annoy again and get more concessions. The road had been much easier than contemplated. The road ahead might be just as easy. What was there to fear? Neither of the rich democracies wanted war. To the East, he could upset the British and French equilibrium with revolts of the Arabs; to the West, there was a chance, a good chance. If he could inveigle Spain, a wedge would be driven. The imperial shibboleth of *Mare Nostrum* could well be raised and indeed moved to an advanced position.

We can hardly believe that in modern times, international morality had become so base that the head of one allegedly upright government, whose state was enjoying friendly relations with the great powers and was accepting their goodwill and their largesse, should at that very moment plot their downfall so deviously, East and West. And the means by which it was to be done were even less worthy. In the West, the liberal government in Spain chosen by the Spanish electorate was to be crushed by force of arms and a government favorable to Mussolini put in its place.

Spain was barely emerging from a medieval system akin to feudal overlordship. The responsibility of democratic usages was being assumed. These ways ran counter to Fascism. Morals in international dealing ran counter to Fascism. Il Duce could not freely and skillfully connive with democracy as an active accomplice. He could not inveigle democratic Spain.

He found friends in Spain. He had previously upset a liberal government in Austria and placed a Fascist government in its place. It could be done in Spain. Fascism through its revolutionary technique could do it.

The penetration into Spanish affairs began as far back as 1934. This was before he had fought the Ethiopian war. He was planning then to annoy the British and French while openly avowing a common front with them in other international affairs. Confidential diplomats, military men and even Italian clergy were sent to Spain to sound out the methods and chances of overthrowing the liberal government. These Fascist emissaries easily met willing listeners in the hidebound aristocratic class, the military caste and amongst powerful Spanish prelates. It may as well be said that they actually came to terms with General Barrera and Don Rafael Olazabel and other Spanish "traditionalists." At least, they encountered elements very amenable to agree and to do business with them.

From the very beginning, Italian arms were plentiful

in Spain. When General Francisco Franco began the insurrection on July 18, 1936, in Morocco he was supplied with Italian airplanes, rifles and ammunition. Spain had little or no air force and what existed at the time of the outbreak was in the hands of the Loyalists. The meager organization of the Spanish armed forces convinced Mussolini that any campaign he could organize in Spain would end in a cheap and quick victory. He was convinced of the efficiency of his own forces after the victory in Ethiopia and was sure that they would make a thorough liquidation of the poorly equipped and undisciplined Spanish soldiers and sailors.

He was on the way to create another Mussolini puppet in Spain. Franco readily conceded everything which would bring him the necessary supplies. Equipment in Italian arsenals which had been intended for Ethiopia and not needed there was easily diverted to Spanish ports. All the airplanes Il Duce could spare were sent. He shipped vast quantities of tanks and armored cars and thousands of trucks even before the insurrection was on the way. These were all manned by men who had received training for or in the Ethiopian campaign.

Italian air bases were established in the Balearic Isles. A very heavy air traffic developed from the Italian mainland to the island of Minorca. The organization of the expedition was proceeding on a thoroughly efficient military basis. On November 25, 1936, Mussolini issued a secret mobilization order for fifty thousand Italian troops to be sent to Franco. These were quickly assembled and the necessary transport provided. They reached their destination within three weeks.

Now while all these preparations were going on, Italy officially maintained an attitude of complete ignorance and unconcern with what was transpiring in Spain. Officially, it was announced that a policy of hands off had been adopted. Since it was definitely an internal affair for the Spanish people themselves, why should anyone interfere? And not alone were there pious manifestations of this aloofness; there were categorical announcements that there was not a single Italian regular fighting in Spain. Whenever confronted with the incontestable fact of their existence, the official answer was that these soldiers were in Spain as private volunteers and the Italian government was having nothing to do with them.

Spain became an international problem. Foreign intervention developed into an issue. The British government called for a conference in London where a non-intervention committee was established to control the shipments of arms to Spain and to guarantee that neither the Insurgents nor the Loyalists were being aided by outside governments. By this time the situation had become much more complicated because Hitler had openly supported Franco with both arms and men. On the other side, Russia was helping the Loyalists, and Leon Blum, who was then premier of France, was accused of supplying French munitions to the Spanish left.

Now in this confusion, each side openly charged the other with violating the non-intervention pact. In this charge and counter-charge, it was easy enough for Il Duce to blanket Italian participation with Franco by accusing Russia of illegal shipments. Great Britain desired to localize the conflict in order to prevent repercussions leading to a European conflict. But the British role was far too ephemeral amongst forces which acted with stark realism. When Britain demanded of Italy that non-intervention be maintained, Mussolini pointed to Russia and France and said, "Tell them."

But of all the participants, it was Mussolini who had set out with a determined and accurately planned expedition to win Spain more for Fascism than for Franco. He saw in it an effective blow to England and France. He expected the Balearic Islands to pass into Italian hands. He would thus possess air bases which diametrically crossed the French routes to North Africa. Besides he would be in easy bombing distance of Gibraltar. Other even greater possibilities he could foresee. A hostile Spain could make it extremely difficult for Great Britain to hold Gibraltar. The command of the Straits passed to whosover controlled Spain. *Mare Nostrum* was reaching reality.

While the staffs of the army, the navy and the air force had been ordered to prepare, reinforce and maintain an Italian expeditionary force in Spain, the Italian people were kept in utter ignorance of the undertaking. The Italian newspapers printed nothing about the preparations. The press maintained the Simon-pure attitude that it was an affair for Spaniards. Mussolini ordered it to play up full adherence to the London plan of non-intervention, though many reporters were either serving in Spain as soldiers or were covering the civil war as correspondents. The only references to the delivery of arms to Spain were the loud wails in editorials when a shipment of French rifles would be discovered or a Russian plane was shot down. Then the perfidy of the French and the Russians would be held to the open view of an allegedly shocked Italian public.

And during all this, the recruits intended for Ethiopia were being advised to accept service in Spain or were sent there without acceptance. Units which had returned from the colonial expedition with "such glorious achievements" wanted to go to Spain. All that was necessary was to change the insignia of their regiments in the Italian army to that of the various "Arrows" which distinguished the "volunteers" in Spain. The pay, the prospect of booty and the abundance of real or illicit romance satisfied these heroes that the Spanish expedition was a soldier's paradise. When they came home on furlough, they strutted about the streets of the large cities twiddling their swagger sticks, objects of patriotic admiration and of legitimate attraction to their own women. It was the way the populace knew that Italy was fighting in Spain. But with all these unmistakable evidences of participation, the diplomats, the foreign service, the press bureau and the newspapers claimed vociferously that Italy was above interference in Spain's internal affairs.

The fact that on November 18, 1936, the German and Italian governments, feeling that Franco was now firmly established with their help, announced the formal recognition of his rule as the *de facto* and *de jure* govern-

ment of Spain, was only a means of putting the insurgents in a slightly better light. The effective help was
already in full force and was to continue in full force
until a final victory would be achieved.

To make sure that Britishers were observing the letter
and spirit of non-intervention, the British parliament
passed the Foreign Enlistment Act which prohibited any
British subject from offering his services to a foreign government. The French government did the same.
Count Dino Grandi, Italian Ambassador to London,
promised that Italy would pass a similar measure though
he was always careful to assure everyone that officially
Italy had no soldiers in Spain.

And even while he was giving these assurances, Italian transports and supply ships were being loaded to
reinforce the expeditionary forces. The fortunes of war
had not turned rapidly enough in Franco's favor. A big
offensive was being planned to bring the fight to a quick
decision. Since Il Duce had expected a far easier campaign when he began the enterprise, he now increased
his forces and the equipment to a hundred thousand
men. He sent his best generals and assured Franco
that the victory would be theirs before the end of the
spring.

When everything was set for the final smashing
offensive, that triumphant trip through Lybia was
planned for Mussolini to proclaim himself "Protector of
Islam," though he had counted on doing it with far
more bravado than he did. He missed nothing when
he did it, but he also expected that during the trip he
would have been able to add to the claim of "Conqueror

of the Lion of Judah" that of "Master of Spain." Enroute to the solemn investiture on a new Italian cruiser, he was receiving reassuring messages that his arms were ready to deal the final blow, to break the power of Loyalist Spain and to march into Madrid and to victory over the Loyalist "outlaws."

Buoyed with imperial grandeur, he sent a message from his flagship to General Mancini, his commander-in-chief in Spain, exhorting the invincibility of Italian military power and glorifying in his complete confidence of a crushing conquest.

"I am receiving on board my Flagship *Pola* enroute to Lybia, the communiques on the great battle in progress in the direction of Guadalajara," the message ran. "I follow the fortunes of the battle with a tranquil soul. I am convinced that the enthusiasm and tenacity of our legionaries will sweep away the enemy's resistance. To defeat the international forces will be a success of the highest value, political value included. Let the legionaries know that I myself am following their action from hour to hour and that it will be crowned with victory.

Mussolini"

Guadalajara is today a name which dims the glory of Italian arms. Justly or unjustly, it is coupled with the trying disaster at Caporetto. Proudly on March 8 their swiftly moving tanks, armored cars and trucks loaded with mobile infantry numbering nine thousand men swept forward as an irresistible avalanche to open the way for the main body of the command. They captured town after town and were driving along near Guadalajara on the road to Madrid, eager to reach that much-desired city. Through stretches of undefended plain they hurtled in happy faith that victory was in sight. Snow and sleet were beginning, however, to make the going harder.

On March 11, a driving rain beat down upon their irresistible machines. Suddenly, a withering fire was opened on them, the attack of the International Brigade, composed of Americans, British, French and even anti-Fascist Italians. What appeared as an impenetrable line of moving steel floundered in confusion and in mud. The armored juggernauts were stuck. Devastating volleys from the brigade's rifles and machine-guns devoured their mobile infantry. More waves of the brigade came forward. The caravan of metal must give way. The Italian infantry turned about. The sorry remnant of the invincible column of iron was immobilized in mud. The survivors fled on their trek to the rear. Three hundred of them fell and two thousand were wounded. The way to Madrid was blocked. Crushing defeat was their fate.

Mussolini received the news. He was still conqueror of Ethiopia. He still proclaimed himself "Protector of Islam." But he was not "Master of Spain."

Italian prestige in Spain plummeted. But something had to be done to save face not so much for Franco as for Italy. The prospect of a Loyalist victory could not be tolerated. It would effectively eliminate all Italian influence in the very country Mussolini needed to advance his imperialist policy. He called for more effective help from Hitler. The Germans came. A campaign of great military precision and more rigid combat followed. They exploited the opportunity by testing the new arms they were developing in preparation for the great world conflict they had already projected. They sent dive-bombers, bombarding planes equipped with target sights, new equipment in mechanized units and heavy guns. They made the first practical tests of the weapons employed in the great mass attack on Poland on September 1, 1939.

The war went on. More campaigns were fought. Another winter came and still Madrid held out. During all the swayings of the Rebel and Loyalist armies, Mussolini still kept up his duplicity but tempered it with equivocation. After months of double dealing, of promises and unfulfilled pledges, the British were finally moved to act. Even then it was only in the diplomatic field.

Britain insisted that all Italian forces in Spain be withdrawn. They were still called volunteers even though they were equipped with such expensive military weapons as airplanes, submarines, cruisers, tanks, artillery and trucks. Italy finally agreed to withdraw her forces. For what it was worth, Mussolini reaffirmed that he had no territorial or political claims in Spain. The agreement took place in February, 1938, when the insurgents had finally struck a deathblow against the Loyalists on the Aragon front. The victory of Franco was assured. Italian troops stayed on, however, and occupied the place of honor in the great victory parades in Barcelona and in Madrid.

And then it had taken Franco until April 1, 1939, before he entered Madrid.

When it was all over and victory was won, who cared how? Mussolini was not one to hide victories. He claimed this one, too. It was not enough to have the Italians occupy the place of honor in celebrations at Barcelona and Madrid. Parades glorified the legionaires in Naples and in Rome. Il Duce made it clear that without them the Franco victory would never have been achieved.

Out in the open now came the extent of the Italian effort in Spain. In June, *Forze Armate*, the official organ of all Italian armed forces, eulogized the achievements of Italian arms and enumerated the items in the gigantic expedition undertaken to erect an Italian puppet in Spain. It especially described the efforts of the Navy, which gave the key to the Italian outlay. It said:

"For more than thirty-two months, the activity of the Royal Navy remained almost unknown. Now that the operations are over, the Navy can abandon its delicate reserve.

"To give an idea of the task to which the Navy was subjected in the period from mid-December, 1936, to mid-April, 1937, which was a period of most intense activity, it is enough to recall that in those four months about 100,000 men, 4370 motor vehicles, 40,000 tons of material and 750 cannons in 52 ships which made 132 voyages were transported to Spain. For the protection of the ships, it was necessary to employ 30 war vessels, which made 134 trips.

"Once the expeditionary corps was debarked, we were required to keep it supplied, to feed it and to assure a logistical link with Italy. This work, carried out uninterruptedly until the end of military operations, exacted an effort that can be summed up as follows:

"The number of troopships was 17. The trips made were 55; boats transporting material, 68; trips made, 134; hospital ships, 4; trips made, 29; sick and wounded transported, 14,858; war vessels employed, 40.

"Beginning Nov. 1, the war missions of legionary submarines began the task of damaging and threatening the Red supply traffic in the Mediterranean. The moral and material effect of the submarine menace was immediate. Traffic was suddenly reduced very considerably, charter and insurance rates on ships rose to the skies; routes had to be changed and lengthened with much loss of time, energy and money. Supplies became uncertain, difficult and dangerous."

It was natural for Mussolini to expect some recompense for this overwhelming contribution to Franco's success. El Caudillo, however, suffered a certain embarrassment because he could not balance what was supposed to be a spontaneous uprising of the Spanish people with the fantastic military assistance from Italy needed for his victory. This, too, was without taking into consideration the contribution of the Germans. The Nationalists had made much of restoring Spain to the Spaniards but from what Mussolini said he had done, he made it appear as if there were but few Spaniards in it at all.

Now the quicker Franco could get the foreign elements out, the better could he establish his right to a Spanish victory. Hence it was necessary to use a polite regard for old friendships but to offer simultaneously a very unmistakable good-bye. And the Spaniards themselves were strong for returning to their old national ways. Under these circumstances, it was difficult to devise anything concrete which could be done for Mussolini or for Hitler either. Franco could not risk concessions. He certainly could not allot the Balearic Isles to Italy without a Spanish protest. It would defeat his own cry of Spain for the Spaniards.

When the Rome-Berlin Axis asked for his adherence, he could only give them assurance of identity of views. He has kept saying this. He has not made any concrete step toward intervention in the present struggle, even though he is entirely indebted to them for his position.

Since there seems to be nothing Spain can give expediently, Mussolini has sent Franco the bill. Now, we are permitted on the inside to see how the enterprise was undertaken for the great ideology of Fascist principles. The bill asks payment of 5,500,000,000 Italian lire. This is approximately $280,000,000. The Mussolini account notes that in reality the total sum expended was 7,500,000,000 lire, which would be some $350,000,000. This is a way of saying that Franco received a good bargain. Il Duce will accept payment in twenty-four monthly installments.

Mussolini itemized the bill as follows:

Air Force

763 airplanes
1,414 airplane motors
1,672 tons of bombs
9,250,000 rounds of ammunition

Land Forces

        1,930 cannon
       10,135 automatic guns
      240,747 small arms
    7,514,537 rounds of artillery ammunition
  324,900,000 rounds of small arms ammunition
        7,668 motor vehicles

Naval Forces

    91 Italian warships
    92 Transports and supply ships

With these fantastic figures, the veil of Fascist trickery in Spain has been lifted. The early soundings and penetration by confidential emissaries undertaken secretly and the eventual equipping of the Franco forces exposes still another machination in the Mussolini technique. Spain proved a ready subject for his schemes of aggrandizement and was conducted into the tragic fate which tormented her people for nearly three years. Without Mussolini, the Spaniards would never have been embroiled in the agonizing strife which has laid them prostrate.

But though Franco won, Mussolini lost.

The Duke of Wellington once said:

"There is no nation on the continent of Europe where foreign interference will prove the aggressor's downfall as in Spain."

El Caudillo knew it.

Mussolini knows it now.

CHAPTER XV

CIGARS, CIGARETTES AND STOOGES

A new man was running the cigar stand, a new proprietor. Frank Rea, who was my first assistant and a loyal trooper, and I always bought our smokes there. It was next door to the office. The old proprietor had treated us as he treated everybody else, surlily, as if customers should be watched. They might snitch a box or pack. He just sold cigars and cigarettes and made friends with no one. He never smiled. The new proprietor was younger, dapper and pleasant. He greeted us by our names with a deferent "Signor." We were glad to buy our smokes there now.

We became so friendly that we passed from weather to women and that was friendly indeed. We called him Mario. His name was Mario Bruno. We became so friendly, too, that we made occasional allusions to "lui." "Lui" was always Il Duce. Tourists called him Mr. Smith but Italians always said "lui." The dapper young proprietor forever smiled and agreed. One day when Rea was with me, I told the latest one on "lui." It was where he approached the gates of heaven and St. Peter would not let him in because God could be a vice-president for no one. Mario smiled but not as usual. He said "Gia," in a kind of objectionable way. It was like an okay with a rise on the end. Something was symptomatic.

When we returned to the office, I asked Rea about it.

"Mario is on the OVRA," he said in a low, warning monotone. "That's why he's got the cigar stand. They put the old man out so as to get Mario the place."

I knew then why Mario was young, dapper and smiling. I knew why he said "Gia" with a rise on the end.

He was the stooge the police had picked to watch the foreign correspondents and the Italian ones as well. We all had offices around that neighborhood and bought our tobacco there.

We could get sore because the old proprietor had been eased out. We could register a silent protest by not patronizing the stand. There were other stands. But would it have mattered? All the cigar stands seemed to have changed hands. The sale of tobacco was a government monopoly and the police thus had some right in them. As it worked out, practically every cigar stand was a listening post for the secret police.

Most of the smoke stooges worked like Mario, quietly, unobtrusively as if they knew nothing was going on. When Mario heard a customer remark something off-color, he noted it. If the remarks were nasty a second time and a third, then Mario told his district leader, quietly, unobtrusively.

The customer was watched, gum-shoed and occasionally framed, perhaps by someone he always thought a friend. They might find nothing condemnatory. If they did, he was warned. He was still followed, gum-shoed and framed. If they got something, he was hailed before the regional Fascist committee and sent to the islands. He would have had numerous warn-ings before the island trip occurred and in most cases he chose freedom by silence, for that was freedom in Italy. The OVRA worked that way. It was all under cover to make it look on the surface as if everything was lovely in Italy under Il Duce.

The OVRA originated primarily in the too-frequent attempts on Mussolini's life. There had been three attempts in one year culminating with a near-hit in Bologna, where frenzied Fascists lynched a Fascist youth, mistaking him for the assassin. The mistake was so grave that no mention has ever been made of the true would-be assassin.

Mussolini was rattled. He called Luigi Federzoni, then Minister of the Interior, and asked him to find a man with sufficient grit and cupidity to prevent these attempts. Crispo Moncada, he who was undisturbed by the twenty-four shots fired at Consul Haven, was chief of police at that moment. He was fired.

"I have the man," replied Federzoni. "He is Bocchini, prefect of Genoa."

"Send for him," curtly commanded Il Duce.

The next day Arturo Bocchini was received by Mussolini. He guessed the reason. Everyone knew the problem. Protect Il Duce!

"Can you nip these attempts?" challenged the chief.

"Within a fortnight," replied Bocchini.

"Then you are Chief of the Italian police," said Mussolini.

"Excellency," returned Bocchini, "I can only undertake the task on two conditions."

"Well?"

"I must ask full powers in all police matters and a budget twice the present amount."

The amount was a secret, but from a hundred or so men detailed as body-guards for Mussolini, Bocchini increased that organization to 12,000 men, known officially as the *Squadra Presidenziale* ("Presidential Squad"). To recruit it quickly, Bocchini called in plainclothesmen of the regular police force from all over Italy. This was his first measure, put into effect immediately. To make good he had to beat any other attempt on Mussolini's life.

Every man in this force was in plainclothes. When in action, the squad was flung out like a long rope, curving and twisting along the routes where Mussolini was scheduled to be. Every day it was newly strewn. And no one was supposed to know they were police. But like their colleagues everywhere in that lampooned profession, everyone knew it. Their particular plainclothes made them particularly conspicuous. They tried to appear as if they were just strolling along. Each was stationed only thirty or forty yards from the other, which is not much of a stroll. Wherever Mussolini moved, twelve thousand "dicks" just loafed or promenaded along.

On some of the routes, where Il Duce made a daily trip, Bocchini put them in even less ostentatious attire. On the road to the Duce's private swimming beach at Castel Porziano, fifteen miles from Rome, they were dressed as workmen supposedly fixing the road. Such highly trained investigating experts despite their garb never soiled their hands in labor or sweated their brows in toil. They loafed again, fearful of anyone malicious enough to bother Il Duce and nuisance enough to disturb their calm.

With so many at his disposal, the Italian police head scoured the buildings where Il Duce was scheduled to appear. He investigated all the approaches. Even the sewers were searched for hidden time bombs. The history of each tenant in an apartment house near a presidential appearance was thoroughly scrutinized and catalogued. One may not have had a police record but one always had a record at the police. When Mussolini made an official visit to the Foreign Correspondents' Club, the buildings for blocks on both sides of the street were searched for any designs on dictatorial inviolability. And, on the night of the function, fifty of Bocchini's men appeared in evening dress to mingle with the crowd and to nip any annoyance initiated against the Head of the Government. This was a normal procedure wherever he went — the theater, an inauguration, a concert, a sports event or even a public religious gathering. Churches were not exempt from searches. The wardrobes of the twelve thousand "bulls" approached the Menjou. And more, they even impersonated priests.

Under Bocchini's administration, six attempts were made in fourteen years, but every one was nipped before a shot could be fired or a bomb thrown.

With time, Bocchini put in his second great inquisitorial reform. This was the OVRA. Announced as the *Opera Vigilanza Reati Anti-nazionale* (Organization for the Vigilance of Anti-national crimes). It was designed primarily to work through the Fascist organizations. It was supposed to be voluntary. The latter was facade. Even though it was little which government officials doled out to the volunteers, it was graciously received and the secret kept.

The OVRA began with the formula that everyone in Italy was under suspicion. It was even charged, but let us say jocosely for the sake of generosity, that high Fascist dignitaries, cabinet ministers, priests, cardinals and even members of the Royal family were covered by the OVRA. Subtle Italian humor did not even excuse Il Duce for failing to exempt his beloved brother Arnaldo and his son Vito.

Now, just as Mario watched all those who came so innocently into his cigar store, so all the members of the OVRA worked unostentatiously for the safety of Il Duce. OVRA agents were given jobs as janitors. In every large building, the superintendents were the district lieutenants. The activity of every man, woman and child was registered and indexed. No countermoves against Fascism could get under way. Not that they were nipped in the bud. They were never allowed to bud.

Waiters in restaurants were recruited. Especially was this noticeable at the outdoor cafes immediately facing the Venice Palace. The plainclothesmen would pace their usual beat before the place. When customers on whom a dictatorial vigilante wanted just a slight line sat down he gave a wink to the waiter. Depending on the customers' conversation, the waiter gave a backward or a forward turn of the head. If it meant watch them, they were watched with the due consequences of their intentions, if any.

The activities of the OVRA were not alone confined to Italy. They were widespread through North Africa and the Near East. Here they were to report to the Italian consulates any information which might be useful to the Fascist government. They also watched for any anti-Fascist activities. Before the present war, Italian waiters on the Riviera listened to the conversations of French officers. In Istanbul, they busied themselves around Turkish officials. In Athens, they watched the Greeks. But most of all, it was at Cairo, Jerusalem and Alexandria that they stretched their ears for the conversation of British officers taking perhaps a quiet afternoon tea.

Now with his tightened professional police and the OVRA, Bocchini had a blanket coverage of every individual's moves. He knew the record of every man and woman, Italian or foreign, living in Italy. No Italian was ever appointed to any official position unless the report of the OVRA was first handed to the appointing officer. The police penetrated every human activity. No one could move without their knowledge. One must always be available. The conduct of each citizen whether he were businessman or worker, artist or professional man was known in detail, from day to day, by the enveloping agents of Bocchini's creation.

When anyone was caught in any kind of anti-government design, it was usually made out that he was attempting to overthrow the regime. This was severe.

The perpetrator, even though to us he had committed what in a democratic state would be just common political opposition, would be slapped into jail and guarded more closely than if he were the most hardened criminal. I attended the trial of Mrs. Adolfo de Bosis, an American woman, widow of an Italian poet, who with two Italian intellectuals, Renzo Rendi and Mario Vinciguerra, was charged with conspiracy to overthrow the state.

Such cases are tried before a military court, composed of officers of the Fascist militia. The sentences are heavy, very heavy, often death. Rendi and Vinciguerra were brought into the courtroom chained hand and foot and to one another. Mrs. de Bosis was escorted by carabineers. The chains were removed from the two men and they were placed with other defendants in an iron cage. The woman was allowed to sit on the outside of the cage. The charges were read with unintelligible rapidity. The evidence had previously been heard by examining magistrates and this too was read. Each man was asked his reason for committing the crime. Mrs. de Bosis was also given a chance to reply. It could not be argued that they believed in free speech. They were condemned before any defense could be made. Only one hour was taken up in the hearing of the case. Mrs. de Bosis retracted and was acquitted. Rendi and Vinciguerra stood firm. They were both sentenced to fifteen years of confinement, which only the hardiest physique could withstand.

Ordinary political offenders are shipped to the

islands. These are sentenced by regional Fascist committees working through the OVRA. Often such offenders have only been talking too loud or have said disparaging things of Il Duce. They are not crimes at all in the democratic practice. Mingled with them are procurers, loan sharks and physicians guilty of illegal operations, for, by some Fascist quirk of reasoning, they are regarded as on the same plane as politicians who object to the regime.

Your reporter visited the island of Lipari where the largest colony of political offenders is kept. I have not heard of any other reporter who succeeded in landing on that forbidden shore. The island is off the coast of Sicily, a short distance from Messina. As I took the steamer, a group of prisoners were herded aboard. One need not have been told who were the political offenders, the procurers, the loan sharks and doctors. One could easily guess.

It was a sad sight to behold them all, their hands and feet in chains and each chained together with heavy strands. I shuddered. The political offenders were the saddest of all. Their faces showed knowledge. They were not ward politicians who change with the wind and could doubtless save their skins. Some were university professors, some were as ascetic as cloistered monks. And yet before me, here they were chained for having political opinions at variance with the dominator of Italy.

The trip over to the island took two hours. At the wharf they were awaited like so many head of cattle. Carabineers in charge of them handed the documents of their particulars to the chief of police of the island. They were led up from the wharf and disappeared into a barracks. Finally, their chains were removed.

I talked with the Lipari chief of police. His career depended on preventing any one of these men from escaping. Only just a few months before, three swam at night to a waiting launch and got away to North Africa. Now, the regulations were rigid. He told me that he began with the imperative goal of no possible escapes. The prisoners were allowed freedom about the village but could not approach the sea. At the village limits, they were also turned back. This was certainly not physical imprisonment. He was overcautious, however, in insisting that each prisoner make known his presence every two hours during the twenty-four.

At its very worst, the Italian method of treating opposing recalcitrants has never approached the fiendish cruelty of Nazi brutality. Race hatred is an importation. Beatings occurred for those heroic spirits who constantly defied Fascist authority. They were often hauled before the Fascist command and confined in a sort of dungeon on the hill overlooking the harbor. Prisoners told me of one man who was so badly treated that he died in the camp hospital. I asked about him. Lieutenant Gravina, the acting commander, replied he had died of tuberculosis. Likely, he was beaten and had tuberculosis both.

For those who obeyed, however, the physical suffering was not great. Married men were allowed to bring their wives and to take a house in the village. Some of them brought very elaborate furniture and victrolas since radios were prohibited. They could make themselves comfortable within their means. The government allowed them ten lire a day for subsistence, which is about fifty cents. Those who could not afford to bring their wives lived in the common barracks where a hundred men were accommodated and joined in a common mess of their own.

The two-hourly answer to roll-call worked greater hardships on the married men than on the single ones, especially at night. In the barracks, a guard entered and checked off the names of those in bed. He did not awaken them. But when a married couple took a house, it was required that the husband get out of bed, stick his head out of the window and show himself to the guards. I told the chief of police that I thought this a rather strict rule since it was very difficult for anyone to go far with the island surrounded by the Mediterranean.

"Three escaped a month ago," he snapped. "As long as I am here there will be no escapes. It is not my affair if they are married. They must report. We want to know where they are. There can be no more escapes."

I knew some of the political prisoners. I especially wanted to talk with Carlo Silvestri, a Milanese newspaperman. We had covered the Cocchi trial together. He had been sent to the island for writing anti-Fascist articles and — talking back. He lived in a house at the end of the village not far from the sea. I rapped at the door. He stuck his head out of the upstairs window thinking, of course, it was the guard. He saw me but did not recognize me. He was confused to consternation.   Living under the threat of additional punishment, to him some new catastrophe was upon him.   He was jittery, truly off.   After a few moments, he came back to himself and asked me into the house.   His wife was present.

Strict rules had become an obsession in his mind. He had been an intimate friend of Mussolini and showed me affectionate notes which Mussolini had sent him.

"Mussolini may rise to be as great a man as Napoleon," he said.   "But he will never change the love of individuality and freedom in the Italian people.   He will certainly not change mine."

The spirit of grimness to his convictions was deep. We arranged to meet again the next day when he would collect the intellectuals for a meeting in the library which the prisoners themselves had set up.   Despite the fact that several of them were college professors, the books sent to the library from friends were censored by a police detective whose knowledge of history and philosophy was bounded by police orders and the sports pages in the newspapers.

At noon the next day, the library, a dark little room opening on a narrow street, was full of learned men. Some spoke with vehemence, others with softness. They objected to the rules imposed.   They found fault with the guards.   They said it was wrong to prohibit them the waterfront.   But it was not those things which were keeping them prisoners.   Many of them could have kept themselves cooped up in one room for weeks provided they had their books of the great thinkers and could speak and write what their souls wished to reveal. Here was the great imprisonment for these learned men. They tried to find fault with the physical restrictions but these were not sufficient to stir any sympathy in a world hardened to much greater brutality. They could walk, eat, amuse themselves but they could not read, study, or express their heart's convictions. Silence was their prison.

Some called it the devil's island. Silvestri said it was not a devil's island.

"Mussolini should understand," he insisted, "that we ought to be treated with greater humanity."

When I returned to Rome, I spoke to Mussolini about the two-hour call.

"It is not a hardship," he said and turned away.

His plan was to force these men to accept Fascism. Many he succeeded in conquering. These went back to the mainland to be silent. They went back to the mainland to be their own prisoners. Silvestri, friend of Il Duce, never wavered, was never conquered.

One day, a procurer engaged me in conversation.

"You know who suffer most here?" he said.

"Who?" I asked.

"The young fellows between twenty and twenty-five. They can get no girls. I see it in their eyes. It's sad," he said.

The island had not changed him.

Within the Axis, police officials from each country visit the other. Heinrich Himmler, Nazi police chief, studied Bocchini's methods and copied much from the Italian. But the Germans did not possess the fine Italian hand. Vicious brutality was added to the torment of surveillance and suspicion. As Hitler began to rise in power and to overshadow the founder of Fascism, German officialdom became more active in Italy. There were exchanges. There was more the suggestion of improving Italian police methods, ferreting espionage and smartening up the Italian system of military intelligence.

Gestapo officials poured into Italy, students from universities camped in Rome, Florence, Naples and Milan. The number of German newspapermen was increased. Their corps was double that of any other country. German professors visited the schools and colleges. Technicians inspected the industries. And, under the guise of cultural and military cooperation, hundreds of German experts became attached to the munition factories, to the army, the navy and air force. By this gigantic mass of German penetration, Italy was blanketed by a German net of police. The whole country might have truly been called completely Nazified. In Rome alone, it is estimated that today there are five thousand German agents.

And added to this Nazi streamlining, which conforms little to the character of the traditional Italian trait of trying to make life easy, comes the smartening of the Royal Carabineers. This corps which by its nature responds singularly to Italian needs must also be Nazified. The unit is over a hundred years old and was thought exempt from any necessity of foreign blitzing. But Himmler suggested that it be smartened so as to be able to cooperate more closely with the Nazi Storm Troopers. This met frowning disapproval by King Victor, whose royal house had depended for its defense for the past century on the efficiency of the Carabineers corps. As a protest against this last Nazi infiltration, he was absent from the 1940 celebration of the anniversary of the founding of the corps.

Saddest of all in this spearhead of German penetration was Bocchini. He was a tall, handsome, massive Neapolitan, who, though his approach to problems ordinarily was meditative and methodical, had in critical moments that very desirable trait of being decisively quick and mentally vital. A lifetime was passed in the Italian civil service which he had made a career. He had risen to the rank of prefect through the sheer merit of his accomplishments. As we have seen, he was designated national police chief because of his energy and intellectual equipment. He was the only official in Italy who was received by Mussolini every day without exception. He gave the daily report on the state of the nation. Few public officials ever retained the confidence of Il Duce as long or as unshaken as Arturo Bocchini.

He had been apprehensive of the systematic boring which the German partnership imposed upon Italian life. Disagreements with the bold arrogance of his Teutonic colleagues embittered him against their claim of command. His own policing of Italy had solved Fascism's safety. It was inevitable that friction between him and Himmler should result. Bocchini died on November 21, 1940 before he had reached sixty. He was in prime health. Suspicion clouds the death as not natural.

Italians have watched with perplexed eyes the increasing domination of the senior Axis partner in their internal affairs. Successive defeats in Africa, in Albania, in the air and on the seas impose silence. Dependence more and more on Hitler is imperative. The Nazi grip becomes tighter and tighter. The great dream of empire fades slowly away.

In a recent demonstration, one Italian shouted,
"Hurrah for Mussolini, founder of the empire."
"Hurrah!" answered another, "but what empire?"
"The German empire," returned the first.

CHAPTER XVI

NOT IN THESE CLOTHES

No single individual has brought greater joy to the Vatican in our times than did Il Duce when he signed the Lateran Treaty in 1929 ending the fifty-nine-year quarrel between Italy and the Holy See. Contrariwise, few men in modern times have attacked the Roman Church with more acrid vehemence. As a youthful revolutionary, he had dreamed in perhaps equally youthful exuberance that he would destroy the papacy. In maturity, the dream often showed evidence of recurrence, but expediency was better politics.

We have seen how he adroitly neutralized the Catholic party by granting quite unpolitical concessions to the ecclesiastical authorities such as allowing the cross on the public schools, placing a crucifix in the Coliseum and protecting religious processions. These things meant much to the clergy but they meant nothing to him except that by them he was able to destroy many of his political enemies.

In religion as well as politics he was as acrobatic as the man on the flying trapeze. He somersaulted from orthodox to heterodox, from mystic to agnostic with the greatest of ease. Before he got to power, he was an atheist. With power, religion cloaked his backsliding past. He got married in the Church. In civil and religious ceremonies, he sat in the seat of the mighty, usually elaborately caparisoned. He learned the forms.

Through his instrumentality, chaplains were assigned to all civil and military institutions. Often on his authority, government funds were appropriated for church repairs. Making official visits to provincial towns, he would always grant a priest's request for a donation. In the villages he constructed in the colonies and in the reclaimed marshes, he took especial pains to oversee the erection of a church. Its architecture must be good.

But his religion was political. He only attended religious functions in a public way. Otherwise, he never went to church. It may well have been that these public ceremonies coincided with the time he wished privately to be devout. We must in all delicacy not trespass here and leave his predilection for being seen and wearing grand uniforms in church to Il Duce and his conscience.

He had a limit, too, in these public devotions. When in his elaborately embroidered uniform of Prime Minister he knelt at the tomb of St. Peter, a part of the ceremonial of his only visit to the Pope, he waved the photographers away saying that the time to pray is not the time to be photographed. With many other men, we could call this contrite modesty but with Benito Mussolini we are constrained to doubt the sincerity of such humbleness. Besides, the Pope had often allowed photographs of himself in the act of prayer.

At another time, too, Il Duce stopped short of manifesting too much outward reverence. In his same resplendent uniform, he attended the wedding of Princess Giovanna, daughter of King Victor, to King Boris of Bulgaria in the basilica of St. Francis in Assisi. The royal party in their gay gowns and gaudy uniforms went to the crypt to pray at the tomb of the saint as an act of humble veneration. Il Duce did not enter the crypt. A friar approached him timidly and invited him to kneel in penitent submission before the remains of Italy's most revered patron. He was momentarily perplexed but his mental agility rescued him again. He made a gesture to his heavily laden gilt garb and raised his sheathed ceremonial sword to the level of his waist.

"Not in these clothes, reverend," he replied as if he had learned from Ecclesiastes that there is a time for everything. Supposedly, he had suddenly found humility but could not practice it because he was wearing the wrong robes. He intended to dress down to St. Francis.

It was characteristic of his impetuous nature that after the jubilant signing of the Lateran Treaty, he quarreled violently with the Pope. It was mainly about whether Catholics should discuss politics in their religious clubs. We know how disagreements come in all human relations but to Mussolini such a misunderstanding should be accompanied by a proper display of his enraged sensibilities. Without any forewarnings, Italy was engulfed in a movement of organized violence. Catholic clubs were sacked and portraits of the Pope were torn from walls and burned. Religious students were clubbed. Placards appeared with the slogan, "Death to the Pope."

Pius XI, then reigning, was aroused and took the offensive. He was a dynamic match for Il Duce. True, their weapons were different. The Fascists applied their terror. The Pope fought terror with religious fervor. Mussolini knew that lesson. He had once told your reporter that Bismarck was beaten by the church because its spiritual arm was impervious to bullets. He could not continue his terror politics when he had earlier learned that bayonets cannot fight faith. In a month, the terror politics ceased.

It was only a week or so later that the Italian ambassador called at the Vatican. Mussolini had had enough. The envoy presented a formula in which Il Duce must now save his face. He would stay out of strictly religious affairs and the ecclesiastical authorities and the Catholic Clubs must stay out of politics. It was all done with a great flourish but nothing was changed. The Pope had been firm, defended his rights.

But on February 10, 1939, Pius XI died in the midst of another quarrel with Mussolini. He was nearly eighty-two and had previously suffered a most devastating illness which only his tough fiber had overcome. Despite his weakened condition, he was still fighting. He had called all the Italian bishops to a consistory in the Vatican palaces where he intended to exhort them all in a movement against Mussolini for his anti-Jewish decrees. Age, weakness and overwork were finally too much for a spirit which had refused to die but Pius XI died fighting to the last breath.

On March 4, Eugenio Cardinal Pacelli was elected Pope and took the name of Pius XII. Your reporter had known this gentle and suave diplomat. He was quite the opposite in temperament from his predecessor. Pius XI was gladiatorial, defiant, commanding and uncompromising; the new pontiff was persuasive, consoling, appealing and conciliatory. It was fateful that a man of such contrasted virtues should have been called to such a task at the very moment when world affairs were steadily developing toward a tragic crisis.

I recall our sitting together on the terrace of the Villa Falconara, overlooking the blue waters of the Mediterranean at Civitavecchia, forty miles from Rome. That afternoon he had officiated at the baptism of the daughter of the late Guglielmo Marconi, inventor of wireless. It was spring of 1931. The other guests had gone out on the Marconi yacht.

"How beautiful and calm the sea is," he said, as he looked out on the vast expanse which was as still as a pond.

"Yes, it is all so calm and peaceful," I replied. The whole scene was placid, and just as placid as the motionless sea was Eugenio Pacelli. To be calm and meditative was an outstanding characteristic in his personality. Whether sitting at his desk, officiating at a sacred function, driving to an appointment or taking a relaxing walk, meditation and prayer was an overpowering habit which ruled his life.

He had been through the last war. It was he who was chosen by Pope Benedict to deliver a peace proposal to Kaiser Wilhelm II in 1917. He had remained in Germany after the war. His house was invaded by Communist bands who demanded surrender. Boldly he faced them in his archi-episcopal robes and warned them that they stood on extra-territorial ground. He ordered them away. They left him unharmed.

If any man can be called an expert on Germany today, it is Pius XII. He had lived there for fifteen years, had conversed with the lowly, held conferences with the highest authorities and had travelled through the land. The concordat between Germany and the Holy See had been drawn up by him. It took Hitler only five days to forget that it had ever been signed. He has broken it ever since.

South America welcomed Pacelli on October 9, 1934, when he was the papal legate to the International Eucharistic Congress. No foreign potentate visiting the Southern hemisphere had ever been received with such enthusiastic acclaim and elaborate ceremonial. Cannon boomed a royal greeting. Flags, parades, cheering and official pomp glorified his presence. In 1936, Pope Pius XI had sent him to visit the United States. Here he traveled over six thousand miles by airplane, visited all of our large cities and talked with nearly all the Catholic bishops and archbishops. He was a guest of President Roosevelt at Hyde Park. With such an encompassing view of the world, he ascended the throne of St. Peter, one of the most richly equipped pastors to be invested with the papal robes. He speaks six languages.

When he became Pope, he had no illusions about the seriousness of the world situation. He foresaw war. As much as his spiritual office could, he tried to turn a war-bent world. The Nazi trend, however, was inevitable. When he found on September 2, 1939, that Italy had declared her neutrality, he cherished a ray of hope. He might use Italy as the basis for a peace offensive.

To further any possibility of success in these pacific

aims, President Roosevelt announced a cooperative effort and appointed Myron C. Taylor, former head of the United States Steel Corporation, as his own personal representative to confer with the Pope. The presidential envoy was given the rank of ambassador and took up his residence in Rome. Taylor had met the Pontiff on the latter's visit here in 1936. Pius XII, then as Papal Secretary of State, had been a guest at the Taylor home in New York City. Messages of undisguised satisfaction came from the Holy See through Msgr. Francis J. Spellman, archbishop of New York, stating that the Pope was glad of the cooperation and especially of the appointment of Taylor. The mission started with sanguine hopes. Even though the prospects for peace were remote, any effort was regarded as worth encouragement if there existed the slimmest chance of restoring the world to its harmonious pursuits.

At that critical moment, Mussolini stood on a rickety pedestal. He had rattled a sword for years, but that same sword was now old and rusty. The great dictator who had boasted eight million bayonets, five thousand airplanes and three hundred warships had no supplies, no munitions and no equipment. He may have had bayonets, but he had few rifles on which to put them. His troops were poorly clad and many thousands had no shoes. Cities had no anti-aircraft defense. There was no oil, coal, copper, cotton, manganese, without which war could not be fought. Italy was at the mercy of any power with modern machines. Under these circumstances, he began to like peace.

To assure the world of his neutrality, he recited poems

and sang paeans on peace. He said that Italy was not thinking of war, could not bear to hear the sound of the word and would not ever mention it. Italy was building the greatest world's fair ever planned, the Great Olympiad of Civilization, which he would inaugurate in 1942. The Italian people were peaceful people and desired above all to follow the pursuits of peace rather than be embroiled in the quarrels of others, he declared. It was neutrality for Italy. His bluff had not yet been called.

He theatrically demonstrated neutrality. He never lacked the ingenuity required for that worthy art. He arranged for a peace visit of King Victor to Pope Pius XII. This took place on December 21, 1939, in a somber and tranquil atmosphere propitious for such a noble and lofty aim. The newspapers printed columns about the visit of peace. More poems were recited, more paeans sung. King and Pope conversed for a half-hour and the sole topic was peace.

Then to give further solemnity to the sublime goal, the Pope had announced that he would return his visit to the king on December 28. This broke all precedent that a pope should visit the king. The Pontiff, however, was sincere in making this gesture. It was a supreme effort to bring peace among the nations. Italy was the shining example of a peace-loving state determined not to be a party to the horrors of war, either to inflict them on others or to suffer them herself. The papal visit was proclaimed around the world. The Holy Father hoped that Italy would be the spearhead for a world-wide spiritual offensive which would restore concord and goodwill amongst men. Again king and Pope conversed for half an hour and again the topic was peace.

Mussolini should have been there. He should have worn his golden swallow-tail. Protocol required that he pay homage to the Sovereign Pontiff. He was absent.

It was quite logical for people all over the world to wonder why Mussolini was not there at the side of his king. But it was all explained. Il Duce would make a solemn pilgrimage to the Pope during the early part of January, date and time to be arranged later. But between the visits, the Pontiff had proclaimed a five-point peace program which meant the restoration of the status quo ante. Poland should be reconstituted. International difficulties should be settled by a peace conference. The Pope condemned aggression, atrocities, contempt for international law and anti-Christian propaganda, which naturally pointed the finger at Germany and Russia. He thought that Italy would be the first to join the peace parade.

But Mussolini was in a dilemma. He schemed to make it appear that he joined the Pontiff so as to hide his hopeless state of unpreparedness. He did not want to be attacked by France and England. They had justifiable grounds. He had signed a military alliance with Germany. He wanted to stave off any thought of attack. He continued very much for peace but he could not accept the Pope's five-point program. It was against Hitler. Knowing nothing of Il Duce's cunning mental reservations, Pius XII wrote a formal letter to the king and bestowed his blessing upon "the illustrious head of

the Italian government and its ministers." This meant
Mussolini. He accepted the blessing. He wanted the
Pope to believe him a man of peace. He wanted
the world to believe him a man of peace. He was
not yet prepared.

To cover up his breach of etiquette on the papal visit,
therefore, he caused it to be noised about that he would
make a solemn pilgrimage to the Pope on January 9.
This would show him a man of peace. But he con-
tracted a cold. The pilgrimage was postponed until a
week later, January 15. He had another cold. It was
postponed indefinitely.

But he did not uncover his real direction to the Pontiff. He kept talking peace. He wished the world to
believe that he was a man of peace. In February, however, he was feeling a little stronger and now instead
of the out-and-out peace talk, violent press attacks on
the "decadent democracies" appeared. Now, to allay
the Pontiff's fears that he was veering away from neutrality, he approved the visit of General Ubaldo Soddu,
under-secretary for war, to the Pope. The visit was a
token of Italy's desire to remain neutral and to follow
the Pope's desire of the rule of reason amongst peoples.

But while Soddu carried a word of peace, the Italian
newspapers were crying for war. Il Duce thought that
Italian public opinion had now reached the point where
he could give the war fever a little extra injection. The
democracies were more vehemently condemned and
Germany eulogized. It was, of course, perplexing to
the Pontiff to find that while he was the recipient of lip
service on peace, he found an active and effective iron

hand for war. No formal international act, however, had brought war any nearer.

As if still to keep in the good graces of the Holy Father, a visit of Crown Prince Humbert took place. The prince told the Pope of his loyal devotion as a son of the church and had great hopes for the peace of the world. This again seemed to encourage His Holiness in his wishful belief that Il Duce did not actually mean war. But it also did another thing. The visit was exploited by both press and radio to show the Italian people that the Pontiff was on Italy's side. Ominously, nevertheless, Il Duce at that very moment was massing his bayonets along the French frontier. It was made to appear in Italy as if the Holy Father had actually given his approval to this threatening Italian military action.

The *Osservatore Romano*, the official Vatican news organ, published a number of pacifist articles during this very period. Mussolini accused the editor of committing an unneutral act. The newspaper was prohibited circulation in Italy. To avoid further charges of violation, the periodical promised to print only the official communiques of the warring nations. On that promise, it was permitted to appear again on Italian newsstands.

On May 29, Pius XII received the new Italian ambassador to the Holy See. The envoy on presenting his credentials made an address to the Pontiff on the loyalty and devotion of his Sovereign, King Victor. In return and still hoping that he was keeping Mussolini and Italy on the road to peace, the Pope blessed the king, the prime minister and the whole Italian nation.

Again the incident was exploited by Il Duce and his editors to show how closely bound were the views of the Holy See and belligerent Italian policy. These were tragic days. The Battle of France was proceeding to its sad conclusion. Il Duce was watching the turn of events hourly. On June 2, the Pope issued an appeal to the nations to humanize war in the interest both of combatants and non-combatants. In the message the Pontiff extended "his paternal love to the Germans and the Allied peoples" as well.

France was failing. Her armies were becoming demoralized. Il Duce felt sure that the Italian forces were strong enough to vanquish the exhausted French if they dared rise in their final agony to march against Italy. The weakness of the enemy and the strength of the great ally, Germany, had suddenly transformed the unprepared Italian army into a warlike and conquering host. Now the courage and military prowess of Italy was glorified in the pages of every Italian newspaper. Il Duce of peace had become Il Duce of war. On June 10, he opened hostilities. Italy attacked its prostrate neighbor.

Pius XII was perplexed.

Mussolini asked all Italian bishops and archbishops to bless Italian arms. He commanded that they support the war policy. They had taken vows of patriotic devotion. All of them fulfilled those vows. Several of them published pastoral letters exhorting their flocks to give all their strength and prayers for the success of Italian armed might.

Cardinal Schuster, archbishop of Milan, visited the

military encampments and delivered addresses to the soldiers, firing them with patriotic fervor in the fight. "God is on our side," he said. He distributed religious medals to the soldiers as a token of divine protection. The archbishop of Gorizia urged the faithful "to lift our reverent thought to the ever victorious King and Emperor and to the undefeated Duce. May God bless and protect him." On June 27, thirty Italian bishops sent a message to Mussolini exhorting him "to crown the unfailing victory of our army by conquering Palestine, thus to bring concord amongst the civilized peoples of pagan and Christian Rome."

Since there was conflict between the papal efforts for peace and the policy of the Italian bishops and archbishops, the Holy See endeavored to show in a published statement that its own inherent authority extended over the whole of the Universal Church throughout the world. The Pope's responsibility and power could not be affected by the action of any local ecclesiastical authorities. It was the aim of the Holy See, it said, to remain decisively impartial in all its efforts with the belligerents. Its mission, above all, was a mission of peace, the reign of Christ on earth.

"The attitude and responsibility of the Vatican are entirely separate from that of the Italian clergy and Italian Catholics," the statement concluded.

Both the Italian and German newspapers joined in new endeavors to make it appear that the Pope was on their side. Reports were circulated by them that Pius XII had urged Europe to accept the "new order." They published stories of the Pontiff's disapproval of democracies. Hitler was making friends with the Holy See, they said. France had been urged to sign an immediate peace with Germany and Italy in the interest of humanity and to avoid complete ruin, they announced.

All these crafty ruses were strenuously and categorically denied by the Vatican. At the moment the reports were being spread with the most carefree abandon, the Holy Father addressed a gathering of pilgrims condemning the tactics of the Axis press.

"An untruthful press is no less murderous than armored cars," he said.

It was a sad realization for the Pontiff. He had stepped down from his lofty throne to visit the King of Italy and to obtain from him his assurance that he was a man of peace. He could recall the promises, of Mussolini, of Soddu, of the Crown Prince and of the Italian ambassador. They were all promises of clay now.

The Holy See was disillusioned. Even the efforts of the United States which had been welcomed with so much joy were unavailing. Taylor returned home in the autumn of 1940.

Il Duce had talked peace but declared war.

Pius XII knew now that Il Duce had never intended to visit him in his golden swallow-tail.

CHAPTER XVII

MANY ARE CALLED . . .

Il Duce commanded not all but a considerable portion of the very finest brains in Italy. When anyone complimented with a job disagreed with him, high or low, political liquidation was the rebel's fate. Besides, when he had drained the soul of some willing genius, he cast him unceremoniously aside. He told me that when Frederick the Great tired of Voltaire, it was explained that an orange should be squeezed and thrown away.

Il Duce often changed his cabinet. Voltaire was never mentioned when this was done. Instead it was said that everybody should get a chance. He told me that he believed in rotation in office though he did not call it by that Jeffersonian phrase. Only a martial phrase would do, hence it was "The Changing of the Guard." And while the guard was constantly changed, no one dared suggest a furlough for the commander. The head man stayed. In nineteen years, he reorganized his cabinet thirteen times. He loved to fire and hire.

Since he had proclaimed it axiomatic that "Il Duce is always right" the guardsmen relieved could only accept his successive changes as the honorable discharge from duty while secretly putting a disgruntled curse on the day he was born. It was glorious to be called to duty but forlornly tragic when invalided home in sound health. While they put on a smile for Il Duce's perfect

judgment, they inwardly boiled with vindictive venom
that he had singled them out for thankless retirement.

Many of his early lieutenants have passed into oblivion either by eclipse or for unforgiven slips.   Death has
been sweet to those who died in harness wearing the
glorious trappings of Fascist officialdom.   The men still
in favor who were with him when he first attained
power can be counted on the fingers of one hand.   They
could hang on only because they were indispensable to
his policies or were better yes men than he could have
otherwise found.   Devotion was an imperative though
not a cherished virtue.

By dictatorial commandment, the general secretary of
the Fascist party sprang to attention at a nod.   The first
to occupy that post was Francesco Giunta, a Florentine,
who, when Trieste was handed over to the Italians after
the first World War, rushed there to exploit any political, commercial, financial or even agricultural im-
positions on the unhappy Austrians.   There he organized the bundles of combat, headed the assault on *Il
Lavoratore*, where Haven lived to tell the tale, and made
himself generally conspicuous.   One day he shot off
his toe by accident.   As general secretary, however, he
never got very far with Mussolini.   He was rough but
not rough enough.   Il Duce relieved him and called the
inflammable Roberto Farinacci.

For drive and action, no Fascist exceeded Farinacci.
He assumed control of the whole region of Cremona
and dictated the business, education and political life of
the community.   He was the supreme master of the
bludgeon and, in case of desirable or undesirable

trouble, always carried a club even on a leisurely walk. His violent repressions completely eliminated all opposition parties. He took charge of the trial of those accused of murdering Matteotti and rushed the trial through with Neronian flagrance, calling the murderers heroes in that they were able to save their own lives. None of them ever was even sent to jail though sentences were passed as a lasting tribute to Fascist justice.

But even Farinacci was not exempt from dictatorial jealousy. When "his work was done," he was relieved. He obeyed though his rash and reckless nature was never at ease at home. He was also disturbing to Il Duce. Reproved, he saluted. It always saved him.

He began the anti-Semitic campaign in Italy as far back as 1936. This campaign continued through 1937 and 1938. Finally Mussolini as a show of loyalty to Hitler decreed discrimination against the Jews. Farinacci was picked out for distinction in this regard and was made a Minister of State, a title honorable enough but without power or governmental function.

He has been violently anti-British and has often attacked the Vatican. In September 1938, he led an Italian delegation to the Nuremburg congress. He was accused as a slacker during the first World War, hiding behind a job as a railroader. In the Ethiopian war, he was wounded by his own hand grenade in the arm while out fishing on one of the African lakes. He came back with both wound and medal.

His place as general secretary was taken by Augusto Turati, of Brescia, who wanted to become a cabinet minister. Following Fascist intrigue, those whom he had antagonized decoyed him into trap after trap, where it was woman after woman.   Since Il Duce eventually was seeking a pretext, he looked with horror on the carnal promiscuity and sent him off to the Island of Rhodes to reflect and recuperate.

Then came Giovanni Giuriati.   Here was a loyal and sincere devotee.   He had served under D'Annunzio. Many bundles of combat originated at his organizing skill.   He was a war hero, a reputable lawyer and added to the lustre of the party by being born in re deemed Zara in Dalmatia.   His first post was Minister of the Liberated Regions.   Then he was made Minister of Public Works.   Later Il Duce made him General Secretary.   But he was to suffer the fate of a whipping boy.   When Mussolini quarreled with Pius XI, Giuriati was blamed.   Innocent, he said it was all his fault. He was banished from Party Councils.   Mussolini said he never wanted to see "that scoundrel" again.   Then he gave him the Collar of the Most Holy Annunciation and made him a cousin of the king.

Achille Starace followed.   He was amiable to the boys and affable to Il Duce.   He always said "yes."   It was he who started the great Italian sports drive.   He headed the Olympic Committee and appointed every sports official throughout the country, professional or amateur.   The great sport spectacles — prize-fights, football games, horse-racing — which drew millions annually, were all of party manipulation.   And what a chance!   He held the secretaryship longest and most profitably.   Graft and corruption flourished so magnificently that Mussolini thought it enough.

He was paid off for his devotion. A number of sophomoric elaborations originated in his fertile though somewhat immature brain. He abolished the handshake, prohibited the wearing of ties and introduced the circus athletics for regional secretaries such as jumping through burning hoops, riding down precipices and playing football on motorcycles. He tried an ill-fated experiment when he proposed to copy the *Heil Hitler* with a *Saluto al Duce.* Il Duce warned him that Fascism never copied.

Ettore Muti, lover of iron discipline and frenzied repression, replaced him. The graft regime provided the new incumbent great scope for a cleaning. His orders were inexorable. The party was ordered to come back to its great and revolutionary mission. He was acclaimed a war hero. He was Ciano's bodyguard in Ethiopia. In the Spanish Civil War, he was credited with having shot down 150 Loyalist planes, probably the entire Spanish air force. He was sent to the Albanian front when Italy invaded that country. His return occurred "only when the job was done." He was again sent across the Adriatic when the invasion of Greece started but no stories of falling British or Greek planes have burned the Italian telegraph wires. He returned without the job being done.

Now, while the party was the backbone of Fascist power and insured domination over the mass of the Italian people, the government was a wider and more effective organ for the nation. The choice of men for cabinet positions and other important posts fell upon the most capable party members. Often it was neces-

sary for Il Duce to call in non-Fascists for some technical or unusual assignment. Within the party, he
could not always find the suitable specialist. And in
government, too, his system of handling his collaborators
remained the same.

His first cabinet was composed of outstanding personages. He asked them to join him in the name of
national unity. This was a strong appeal. For national
unity, they helped him. He played a clever card. It
looked as if he had rallied the whole country under the
sway of Fascism, for these great celebrities seemed to
give him the stamp of approval. He appointed General
Armando Diaz, the World War commander-in-chief
and a great popular hero, War Minister. Admiral
Thaon di Revel, naval commander-in-chief in the
World War, was made Minister of Navy. He secured
big names in finance, education and political adminis-
ration. It looked like national unity. Everyone was
pulling for the Fascists.

But before the first year passed there was disagreement. The big names began to leave the cabinet. It
was always announced that "they had now finished the
mission for which they had been called and had resigned." Then came the reshuffle. Il Duce began to
draw on the amenable brains of the country, each to follow the unbreakable rule that if they were overwhelm-
ngly good they stayed. It was imperative that they
should be yes men.

In this quite personal process, he had many fits which
gave those around him many starts. A cabinet minister
would prepare a report for a cabinet meeting and as he

left his own office to attend, a messenger might easily come from Il Duce to announce that another had taken his place. He did not lack variety in staging these summary dismissals. Once I was sitting across the desk from Alberto de Stefani, at that moment Minister of Finance. He had just shown me the entire exhibit he had prepared to present to our Treasury Department in Washington asking for the reduction of the Italian debt. We had gone over it and I was then ready to leave with a two-column interview. His secretary announced that Roberto Farinacci was waiting. We were saying goodbye as Farinacci entered. I heard him say :

"Il Duce told me to tell you that your job is finished. Count Volpi will be here in a few minutes and will take your place."

De Stefani walked out of the Finance ministry that afternoon completely crushed. He was being deprived of the credit for a report which he himself had prepared on the funding of the Italian debt to the United States. He was scheduled to leave for New York within a few days. He was told to stay at home. Volpi went. On de Stefani's work, Volpi came back a hero.

In his turn, Volpi took a more stinging rap. When Il Duce tired of him, he was even more crudely dismissed. He received a letter by routine messenger. I read :

"Your work as Finance Minister is now complete. You can consider this letter as having accepted your resignation. Mussolini."

Many of the Fascist ministers never knew they had been removed until they read it in the newspapers.

Grandi was called to Il Duce's office about seven one evening. Il Duce received him very soberly and handed him a sheet of paper. Typewritten, it read:

"Dino Grandi has resigned as Minister of Foreign Affairs. He will take up an important diplomatic post."

"What do you think of it?" asked Il Duce.

"Whatever Your Excellency does is always well done," replied the amenable Grandi.

"Good-bye," said Il Duce.

"Good-bye," returned Grandi.

Giuseppe Bottai, as Minister of Guilds, was making an inspection tour. While he was haranguing a group of workmen on Fascism, a messenger arrived to tell him he was relieved. He descended the platform with less authority than the workmen he addressed. A Minister of Public Works was making an inspection of a great dam which bore Mussolini's name. He received a wire he was discharged. Mussolini himself desired to inspect the dam.

No time is given to wind up affairs. You go out just as unceremoniously as you come in. The tree of power is pruned as a gardener trims the hedge. Snip! Snip! Snip!

Of the men who started with him Dino Grandi, Giuseppe Bottai, Roberto Farinacci, are the only ones who are now in popular view. There are many, many mercilessly forgotten. Cabinet ministers, party secretaries, ambassadors, prefects and even strong-arm men are informally smothered. One squeezes the orange and then throws it away.

Since the all too suspicious death of Balbo, it is

Grandi who remains the one figure who has been abl
to weather all the caprices of Fascist policy both domes
tic and foreign. He has done it by obeying Il Duc
and by submerging his own opinions for those of th
great master.

Dino Grandi was the suave, bearded and fashion
plate diplomat who visited President Hoover in 193
and won what could be called a triumphant acclain
everywhere—front-paged, lunched, dinnered and lion
ized. His morning coat and striped trousers seeme
somehow to place a sanctified mantle over his revolu
tionary past. He was now a polished gentleman.

On his return from the first World War at the age o
23, he walked the city of Milan in search of work. Affa
bly though desperately, he often panhandled the pric
of a meal while wearing a row of medals which unmis
takably were a burden on his courageous breast. Re
turning to his native town Bologna, a law practice en
ticed him. It was a mirage. Instead, he paid mor
attention to organizing the bundles of combat and in
two years had made such headway that he was electe
to Parliament just barely within the age limit.

With the March on Rome, he was Fascist Chief o
Staff and it was he as a Monarchist who engineere
that the King should call Mussolini to form a govern
ment. He was made Under-Secretary for Foreign Af
fairs and after seven years of good behavior was pro
moted to Minister of Foreign Affairs at the age of 34
the youngest ever to grace that office in Italy. His wor
as a diplomatic negotiator was brilliant. He spok
French and English perfectly. He had trained himsel

o be a perfect Foreign Minister — spoke the languages, kept himself slim by an ascetic's diet and ordered his clothes from the only English tailor in Rome.

Like so many of Il Duce's collaborators, he was perhaps too good as Foreign Minister. A change was necessary and Grandi was sent to London as ambassador. He made the great hit of his career. He became the intimate friend of king, queen, baron and publican. He was a figure in England. But Mussolini began his quarrels over new lands. Grandi now was placed between his love for the British and his loyalty to the Duce. He chose the Duce. Now he had to play a double game. He had to tell the British how the invasion of Ethiopia was not aggression.

Then along came the Italian intervention in Spain. Here he had knowingly to tell the British government that Italy was not sending troops to Spain when he knew that they were. He slapped the Russian ambassador's face for charging that Italy was sending men and supplies to Franco. He persuaded Chamberlain and Lord Halifax to negotiate the "gentlemen's agreement" for the Mediterranean in January, 1939. The British were still trusting Grandi.

But when on that Good Friday just a few months later Italy invaded Albania, the British wondered about the gentlemen's agreement. Grandi was discovered. He had double-crossed the British. His work in London was now finished. He was transferred to Rome. The reason for the transfer was given as arthritis but he was then only forty-five. He delivered a speech to the Italian colony in the embassy charging that the British were "lying against the Axis powers." He scoffed at "the decrepit impotence" of the democracies. This finished his work in London.

Mussolini gave him the unimportant post of Minister of Justice which counts little in a country controlled by the OVRA and Gestapo. During the present war, he was entrusted with the task of telling Hitler why Italy acted so impulsively on Greece. Grandi was to say how well equipped the Italians were and that the campaign was to be a pushover. He evidently made an impression upon Hitler for when he said good-bye, the Fuehrer lifted from his desk a shining star which he pinned on the breast of Grandi. It was the highest decoration ever bestowed upon a foreign diplomat.

Of the men mentioned as successors to Il Duce, Grandi looms up and gains as each year passes. His present rivals are Ciano and Farinacci. In poise, intelligence, experience and ability Grandi has the call. If Il Duce could have his way, it would be Ciano. He will always be his son-in-law.

Little recommends Galeazzo Ciano as heir though he is actually groomed to the succession. Certainly young and definitely unsophisticated, this only son of the late Admiral Costanzo Ciano was set to be a play-boy until he married Edda. This changed everything. We might say before going further that Admiral Ciano was a first hour loyalist to Mussolini and was perhaps repaid many times over even without having his son chosen the heir designate. He became one of the richest men in Italy after having held the post of Minister of Communications for ten years with the whole railroad system, the merchant marine and the telephones under his control. He bought villas, a newspaper, yachts, bundles of bonds and stacks of stock. The son is certainly heir to all these.

As a young university student, Galeazzo had trained for a literary career, more precisely, as a playwright. One of his plays was put on the stage but brought him little renown as it was pitifully immature even though there were signs of talent. He joined the staff of a Fascist newspaper as dramatic critic. A considerable soft pedal has been placed upon these literary meanderings perhaps for the reason that they may not have implied a rugged revolutionary recklessness, though we have the incontestable fact that father-in-law started that way.

When Il Duce began the complete "fascistizing" of the state, it included the Italian diplomatic corps also. Here was a chance for young Fascists to qualify for the foreign service. Young Ciano left literature for diplomacy. We have seen how he was promoted.

He was Minister of Propaganda at thirty. When he entered his first cabinet meeting he was fifteen minutes late. Il Duce scowled. This was not Fascist discipline.

"You are late," roared Il Duce. "I warn you. You cannot sit with us. Take your papers and get out."

He got out and quickly. That afternoon he received an alarm clock with a card conveying an affectionate father-in-law's admonition, "With the compliments of the Head of the Government." Everyone thought it funny. Everyone laughed.

But he became Foreign Minister at thirty-two, even

younger than Grandi. Not entirely without experience
he was a consular clerk at Rio de Janeiro under Gae
tano Vecchiotti, who is at present Italian Consul Gen
eral in New York. He had been, too, consul genera
himself in Shanghai. But when we think that he too]
Grandi's place we can only attribute the change to th
superior qualities of sons-in-law.

In diplomacy, he could not refrain from some out
cropping of the play-boy. His diplomatic efforts cen
tered on the beach at the seaside resort at Ostia. Ther
he basked each season and so basked all the diplomat
assigned to Rome. Each tried to get the place neares
the count. He was the king-pin. Alternating bask
ing with swimming, he learned what other countrie
said they wanted. Swimming, he had no breath whei
Italy was discussed. Under the rose, he was dubbec
by his fault-finding countrymen as the *ministro aquatic*
(aquatic minister), an Italian subtlety implying that h
was perhaps a better merman than statesman. He likec
Breckinridge Long, our envoy from 1933 to 1936.

For winter, he wanted to pick up golf which he had
never played until he had learned that it was quit
diplomatic. The course and buildings at the Rom
Golf Club were rebuilt with government funds on th
excuse that the improvement would help the touris
trade. Now there are no tourists. He plays witl
Italians. There are no British ambassadors any more
The present American Ambassador, suave Willian
Phillips is engaging but, not such a good golfer. In any
event, Ciano's golf was not as successful as his swim
ming.

Galeazzo is so much of a successor that Romans call him "Il Ducellino" (the Little Duce). Suiting action to word, he imitates the dictatorial grimaces, sticks out his jaw and speaks in a staccato vehemence. He stands arms akimbo, hands on hips. When he was getting fat — which was a dangerous omen, for his father and mother were mildly monstrous — he adopted Il Duce's diet of fruit, fish and fowl.

Taking on the mannerisms and bluster of Il Duce, he carried them with him when he went as captain of an air squadron, *La Disperata*, to Ethiopia. He did not give up his post as Minister of Propaganda. He paraded around as if he were the personal embodiment of his father-in-law. De Bono invited him to all the meetings of the High Command. Under Badoglio, however, his dictatorial mimicry received a blow. The marshal detested his display of swank and swagger. He broke into a meeting of the staff at general headquarters one afternoon expecting that each officer would stand when he appeared. Badoglio frowned.

"Captain Ciano," he said with decisive bite, "if you are here as Minister of Propaganda, I wish to state that this is not a cabinet meeting. If you are here as a captain in the king's army, take your place with your squadron and leave for it immediately."

Having trained for a literary career, he had veered toward an Italo-French friendship. It was Il Duce's Nietzschean drive which made him a friend of Hitler and Von Ribbentrop. The Germans made fun of him at first. When he visited Munich for the Axis negotiations, he was feted in the famous Nazi beer garden.

There were murmurings of what Italy had done in the first World War — signed a treaty with Germany and Austria and then joined England and France. After the *Horst Wessel Lied* and *Giovinezza,* the orchestra struck up a gayer melody from one of the popular operettas of the day, "Du kanst nicht treu sein" (You can never be true).

He has not liked Hitler. One reason is because the latter treated him so badly at the Salzburg meeting in 1939. Il Duce had told him to say that Italy could not go into the war for three years. When he told this to Hitler, Der Fuehrer wanted to know whether they were to expect a recurrence of the last treaty with Italy. Ready or not ready, he was making his plans whether England would fight or not. On came the war and Ciano returned to Rome carrying with him the undoubted anxiety of what was going to happen to an unprepared Italy.

Many are the men who have been called by Il Duce to high rank in his rule. Many have been ruined and sent into oblivion by his reckless disregard of others and his unscrupulous insistence on blind obedience to his command. The few who have survived the severity of his regime have done it only through submerging their own ability to his egoistic destiny. His goal was to perfect a wholly Mussolini machine of government so that it would endure manned by the men he chose. This was to be the guarantee that the founder of Fascism would be historically glorified.

Now the aspirants for the mantle of dictator are beginning to chart their course. He does not expect to be

long-lived.   None of his family lived beyond three score
years.   He told your reporter that he thought his own
span of life would be spent at sixty-five.   He is still
young enough to see and certainly suffer great changes.
The specter of Hitler or the specter of defeat are not
pleasant to contemplate.   It may never be Ciano,
Grandi, or even Farinacci.

CHAPTER XVIII

SERGEANT WITH A MARSHAL'S BATON

In 1910, Sorel doubted the depth and stability of Mussolini as a revolutionary. He prophesied that young Benito would some day wrap himself in the Italian tricolor and brandish the sword of a chauvinist. Sorel detected the martial strain. Until that time, Benito had condemned wars as the invention of the capitalist class. He preached that they prolonged the enslavement of the workers who did the fighting anyway. He was sent to jail for anti-war incitement. But Sorel perceived a subtle difference — Benito was against wars because they were not his own wars.

In 1914, the world conflict uncovered his belligerent bent. He wanted workers to join so that they could seize the arms and then overthrow the capitalist class. It was then the Socialists expelled him. He went to war anyway and became a sergeant. The whet for martial movement spiced with revolution possessed him. Fascism was one result. Fascism was military with its squadrons, legions and battalions.

He could well have dreamed of commanding large masses of armed proletariat as Trotsky had done. He certainly dreamed it. Among so many other things done on assuming power, did he not order a horse from the Ministry of War so that he could learn to ride? A commander must ride a horse since a commander must parade. Riding daily in the great public park in Rome, the populace could see that he had great talent. He could ride a horse — something most of them could not do. It would remind them that he could lead an army.

And then from the very start, the talk about a strong army, a powerful navy and a big air force began. New uniforms came into existence and the whole nation, much against its inclinations, was ushered into a military atmosphere. He collected uniforms for himself. He wore them whenever he possibly could. Spurs on the boot was the order of the day.

Though at first he could boast no military prowess because he had only held the rank of sergeant, he created the very elaborate rank of honorary corporal of the Fascist militia, perhaps in a Napoleonic tradition. It was a happy thought because it signified both honor and soldiery without any necessity of being worthy of either.

He had difficulty, too, in getting any regular army men to assume command of the militia. He assumed command himself. He could wear another uniform — commander-in-chief of the Fascist legions. Accordingly and quite conveniently, he took the rank of general. He gradually beautified this uniform with golden stripes and gilded trinkets. The final touch was put upon it when he ordered an eighteen-inch aigrette for his helmet and stuck it straight up in the air. It looked so very military that he allowed it for the other generals as well.

He inspected the army, the navy and air force every year. Through July, August and September, he was present at all the grand maneuvers from the very first day until they ended. The army often undertook the problem of beating back the Germans, the French or the Yugoslavs in the Alps or of meeting an invading force in the South, presumably the British. In these wars, the defending forces always won, the communique said. The convoying of troops to North Africa was a favorite exercise. This is bothering the Italian fleet today, but in other days the convoy always "succeeded in evading capture by the enemy forces." In the air force, he ordered Balbo, whom he had named to command very early, "to darken the sky black with planes." With all this military touch and activity he was learning to be a soldier.

Of course, with his impulsive and self-willed character, the military men were bound to play an important part. As we have seen, he used military men to good advantage in forming his first cabinet. But they have always given him an itch for which scratching was not a cure. Their loyalty was first sworn to the king. He could not exact from them the undivided devotion which he claimed from the rank and file of the Fascist party.

Early in his regime he had trouble about the true status of the Fascist militia in relation to the regular army. The militia was his favorite for he purposely tried to train it as a personal force. Men and officers swore allegiance to him. This caused such an uproar that the oath was finally modified to include the king. He failed then to build up this personal army. He tried to win over the men of the regular army command. It was a difficult undertaking. He could win them over

to him as Prime Minister but he never did succeed in
divorcing their loyalty to the king.

We may say here that every so often there were little
signs in his speeches to his cohorts that he harbored a
strong desire to power over the king and even for the
elimination of the monarchy. As we learned he was
outspoken in this when young. In these days the old
aim cropped up. I once saw a film he had made which
showed the cavalcade of the regime. In one scene he
said, "I did not consider this the moment when I should
move to possess absolute power." This film was never
shown publicly.

He did have a handful of Fascists who could aspire
to high rank in the army and the navy but they had
neither the distinction nor the rallying qualities of great
leaders to create for him a personal military following.
To be sure, Balbo built up the air force. He had inculcated into his command a sacrificial devotion to the
person of Il Duce. Colonels of the air force had told
me that if Mussolini would ask any one of them to take
the life of their father, they would obey. But the air
force was relatively low in personnel and ineffective
against any movement insurrectionary enough to contemplate the overthrow of the monarchy.

In the army was one general who reversed the usual
military loyalty. As a rule, they paid sincere devotion
to the king but lip service to Mussolini. General Ugo
Cavallero paid sincere devotion to Mussolini and lip
service to the king. He was early a supporter of the
Fascist regime. His chief merit as a soldier seemed

summed up in his ability to write the official communiques. He conceived himself as a military man of letters. He had been secretary to General Diaz in the first World War and had been entrusted with the editing of the high command's announcements. He is reputed to have written the final communique of the victory, considered to possess some literary flair though it was the military merit which gave Italy Trent, Trieste and the Dodecanese. With the merit, he had nothing to do.

As a conversational companion, I always thought of Cavallero as one of the most polished individuals it was possible to meet. Besides possessing a somewhat wide knowledge of literature in many languages, he had a most happy faculty of being able to be humorous over everything and to smile throughout a whole evening. He was such a one as would constantly be invited to dinner because of his gifts as a *causeur* and his diverse worldliness, a sterling asset for one who is more often in a salon or reception hall than on the battlefield.

Because of his devotion to Fascism, Mussolini chose him as his first undersecretary for war. Later, it was somehow suggested that he should make some much needed money. He was assigned the post of president of the Ansaldo corporation, which builds battleships, makes guns and manufactures munitions. Stories of corruption abound in regard to Italian battleships, guns and munitions. Cavallero was able to replenish his fortunes. Patiently, he could await a turn.

It came. When Mussolini finally quarreled with Badoglio in December, 1940, he sent for the great litarary general and appointed him Chief of Staff of the Italian army. Then, too, things were going from bad to worse in Albania where the slender but courageous Greek army was putting whole Italian divisions to rout. Instead of commanding the metropolitan forces, Cavallero was sent to Albania to organize an Italian offensive. He failed in several attempts. It was not quite fair of Mussolini to expect anything sensational since the Chief of Staff operated a typewriter better than a tank. It should not have been required that his spick and span uniform be messed up in the mountain mud of the Albanian Alps. I can also say from personal observation that there was not a single salon or reception hall where tea could be served in the whole of the country. It was a bitter struggle.

Other Fascist generals have fared no better. We have already learned how De Bono came to delightful grief in the Ethiopian campaign by finishing his career with a disorganized army but a promotion to field marshal. Attilio Teruzzi was, for a while, chief of staff of the Fascist Militia. His campaigns finished with many medals and bric-a-brac though his luxuriant beard had never even been singed. Bergonzoli, also poetically maned, trimmed his hirsute growth so that it quivered. Thus was he nicknamed "Electric Whiskers." They were of some account, for he fought well against the unarmed blacks, though against the whites they failed him. General Wavell mopped him up with all his floss and fringe in three weeks. Starace commanded a division on the Sudan border with little dazzle or glory. There was fine fishing at Lake Tana, they said. Telling of the catch was a wide array of stars, crosses and braid, generously bestowed on all friends of Il Duce. There are others who can count the same degree of achievement. It is picturesque to watch them parade along the Via dell'Impero looking so proud but perhaps not too unworthy, wearing the bronze, the gilt and the brass. Few are fooled and, least of all, the Italians.

To the generals of the regular army could be attributed many major displeasures for Il Duce. Some of them have fought him from the very beginning. First was he who, we learned, ejected D'Annunzio from Fiume and is now Italy's highest ranking soldier, Marshal Caviglia. He did not like the tinkering with the regular army by the militia. Acrid words were hurled at Mussolini by the aging though active marshal. He was a member of the Italian Senate, too, and could thus speak his mind without being sent to an island.

Caviglia, before Il Duce came to power, was officially hailed as "the hero of Vittorio Veneto," the decisive battle of the World War for Italy. Wearing such a glorious halo, the Fascists found it difficult to attack him. They planned, however, to remove the halo. They issued orders that Caviglia was never to be referred to as a hero. Never was there a word in the Italian press relating to his glories. Never was he called upon to officiate at patriotic ceremonies or appear before the public for any reason whatsoever. Though more soldier than writer, he *was* a writer. All of his achievements have been published in books. He has written a dozen himself. He was one who urged Italian neutrality today. Modern warfare is more industrial than

military, he said. Italy did not have the economic resources to fight the war, he claimed. He is remembered
now.

Other regular army generals called in for collaboration have adhered scrupulously to their monarchical
oaths. They have guarded tactfully but effectively
against encroachments of the king's command. General
Vaccari built up the defenses along the Austrian and
Yugoslav borders. General Clerici reorganized the
forces to meet the limited Italian budget. General
Baistrocchi introduced the mechanized division. It
was not as powerful as the German panzer division.
Having limited motorized equipment, he tried to combine cavalry, bicyclists, armored cars and tanks. Its
in efficiency has been shown by the sorry efforts in the
Egyptian campaign.

But principal in this inside drama between king and
dictator was Marshal Badoglio. As a soldier we have
seen how he has obeyed implicitly all the king's com-
mands. He never allowed misunderstanding in his
allegiance, first to the king and then to the ministers as
officers of the crown. There was never any Duce of
Fascism as the ruler of Italy for him. He held office
under the crown.

Badoglio is hailed as Italy's greatest soldier. In appearance, he is almost the double of the late Knute
Rockne, the coach of Notre Dame university. Though
he is soft spoken and affable, he is a stern disciplinarian
and possesses no small measure of quick and unequivocal
decision. His training started in the Military Academy
of Turin and took him through the Italian East African

campaigns of 1896 and 1897, and the first Lybian war. By the first World War, he was an officer of known achievement.

Badoglio was assigned in 1915 to the staff of the Second Army Corps when Italy joined the allies. In 1916, he led the assault on the Austrian stronghold of Mount Sabotino and conquered it. Promotion to brigadier-general was the reward. In 1917, after the Caporetto disaster, he was called as assistant chief of staff to General Diaz. This was evidence of royal confidence in him. The Italian army was reorganized under his guidance. He prepared the plans for the final Italian offensive on the Piave, and on the defeat of Austria was appointed chief of the Italian delegation to negotiate the armistice. He was then forty-seven.

He was chief of staff of the Italian army before Fascism came to power. In 1921, on a mission of goodwill, he was sent to the United States. Thousands of Italians waited for hours for his ship to dock in New York Harbor. A tour of the entire country followed. It was prohibition then. Asked what he thought of it, he replied,

"I have never taken spirituous liquors in my life. I would not now begin. But light wines appear necessary to me. In the Italian army, where we always serve them, I have never seen any drunkenness."

When he returned to Italy, he found the Fascists rising to threaten. He was called into consultation by Prime Minister Facta. It was the moment when Mussolini had sworn the violent seizing of power. On

October 7, 1922, Badoglio unqualifiedly assured the cabinet that depending on the ministry for his orders, he could very quickly dominate any situation which the Fascists could contrive to create.

"After five minutes of firing," he told them, "the whole of Fascism will collapse."

This brought vehement words from Mussolini who was then just waiting and watching events in his newspaper office in Milan.

"We do not believe that the vile intentions of General Badoglio will materialize," he wrote. "The National army will not march against the Black Shirts. In spite of all he has said, we have the firm confidence that General Badoglio will avoid the useless attempt of becoming the headsman of the Fascist revolution."

When the March on Rome was actually being organized, Badoglio was called by the king. The sovereign asked his advice on the maintenance of public order.

"Sir," said the Italian Chief of Staff, "assign to me a single battalion of the Royal Carabineers and I will drive those upstarts into the sea."

The monarch smiled. He heard more advice, and a few days later decided on asking Mussolini to form a government.

Il Duce could not but look with furrowed brow and curled lip at the soldier who held him in such disdain. He could not eliminate him because he was indisputably the first soldier in the land. Besides, he could not cross the king's confidence in him. Traditionally, the

Italian army is divorced from politics. Discreetly Mussolini crept in the shadow of this tradition perhaps to wait for another day.

They got along. Il Duce tried to win the soldier but the soldier was a servant of the king. Various posts were offered him. He accepted the ambassadorship to Brazil on a very special mission. Government and people welcomed him, complimented that such a celebrity had graced the diplomatic corps at Rio de Janeiro. He remained a year and then on the request of the king accepted the governorship of Lybia. There he stayed five years. Returning to Italy, he resumed his post as chief of staff.

During this period of his sojourn at home and now at the age of sixty-three, he took a course in aviation and qualified as a military pilot. We next heard of him through all the turns of the preparation for the war in Ethiopia and how he was ignored until his services were indispensable. When he finally entered the Ethiopian capital, the king showed his appreciation, created him the Duke of Addis Ababa and made him the first viceroy. He stayed in Ethiopia a few months. Because of his health, he was relieved and returned to Rome.

But the impresario was jealous of his star. Mussolini would not let the great artist take a bow even though the populace was clamoring for a glimpse of the hero. Often when great personages visited Rome, a gala performance was offered at the opera. But for the hero of Addis Ababa, there was nothing. What an occasion for the realization in theater as well as fact of the great Verdi opera of "Aïda," coinciding as it does with the

Badoglio conquest of the Ethiopians. No, "Gloria" was not sung for Badoglio.

An official welcome for the hero was tabooed. Mussolini refused any show of triumph whatever. Badoglio slipped down from the train, greeted only by his relatives, his intimate friends and former members of his staff. The Fascist press was ordered to emphasize the idea that Badoglio's contribution to victory was considerably minor to that of Mussolini. The editors were told to show that detailed plans of the campaign came from the brain of Il Duce. The campaign was directed from Rome, they said. Badoglio only had to follow instructions and victory was placed in his palm, they wrote.

Empty tokens of esteem were showered upon him to cover up the jealousy of Il Duce. An official communique announced that Badoglio had received honorary membership in the Fascist party, an honor certainly without significance to the great soldier. The city of Rome bestowed upon him the rank of honorary citizen, a privilege granted many minor personages. This was camouflage to satisfy the popular demand that some public recognition should be given the man who had brought them an empire.

It was quite natural for Badoglio now to wish complete retirement, but the king called him again for the tightening of army organization. The trends of Europe were directed toward war and more than ever now the Italian army should be tuned up for the emergency. Badoglio found that little could be done with the present means because practically all the equipment available had been used up in the Ethiopian campaign. He could only report the armed forces unprepared. On that basis, he advised against the Albanian invasion of 1939. He insisted on Italian neutrality and vehemently condemned the ill-fated campaign in Greece. Finally, on December 5, 1940, a strange communique was issued. It said that according to "a decree in the course of being signed by the king, the resignation of Marshal Badoglio as Chief of the General Staff has been accepted." It was not an unusual Mussolini trick. He had fired him even before he had time to resign or even before the king had time to sign the royal decree.

Despite his unswerving devotion to duty, there are cries in the Fascist press that he failed them when he was needed most. The fact is he does not believe that Italy should have gone to war.

With Badoglio set aside both by choice and circumstance, the only Italian general who was considered to possess any great amount of military skill was Marshal Rodolfo Graziani. His long experience as a desert fighter gave confidence to Il Duce that he was the man to lead the Italian army against the British Imperial Army of the Nile for the seizure of the Suez Canal. Instead, crushing defeat has been his fate. In any other military establishment, he would have been relieved of his command very early and sent away to nurse the reverse the rest of his life.

But Graziani stayed in command. It is difficult to say whether he owed his great loyalty to the crown or to Il Duce. Sure it is that his career was made because he was a favorite of the dictator. His brother-in-law was Mussolini's private physician. The decisions required of Badoglio as between king and dictator had never been exacted from Graziani. We cannot tell what he would have done had he had to face that crisis.

He had started out a lawyer but never practiced. At twenty-two, he passed the military examinations and was sent as a lieutenant to Italian East Africa. He was there nine years. He entered the World War as captain, had three and a half years of active service, and at thirty-six he became a colonel. He saw service all along the front and was twice wounded. After the war, he was demobilized but returned to the army when Mussolini came to power. He was sent to Lybia and there his experience as a desert fighter began.

His campaigns consisted chiefly of raids into country occupied by Arab tribes. Resistance, while fierce, was no match for his better equipped units. He conquered Fezzan well into the interior and received the congratulations of Marshal Lyautey, then military governor of French Morocco, who praised "the military genius of my Latin brother." He had also fought a combined action with General Archibald P. Wavell, who was his adversary as commander-in-chief of the British Imperial Army of the Nile. They were both cited as joint conquerors on the Kufra Oasis. To celebrate the occasion, they exchanged daggers on which was inscribed, "United, we are masters."

Promotion raised him to the post of vice-governor of Lybia under Marshal Badoglio. Then he began the cruelest mass murder in colonial history. It is difficult to understand why the campaign was necessary since

Italy's North African colonies had been reported in perfect calm for years. Graziani, however, inaugurated a system of inhuman annihilation of the Arabs. He originated "the flying tribunal." This military court went through village after village ordering wholesale massacres on the most insignificant provocation. Men, women and children were herded into enclosures and mowed down by machine-guns. Hundreds of villages were razed to the ground. It was not without some foundation that the Arabs had called him "the butcher."

In the Ethiopian war, Graziani led an army from the South while Badoglio was operating from the North. He encountered great difficulties at first but succeeded in penetrating two hundred and fifty miles into the interior to capture the stronghold of Neghelli and to defeat Ras Desta, son-in-law of Haile Selassie. When Badoglio resigned as viceroy, he was appointed to replace him.

In February, 1937, an attempt was made on his life when in Addis Ababa a bomb was thrown at him. It exploded twenty feet from where he was standing. There were marks of thirty-eight splinters on his uniform. His temper was up. He ordered the bloodiest human butchery of modern times. It made even a week's work in Lybia seem like a street fight. The natives were herded outside the city. Huts were burned and their occupants massed for the kill. Hour after hour Italian soldiers flaming with blood lust perpetrated the most revolting tortures.

Streams of red flowed in the narrow passageways of the crowded capital. All day long and on into the night, the soldiers of Graziani herded and killed, herded and killed. No native, man, woman or child, within sight of a soldier was spared. Mass murder of the innocent was inflicted with sword, dagger, torch, rifle, bomb and machine-gun. Terrified natives were thrown into the flames. At the end of the long orgy which lasted for twenty-four hours, twelve thousand Ethiopian men, women and children had been slain. Then they herded the survivors to bury the dead without record or regard for family ties. It was the price exacted for a missed aim, the soiled uniform of Marshal Graziani.

His reputation as a desert soldier had been won on lesser episodes than this but episodes such as this nevertheless. His career is summed up in the massacre of unarmed and defenseless tribesmen. Now, he was Il Duce's choice to lead the Italian army against the British Imperial Army of the Nile. Against trained soldiers, his military skill has been exploded, a myth. He wears five rows of ribbons, many cordons, stars and gilded trinkets. He has finally resigned in disgrace.

And while Il Duce can order the Italian people to cut down their macaroni to one plate a week and have them obey, it is not so easy to order his generals. He has tried to impose his political instincts into the military field. He has aspired to be the general of the generals. Caviglia and Badoglio have spurned his military judgment. He desired to ride upon a wave of military glory. When the generals succeeded he claimed that glory. To show the populace that he had military talent, he requested the king to bestow upon him the highest military decoration of the Italian crown, the Grand

Cordon of the Military Order of Savoy. If there still was to be doubt, he officially offered for the king's signature a decree which nominated him "First Marshal of Italy." This for the sergeant.

CHAPTER XIX

"BENITO, I'LL NEVER FORGET IT"

What was on the inside of the Rome-Berlin Axis?
When Mussolini came to power, he inherited the
muddles over Fiume, Dalmatia, the Dodecanese and
even Albania. Anything could happen and often did.
Basically, however, Italian foreign policy centered on
three fundamentals: inviolability of the Brenner Pass,
the independence of Austria and a zone of influence in
the Danubian basin. Keeping the Brenner frontier
meant keeping the South Tyrol and its 250,000 Austrians of German blood. Insisting on Austrian integrity
signified a buffer state between Italy and Germany with
weaker neighbors all about. Influence along the Dan-
ube was an instrument of economic penetration and international prestige.

In the Mediterranean, Italy kept Britain a friend.
Then Britain supported Italian aspirations. In banquet
talk, it was spoken of as "the traditional cordiality be-
tween two great peoples." Much was said of the help
Great Britain gave during the days when Italy with
Garibaldi and Mazzini was fighting for independence.
It suited both countries to exchange these compliments.
An air of neighborly living hovered caressingly about
them.

But behind it all, sterner factors — commerce, finance,
defense, empire — encouraged if not imposed a friendship. Britain cherished the advantage of having a po-

tential ally in the Mediterranean rather than an enemy. Italy could do more with an amiable England. Italy could not resist a British blockade. Even during the period of the Triple Alliance, Italy's adherence was predicated on the provision that she should not be expected to go to war against England. Italian statesmen agreed that they could get farther going along with rather than going against her. This was the traditional Anglo-Italian cordiality. Mussolini continued the British tie.

As his own foreign secretary, he settled the quarrel with the Yugoslavs by the annexation of Fiume to Italy and the awarding of Port Baross to Yugoslavia. Adjustments were made in Dalmatia, the Dodecanese and Albania. This cleared the air and allowed him to make overtures to France. But France was haughty and had organized the Little Entente—Yugoslavia, Czechoslovakia and Roumania. This was a fresh design to place an ally at the back of their probable enemies, Italy and Germany. Trying to be friends with France did not work. Mussolini then adopted French diplomatic strategy himself. He made an agreement with Hungary as his ally at the back of the Slavs. This was Europe in those vacillating years.

Friendship with Germany was impossible because of the South Tyrol impasse and the German aim to unite with Austria. Germany asked for greater autonomy for the 250,000 Germans living in the South Tyrol. Mussolini answered by prohibiting the German language in the schools, by the suppression of German clubs and the changing of all public signs and notices from Ger-

man to Italian. Tension was created and tension stayed.
On union with Austria, Mussolini countered by keeping most of his army in the north. He was supported
by England and France. No possible avenue was open
for Italo-German rapprochement. It was conflict.
Often it was open conflict.

When the Nazis rose to rule in 1933, he saw a
chance. He could play them against France and England, a game at which he had already shown outstanding skill. The Reich needed friends. Hitler looked for
a smile anywhere. Both began to flirt. They possessed
identical ideologies, they murmured. Il Duce was the
big brother then. Il Duce patronized the new baby in
his dictatorial infancy.

Since the Nazis cried loudly that they had the same
system, the Italians succumbed to the compliment.
Hitherto, Mussolini had said that Fascism was not an
article for export. Now his press and puppets began to
visualize a world won to Fascism or vice-versa. Il Duce
himself expanded both his head and chest and proclaimed from the balcony, "The twentieth century belongs to Fascism."

Officials of one country visited the other. Goering
and Von Papen made frequent trips. They wined and
dined. Toasts were drunk to the great leaders and the
common aspirations of the two kindred peoples. They
were nations going hand in hand with common systems
which were bound to be adopted by the whole world.
Then the Germans sought to learn how to run the system. The Italians swelling with pride showed them
everything from the military induction of three-year-

olds to the swift and decisive liquidation of political
opponents. One was instructed. One was complimented.

Il Duce continued to patronize Hitler, who took it
because Germany was woefully weak. She was not a
very desirable friend since France and England held
such superior power over her. And because she was so
held, no one paid much attention to Il Duce's patronizing blessing. He did not show too much amiability.
Not yet.

The enmity of both France and England was not desirable. He was again complimented in the spring by a
visit from Ramsay MacDonald, Prime Minister of England. He welcomed him personally at the Ostia sea-
plane base on a Saturday. On Monday, he presented
to MacDonald a scheme for the "peace of Europe."
This was right down the road over which the aging
Prime Minister desired to travel. He was always
preaching the "peace of Europe" though had he used a
stronger club for his country he would have made peace
rather than talked peace. He swallowed the pact. It
was the solution. He came for peace and Mussolini
had given it to him in the famous four-power pact of
Italy, France, Germany and Great Britain.

Mussolini rose now as a man of peace and was even
suggested for the Nobel prize. He was not alone big
in his own eyes but now was big in the eyes of British
statesmen. He was preventing another war. He was
isolating Russia, then as now the great question-mark.
All four nations signed the pact on July 15, 1933.
They were looking for a lasting peace by the end of the

summer. The British were glad to welcome Germany
back to normalcy. The French were suspicious. The
French parliament failed to ratify the pact. It never
went into effect.

Hitler had pronounced the policy of all Germans
within one Reich. This was such a dream that few
statesmen paid much attention to it, conceiving it to be
one of his rallying cries to fortify the Nazi morale. It
was so far off that he could not possibly mean it. It
involved Danzig, Memel, the German minorities in
Poland and in Czechoslovakia. Mussolini, too, thought
he could not mean the South Tyrol. He could not
mean Austria.

Their first visit was arranged in May, 1934, at Venice.
Il Duce stood waiting at the Lido airport for the big
Junkers, personal plane of Adolf Hitler. It was a
balmy morning. Everyone was in summer attire. We
watched the big machine circling overhead and slowly
descending. When it landed, the door was opened and
out came Hitler, awkward, timid and pudgy in a brown
gabardine followed by all the Nazi hierarchs in brown
gabardines, on this beautiful May morning in Italy.

To make matters worse, Il Duce wore the uniform of
Commander-in-chief of the Fascist militia, which set
him off a bit conspicuously. Mussolini went forward to
meet Der Fuehrer. We followed Il Duce, who welcomed him in German and asked about the trip. Responding, Hitler said that he had had a wonderful trip
and without smiling was pleased to meet Il Duce. Immediately, the band struck up the national anthems and
everybody was brought to attention. The ceremony

over, Mussolini turned about and led the way to a waiting launch. It was naturally through those who were standing in the rear. Someone remembered that they had not played the *Horst Wessel Lied* and immediately the bandmaster gave the sign and up the Nazi song was struck. With it the welcome was complete. No, not before Hitler had called Herr von Hassel, German ambassador to Italy. He scowled at him and then said, "Why did you not advise me to wear my uniform?"

Now we cannot say that the meeting was enthusiastic. It was friendly. Delight did not scintillate in anybody's eyes. Two strangers met. Mussolini was pleasant or perhaps he would not have inquired about the trip. He had a swarthy, healthy glow. Hitler, in contrast, looked like a pastry cook. They were taken to Venice in a launch. The first conference took place that afternoon in the royal palace at Stra, near Padua, on the mainland.

Mussolini in uniform, Hitler in gabardine met in the richly furnished salon on the second floor of the palace. The doors were closed. The session began. It was fortunate that Il Duce could speak German, otherwise their dictatorial dignity would have been disturbed by the presence of one who took orders. But it was not long before the secretaries and attendants who had accompanied them, heard violent shouts emerging from the dictatorial arena. The pounding of fists, which they hoped was on the table, punctuated loud talk. Everyone heard intermittently a screech of "Österreich." It was "Österreich" this and "Österreich" that; pounding and "Österreich."

Finally, after an hour's shouting and pounding, their door opened. Secretaries and attendants rushed to the door. Each dictator was embarrassed. Each tried to return to the calm which should be shown on personal appearances. Mussolini pulled at his tunic and Hitler pulled at his gabardine belt. Their faces showed the heat of battle but with it also was heat of hate. Il Duce had not succeeded in controlling Der Fuehrer. Der Fuehrer had got nowhere with Il Duce. After they reached their hotels in Venice, Count Ciano gave out a communique stating that they had met in "an atmosphere of perfect cordiality" and that they had agreed on the maintenance of the independence of Austria. Dr. Dietrich, the German press chief, gave out no communique. Instead, he passed the word around the German correspondents that there was no agreement at all on any question and especially not on the question of Austria. Der Fuehrer did not commit himself.

The following day, a review in honor of Hitler enlivened the program. Pouting, Mussolini was a half-hour late. Hitler and his foreign secretary, Baron von Neurath, stood on the reviewing stand first on one foot and then on the other waiting patiently for the arrival of Il Duce. It was a long, long wait. No attention at all was being paid to Hitler. Finally, Il Duce arrived and the two dictators exchanged the greetings of the day. They had not made up but were just going through the scheduled program.

When the review finally passed, it was composed of the most motley group of Fascist militia ever seen. Mussolini had given orders that companies in old uniforms and looking strictly unkempt were to participate in the ceremony. If Hitler had had any respect for Italian soldiery, his opinion certainly was shaken at the sight of this disheveled mass. The review had hardly finished when Mussolini led his guest through the crowd without any police escort from the square to the royal palace. In the midst of the most distracting confusion they ploughed their way through the mobs, — all of it quite in contrast to the military precision which mark events in Germany at which Der Fuehrer is present.

Il Duce had shown him his disdain.

They went through the rest of the program, too. Il Duce spoke from a balcony in the square while Der Fuehrer listened at a nearby window. He said nothing about the great friendship uniting the two countries nor about the common aims which bind the Nazi and Fascist systems. It was all one way, all praise for Fascism. Italy was the country of the future.

The next morning, at Der Fuehrer's departure, the same ceremony was arranged as on the arrival. They played the national anthems and then the *Horst Wessel Lied*. It was like the send-off of a relative who had overstayed his welcome. Smiles were skimpy and begrudged. But they had talked. They had learned something about one another.

A few days later, Starace asked Il Duce what he thought of Der Fuehrer.

"He is a fool," snarled Il Duce. "I will teach him a lesson yet."

The outcome was a violent quarrel between the two

dictators. The Nazis schemed to take Austria anyway. Il Duce had nursed Austria personally. He had handed it money and had been the strong arm for keeping diminutive Chancellor Dollfuss in power. But on July 25, 1934, a group of German and Austrian Nazis stormed the Chancellery in Vienna, shot Dollfuss, fatally wounding him. Others in the building were held incommunicado. Secretaries asked permission for a doctor for the chancellor. The Nazis refused. In intense suffering for over three hours, he bled to death. Austrian police, however, stormed the Chancellery and dislodged the Nazis.

Mussolini was ready to go to war against Hitler. He ordered five divisions to the Brenner Pass. They were set to march into Austria if the Nazis had not evacuated the Chancellery. Hitler then had few troops. He could not risk war especially since France and England were ready to help Mussolini. Both had given Il Duce assurances. The Nazis withdrew from the attempt. Austrian independence remained.

There was very bad blood between the dictators now. Il Duce realized that Hitler was determined to seize Austria. This accomplished, he would threaten the South Tyrol. The foundations of Italian foreign policy, — the inviolability of the Brenner Pass and the integrity of Austria, were menaced. Mussolini watched him. He was enraged. His hate for Hitler increased. He repudiated Nazism. To me he called the Germans a nation of pederasts. He later published it in *Il Popolo d'Italia*. He ordered a press campaign against the Nazis. Sexual perversion was a favorite weapon of attack.

In speeches, Mussolini scorned their culture, burlesqued their dress as tourists, jeered at their whimpers of economic poverty and loudly characterized them as degenerates. In Bari in September, he publicly branded them as barbarians and said that Rome had her Virgil, Cicero and Horace while the Huns were still savages painting their bodies brown. Every organ of Italian propaganda was used to subject Hitler and the Germans to the most violent language. What we marvel at today is that Hitler was so weak he had to take it.

Having done England and France a good service by thwarting the Nazi coup on Austria, Mussolini now considered himself worthy of favor. His help and quick decision were necessary elements to their slow-moving governmental frame-work. Now it was that he looked with longing eyes toward colonial expansion. This was the favor to ask. This was when he worked Laval to give his support to his Ethiopian enterprise. It was noticeable how he maneuvered France against England. He had to have his friend. The campaign threw the whole of European politics into a jumble. We saw finally that when he was in trouble over the international boycott, Hitler came to his help. It certainly was not without motive. He came. It was the birth of the second Hitler-Mussolini comradeship.

Mussolini had weighed friendship with England. By 1937, the increasing rearmament of Germany was confirmed. He deprecated the slow processes of the democracies. He viewed with disdain the unending parliamentary debates on vital defense measures. He

knew of the corruption in French politics. He discerned the disinclination of the British to move toward
war. He watched the movements for peace in Britain,
the United States and the British colonies. He convinced himself on the one hand that the British were a
decaying race; on the other, the Germans, a rising energetic people.

Besides, the intervention he had undertaken in the
Spanish Civil War, designed to strengthen his Mediterranean position against England, had become a great
drain on his resources, already impoverished by the
Ethiopian campaign. He thought it would be a quick
decision but a quick decision had not materialized. Defeat at Guadalajara made German help indispensable.
He asked for it and received it. Again it was not given
without motive. The Nazi dive bombers and bombardment planes had their tests over Madrid and Barcelona.
Hitler extricated him. Hitler saved his face. They
called it "the firm determination of the Italian and German peoples to defend with all energy the sacred inherit-
ance of European civilization." At this point, their tie-
up was first called the Rome-Berlin Axis.

In conflict with hereditary Italian policy, Il Duce's
face was turned toward Germany. He began a violent
and widespread campaign now against the British both
at home and abroad. Every Italian agency of propaganda turned to creating an anti-British atmosphere.
We have seen what he attempted to do in the Mediterranean countries and amongst the Arabs by bribery,
fifth columns, the press and the radio. He carried this

also into the Americas.   Nightly broadcasts were scheduled for both North and South America to show the
justice of Italian aspirations and the perfidy, disloyalty
and inefficiency of British rule, as his propagandists
put it.

And this direct turn he confirmed in his own conscience by a theory on the imperial cycle which he himself had worked out.   It was in reality a translation of
the theory of Professor Vincenzo Pareto whose lectures
he heard as a youth while exiled in Lausanne.   Pareto
in his treatises on government showed that dominion
continues as long as the rulers are virile and possess the
will to command.   After generations of rule, this virility
and will to command degenerate because the ruling
class desires not to be bothered and wishes to continue
in ease.   They begin making concessions.   This
strengthens those challenging their rule.   Concession
after concession is forced.   Eventually, they are over-
thrown by the new virile class which has aspired to rule
and possesses the will to command.   Then the cycle begins again.

This theory gave Mussolini great inspiration in the
Fascist revolution.   He interpreted his assumption of
power as the birth of a new and more virile class.   Now
on the crossroads of his international policy, he saw the
great nations like Britain and France desiring to live in
ease inclined to concede and allow the command of the
world to pass to a newer and more energetic race.   This
new race he conceived as a combination of Italy and
Germany.   They were the new people possessing the
will to fight and to rule.

"We are a dynamic people," he told me. "The Germans are a dynamic people. We will go with Germany."

He had made the fatal decision. Many hours had he spent in counting the gains and losses. He had rejected the sacred friendship of England. Necessity did not impose it any more. Germany was to be his ally. Did that run counter to Italy's claims for an inviolable Brenner, the independence of Austria as a buffer state and the demand for a zone of influence in the Danubian Basin? It did uncompromisingly. He was willing to risk the annexation of Austria and the threat to the Brenner. He was willing to surrender his aims in the Balkans to the German expansionist movement eastward. In return he was determined with the help of Spain and Germany to make the Mediterranean the *Mare Nostrum* and to acquire his Moslem Empire to the Indian Ocean as the new Empire of Rome. This was his choice.

Besides, it was the late General Douhet of the Italian Air Force who had written the first concept of the *Guerra Fulmine* or *Blitzkrieg* as it is now known. He had presaged the attack of the weak upon the strong by the "lightning war" from which the Germans afterwards adopted the *Blitzkrieg*. The Italians had greater need of the *Guerra Fulmine* than the Germans because of their lack of resources. Douhet imagined a great Italian air force, organized in one rapid stride before Italy's probable enemies had time to produce and train the necessary defense. It was to strike on an all-out movement destroying factories, railroad centers and communications of all kinds so as to throw the enemy into confusion and break the morale of the civilian population.

Asked by a foreign diplomat whether he would have any regard for the civilian population, Douhet replied, "First it must be the victory of one's country; then humanity."

Since Hitler had adopted the Douhet theory, it fitted superbly into the Italian concept of war. The only hitch was that the Italians after 1937 were prostrate and would continue prostrate for many years to come. Hitler went ahead. Mussolini wanted to share the great all-out against whoever Hitler was going to attack. Il Duce pointedly became a great annoyance to Britain now.

In May, 1937, the British government invited Haile Selassie to the coronation of King George VI. Mussolini exploded. He ordered all Italian newspapers to withdraw their correspondents from London. The British explained that the Ethiopian emperor was still on their royal list. Further clarification, too, was given when Grandi was told that they could not be expected to grant concessions to Italy, such as the *de jure* recognition of Italy's conquest, when Mussolini was conducting a hostile British policy everywhere. The black monarch graced the coronation in his arch-regal and imperial robes.

The friendship between the two dictators grew so deep that in September an official visit of Mussolini to Hitler was made. At Il Duce's official entrance into Berlin, hundreds of thousands of cheering Nazis proved

to him that Der Fuehrer was sincere.   More multitudes
acclaimed him at the Sportpalast.

Hitler massed a hundred thousand soldiers with full
equipment.   Exhibitions of machine-guns in action, of
chemical warfare, of huge field pieces and howitzers, of
motorized divisions with tanks, armored cars and mobile
infantry scampering over fields at great speed were given
under the most realistic conditions.   For the air review,
thousands of planes, fighters, bombers, reconnaissance
planes and divers, maneuvered and performed em-
blematic enough of what could be done to Paris or
London.

In the five days, he was filled with the crushing power
of the German military machine.   He meditated.   He
concluded that the combined might of 65,000,000 Germans and 45,000,000 Italians would be sufficient to
smash any combination which could be hurled against
it, especially from "the weak and decadent democracies."   He was convinced.   His conscience was satisfied
that he was on the road to empire.

At the chancellery, Hitler showed him a map of Europe.   He explained to him the alternatives of an eventual campaign.   While he spoke, Mussolini noticed that
Austria appeared under the German colors.   He sighed.
He said nothing.   It was the price he had to pay for
partnership with Germany.

On November 6, he signed the Anti-Comintern pact.
To show further collaboration and after strong German
pressure, on December 11 he withdrew from the League
of Nations.   The following February, Chancellor
Schuschnigg of Austria and successor to Dollfuss, was

called to Berchtesgaden to receive the order to evacuate. In March, Hitler invaded Austria. Il Duce could offer no resistance. The British circulated strong protests to all the governments. The French did likewise. Italians themselves were thrown into consternation. Hitler was now on the Brenner Pass. He was not sure that Il Duce would turn at the last moment and accept the help of Britain and France. When he was sure that Mussolini was not going to move, he sent a personal telegram.

"Benito," it read, "Ich werde es Ihnen nie vergessen." (Benito, I will never forget it.)

When this was learned by the mass of Italians who lived with strained nerves expecting Hitler to cross the pass, they laughed. Placards were found in Rome surreptitiously left for public view with :

"Adolf, neither will I. Benito."

Heartrending was the fate of the children of Dollfuss. Mussolini had sworn to Frau Dollfuss on the assassination of her husband that "your children are my children." When Frau Dollfuss appealed to the Italian embassy for safe conduct from Vienna, she was refused admission. Mussolini ordered that no contact be established between her and Italian officials. The French minister took her under his protection and she was taken with her children to the Swiss frontier.

Now Il Duce prepared for the return visit of Hitler to Rome. This was to surpass any official visit made in modern times and with modern machinery. He gave orders for elaborate displays of the air force, the army and the navy. He knew he could not match the German army in discipline and equipment or equal the German air force in modern machines and numerical superiority, but where he did have something was in a grand show place and a substantial navy. For the German army and air force he was going to pay back with fine historic and artistic scenes and a navy. He knew the German staff would be impressed by the latter because it was precisely what they lacked.

It was May again. At enormous expense, he decorated every public building and monument. Owners of private buildings took the hint. Theirs were just as decorated. The great Roman monuments of antiquity were floodlighted. No royal personage ever had such lavishness showered upon him as did Hitler. King Victor welcomed him personally at a station especially constructed for the occasion. He rode through streets of soldiers massed six and eight deep, a hundred thousand of them, along a three-mile route. Mussolini dug up new uniforms for every man in line. With bands, bunting and braid, it was the most costly reception ever given a foreign dignitary in modern times.

On the third day was the naval review in the bay of Naples. All the vessels of the fleet were concentrated. Hitler was aboard the royal yacht. It circled through the destroyers, scout ships, tankers, colliers, cruisers and battleships—a formidable array drawn up for miles along the coast. It took four hours to make the cruise around them. No one told him that three fourths of those vessels were obsolete. No one said that most of them had been used in the last World War. Many of them were former Austrian craft consigned to the Ital-

ians by the armistice. The review did not have one
modern battleship. The newest was twenty-six years
old. Two new battleships have been commissioned
since that time and, — fatefully damaged in combat.

But with all the great masses of entertainment and of
people, there were no cheers for the great and honored
guest. He was left cold. It was so noticeable that
when Fascist crowds were shouting "Hurrah for Il
Duce," Mussolini had to point to Hitler to try and turn
the claque. It was unsuccessful. Though Hitler was
moved by the impressive sights in monuments, works of
art and Fascist staging, he was not moved by cheers. A
German alliance was not popular.

The displays of friendship set the whole of Europe
in jitters. In the hope of slowing the mad race, Great
Britain aimed at some agreement with Mussolini. The
Mediterranean pact was concluded in April and went
into effect in November. It solemnly bound Italy and
Great Britain to respect the *status quo* in the Mediterranean. Mussolini agreed to the pact to gain time. He
was not in earnest. Neither the British nor the French
statesmen understood the real mentality nor the temperament of the two dictators. The latter were united
and anything done either in good faith or bad was directed toward the fulfillment of their imperialistic aims.
That pact was broken on Good Friday of 1939 when Il
Duce invaded Albania.

On May 22, 1939, the Rome-Berlin Axis became an
offensive and defensive alliance. The deed was done.
Hitler and Mussolini swore a lasting friendship to pro-
cure "living spaces" for their peoples.

Did he who had discovered Machiavelli in the maturity of his life follow the advice of his patron?

"And here let it be noted, [wrote the great Florentine philosopher] a prince should be careful never to join with one stronger than himself in attacking others, unless, as already said, he be driven to it by necessity. For if he whom you join prevails, you are at his mercy; and princes, so far as in them lies, should avoid placing themselves at the mercy of others... Whence we may draw the general axiom which never or rarely errs that he who is the cause of another's greatness is himself undone."

CHAPTER XX

ET TU, DUCE!

When Hitler invaded Poland and forced Great Britain and France to declare war on him, the world wondered whether Il Duce would fulfill the Axis "pact of steel" or whether it would be a recurrence of 1914 when Italy stayed out. The pact required Italy in the war. Italy did not move a soldier.

This was not altogether deliberate. Italy could not move. As we have seen, she had no gold, no guns and very little of anything. Her great cities had no anti-aircraft defenses. When the British bombarded Turin, Milan and Genoa even a year later, they were not molested. There were no uniforms, no blankets and no shoes. At the regular annual call of the conscripts, three hundred thousand were demobilized on the excuse that they were needed in the harvest, a work of peace rather than war. The maneuvers of the previous August had conclusively shown that the fighting equipment was obsolete, inadequate, rickety and rusty. One American newspaperman reported that Mussolini suffered a heart attack. It would have been true had it been taken with a sense of humor. Il Duce took it seriously and expelled him.

Mussolini was forced nevertheless to put on a bold front. He excused Italy's cool unconcern with the subterfuge that it was a local struggle. For one who by touching a button could rally eight million bayonets, five thousand planes and three hundred men-of-war, it was not according to type. He announced with a subdued bravado that Italy was going to build a world's fair with giant ferris wheels, merry-go-rounds and a midway. Instead of war he talked peace. Hitler did not seem upset in the slightest. Either from disdain or in complacent self-confidence, he sent a message to Il Duce saying that Germany did not need Italian military aid. He had evidently been informed on the no gold, no guns, no anything.

As events have transpired, we can be sure that had Mussolini had cannon and money he would have entered the war from the first day. It was to be the Douhet system. A fully armed Italy and a fully armed Germany would overcome a partly armed France and a very poorly armed Britain. He would have blared from the balcony that he was keeping his word. They had both calculated in staff talks on a quick decision. He cursed himself for not being prepared.

The war at that awkward moment was not relished. He pouted a little. He was not altogether pleased with Hitler's annexation of Austria and Czechoslovakia because it left him without anything to show to his own people for the Axis tie-up. He discovered, too, that both France and Great Britain were anxious about him. He began to take an inventory of the possibilities. Again he might play. He thought wishfully about Hitler because he counted on great booty by a defeat of the two democracies.

His chief concern was how to gain time. It was then he made it appear to England and France as if there was a chance that he might go with them. He accepted orders for airplane motors, textiles and other manufactured goods. He appointed his own under-secretary of state for foreign affairs, Giuseppe Bastianini, as ambassador to Great Britain to replace Grandi, an act of goodwill. He was declaring fidelity to Hitler but flirting with France and Great Britain. He made the world believe he was on the fence.

The flirtations came out in public view. Hitler told Von Ribbentrop that Italy had better be watched. Der Fuehrer asked Ciano to Berchtesgaden and inquired what the flirtations meant. Ciano laughed them off as innocent, platonic. He explained that Italy could not go to war. Italy had already advised Hitler that she would not be ready for three years, he said. Hitler cocked an eyebrow and hardly mentioned Italy in his speech to the Reichstag on October 6. He had learned that the flirtations had advanced to a proposition. The British offered concessions on the Suez Canal and in trade. The French made overtures to Italy in East Africa and in Tunisia. Something was in the air. The French command removed half its forces from the Italian border. On October 31, Mussolini reshuffled his cabinet and dismissed all pro-German elements.

This made it look as if Italy leaned to the Allies. It was only necessary to make the proposal high enough. A British trade delegation went to Rome to negotiate a commercial agreement. The Italians were offered a chance to get rich. France would give territory, Britain would give trade. Orders for more millions of pounds sterling in trucks, airplane motors and parts were in the offing.

Hitler now turned on the pressure. He was not going to be caught. He wanted a definite Italian stand. To satisfy him, Ciano in a speech in the Chamber of Guilds said the "pact of steel" was inviolable and that Italy would not repeat the World War decision of changing from the German to the Allied side.

Articles in the Italian newspapers boosted every German military success and deplored every Allied success. The British discerned a certain disloyal note in the Italian policy. Accordingly, they now changed their attitude from trying to persuade Il Duce to remain neutral to one of strict accountability. They seized thirteen ships loaded with coal passing through the English Channel from Germany to Italy. The incident, however, was smoothed over on the grounds that the ships had begun their voyage before the blockade restrictions were in effect.

But just as the incident seemed solved, Mussolini decided abruptly to send home the British delegation. It could not meet his price. It departed without having accomplished anything. Instead and as if to serve warning on England, he signed a commerical and cultural agreement with Germany which though it was more show than substance was pointed enough. On March 11, Hitler met Mussolini at the Brenner Pass. Martially, their two armored trains were brought up alongside one another. Il Duce strutted confidently for he was still somewhat of a big boy in the transaction. He

still had a navy, at least on paper. The communique
concluding the meeting said :

"The conversation proceeded in harmony with the
spirit of the pact of alliance and the existing agreements
between Germany and Italy."

Italy was gaining the time.

The invasion of Poland had convinced Mussolini of
the invincibility of the Nazi machine. It was precise,
unified and had one command. This contrasted with
the Allied machine which had few mechanized units,
a negligible air force and a vacillating military and political policy. He visualized power on the one side, inefficiency and disintegration on the other.

In the early spring of 1940, he leaned distinctly over
from the middle of the road. He ordered a still more
violent press campaign against France and England.
This was to whet the mass for belligerent action. The
military policy of the Allies was depicted as full of
blunder and indecision. The invasion of Denmark and
Norway gave him a chance to ridicule their fighting inefficiency. The press laughed at the evacuation of
Narvik and the whole of the Allied generalship. The
direct, withering and dynamic drive of the Germans re-
gardless of pacts or promises fitted admirably with his
own philosophy of international dealing. He gave up
the world's fair.

All over the country there were anti-British and anti-
French demonstrations staged. Two British diplomats
were assaulted in Rome. The situation was so strained
that the British Embassy issued a warning to all British
subjects to return home. Officially, Mussolini was si-

lent but suspiciously silent. At Orvieto in his first utter-
ance during these tragic days, he said,

"The skipper is preparing the course of the ship. He
must not be disturbed. The events which I foresee are
of gigantic proportions. We are convinced of our preparation for their exceptional character. Italy is ready to
face them."

Now war could come any moment. Posters were
plastered all over Italy by Fascist youths stating that
"the collapse of the democracies was certain" and that
there was "incontestable proof of a Franco-British defeat."

Winston Churchill who had already offered Mussolini
the olive branch received the "musty" answer and decided that it was to be war in the Mediterranean.
Premier Reynaud of France told the Chamber of Deputies that he, too, had offered Mussolini a "Mediterranean
understanding which would constitute an indispensable
basis for peace."

Il Duce wanted none of that. He could see "the
great events." He watched the irresistible flow of the
German army. He visualized a defeated France and
a surrender of the "decadent British." He had worked
out his theory mathematically and it could not fail.

Then the invasion of Holland and Belgium came on
May 10. Each day convinced him the German army
was irresistible. Each day gave him great faith that he
was choosing wisely. Every German move was glorified. The mistakes of the Allied command were mag-
nified. There was the break through at Sedan. The
surrender of King Leopold confirmed his judgment.

Now another break through at Saint Quentin. The Germans reached the channel. It was such devastating military success that it was unbelievable. The entire British army was almost surrounded. Then a lull and the memorable evacuation of Dunkerque took place. He ridiculed this and said that it was following the British method of warfare. It was all going according to his own wishes. The Germans were sweeping toward Paris. He could see the end of the war. He could see France eliminated. The French rout began. He could see German victory in sight. It was unfailing. He wanted to be in on the victory. He could not miss this great chance. Victory was his destiny.

His whole fiber itched. He picked the moment. He declared war.

This, too, had to be done from the balcony. This, too, was to be a grand moment with radio hook-ups, loud speakers, and bells calling the people into the public places. Two hundred thousand massed in Venice Square. All the Fascist organizations were there with their uniforms and banners. They awaited his timed entrance. At seven o'clock in the evening of June 10, he was to launch the war cry. The cheering was deafening. "Duce! Duce!" cried out the hundreds of thousands as if he were some pagan pontiff.

He appeared. The acclamations were thunderous. He stood arms akimbo. A dream was being fulfilled. He was leading a nation into a war of destiny. After several moments, silence awaited the dictatorial edicts.

"Fighters of land, sea and air," he bellowed. "Blackshirts of the revolution, veterans of the legions, men and women of Italy, of the Empire and of the kingdom of Albania, listen!"

He paused amid the breathless silence.

"The hour destined by fate sounds for us," he shouted, biting each word. "The hour of irrevocable decision has come. A declaration of war has already been handed to the ambassadors of Great Britain and of France."

The cheering was cannon-like. When silence came he continued.

"We take the field against the plutocratic and reactionary democracies, who always have blocked the march and frequently plotted against the existence of the Italian people."

It was another explosion.

He paused again. Silence returned to make each moment the more anxious.

"Several decades of recent history may be summarized in these words : phrases, promises, threats of boycott and finally the crowning indignity of that ignoble edifice, the League of Nations of fifty-two nationalities.

"Our conscience is absolutely clear. The entire world is witness that the Italy of Fascism has done everything humanly possible to avoid the tempest that envelops Europe but, all in vain."

He then charged that if treaties had been changed, the war would have been avoided. He said that had France and Great Britain listened to Hitler, peace would have been restored. Italy must get to the ocean, he said. The battle was only one phase of the Fascist revolution.

"It is the conflict of poor, prolific peoples who labor against those who would starve us while they ferociously cling to a monopoly of all the riches and all the gold on earth," he kept on. "It is a conflict between two ages, two ideas."

Then he promised that he did not intend to drag other nations into the war and specifically mentioned Switzerland, Yugoslavia, Greece, Turkey and Egypt.

"It depends upon them," he threateningly warned. Then he praised the Axis.

"Italians," he said, "in a memorable mass meeting in Berlin, I said that according to the rules of Fascist morals when one has a friend one sticks by him to the end. This we have done and this we will continue to do—with Germany, her people and her victorious armed forces."

Then he saluted the King of Italy and finally concluded:

"We hail the Fuehrer, the chief of our great ally, Germany.

"Proletarian Fascist Italy has arisen for the third time, strong, proud, compact as never before. There is only one command. It is categorical and it is imperative on every one. It already wings its way and inflames all hearts from the Alps to the Indian Ocean—Conquer!

"People of Italy, rush to arms and show your tenacity, your courage and your valor."

He gave the Fascist salute in a quick, military gesture. The cheering broke out. He made his exit into the palace. He heard the thunderous ovations from the inside. It was another great moment.

Victory was to be a matter of days.

Boasts in the Italian press blared that Italy and Germany would annihilate Britain. Italian planes bombed Malta. Others bombed Aden. Still others bombed Toulon, Bizerta and Tunis. The Italians started an offensive in the Alps. Many hundreds of them were killed in this useless display for France was prostrate. France surrendered. On June 18, Mussolini and Ciano went to Munich to a conference with Hitler on Marshal Petain's message of capitulation. Six days later the armistice with France was signed. Toulon, Bizerta, Oran and Ajaccio were to be demilitarized. The Italians were accorded full use of the port of Jibuti in French Somaliland. A thirty-mile zone along the Italo-French frontier also was demobilized.

The British were left to fight alone. In Palestine, their flank was exposed by the immobilization of the French forces in Syria. The Italian forces in Lybia were free to attack Egypt without fearing any French pressure from Tunisia. The effective support given to Britain by the French fleet was taken away. The British could not use French bases anywhere in the world. The British colonies bordered by French colonies were now exposed to the Axis attack especially in East Africa. These were the dark days for England. A shining dawn appeared on the Italian horizon. Victory everywhere seemed but necessary to seize.

Sanguine and joyous were his hopes in all of Africa. Marshal Graziani was told to gather his Lybian armies estimated at 300,000. He was instructed to prepare an offensive against the hard-pressed British in Egypt. He was to take the Suez Canal and conquer that country to join the two Italian colonies of Lybia and Ethiopia. The British were outnumbered by at least five to one. On July 5, Italian forces occupied Kassala and Gallabat in the Anglo-Egyptian Sudan. Ten days later Fort Moyale on the Kenya frontier was taken. The Italian offensive, though in sporadic forays, had begun.

On August 5, Italian forces attacked British Somaliland on a three-hundred-mile front. They seized the port of Zeila. Adjoining French Somaliland surrendered. They drove on, aiming to seize all British bases on the Red Sea so as to threaten Aden and the Empire line. On August 12, the British abandoned the colony and the defeat was hailed throughout Italy as proof that England was now on her knees. It was reckoned as just a prelude to the greater offensive which Graziani was preparing in Lybia.

Meanwhile, Great Britain recognized Haile Selassie as an "ally." On July 22, he flew from England to the Sudan to rejoin the Ethiopian forces and to continue the fight for throne and country. He was smuggled ashore in Alexandria, Egypt, and hidden in the washroom of the Italian Yacht Club. There British officers toasted him in Italian chianti, found in the cellars. The King of Kings doffed the mufti for the uniform of generalissimo of the Ethiopian Army. To the pilot who brought him from England he gave a gold watch engraved with a crown. "When next you see me I'll be wearing the crown," he said.

On September 14, Marshal Graziani began his march eastward with what was considered an invincible desert force of twenty divisions, with one thousand tanks, five thousand trucks and two thousand airplanes. Two days later they covered seventy-five miles and occupied the fort of Sidi Barrani. This was to be his advance post where he would organize his irresistible dash for the Suez Canal, four hundred miles away. He had only to await weather and to choose the day.

The initiative was distinctly in the hands of the Italians. So sure was the situation in hand, that Graziani was summoned to Rome to illustrate to Mussolini the certainty of Italian success. Il Duce in turn took Graziani's reassuring words with him up to the Brenner Pass on October 4 where the two armored trains drew up again. There he told Hitler that the Egyptian campaign was won and also assured Marshal Wilhelm Keitel, chief of the German General Staff, that Graziani would soon give the Fascist salute to the Pyramids.

To show to his own people that he was doing something Mussolini projected an invasion of Greece also. He thought it would be no more than a trick in legerdemain. Presto! Change-o! He knew the condition of the Italian army did not permit much of a campaign and decided to buy off the Greek government with large sums of money, which in terms of army expenses would only be a beer ration. Accordingly he chose chunky Emmanuel Grazzi, who had served many years as consul-general in New York and was known in our metropolis only as an excellent bridge player, to act as the go-between. Grazzi was his minister to Greece. The amounts set apart for this clandestine enterprise have been reported variously as from $10,000,000 to

$20,000,000. This was big money for Greek government officials. Grazzi decided he had found his men and, what is more, the money was paid over.

Meanwhile Mussolini had called Marshal Badoglio to a conference. He told him that he wanted to take Greece and desired to know the cost. Badoglio replied that it would take ten divisions and there were only seven divisions available. Besides, Badoglio said, it was bound to be a hard campaign. The winter was approaching and the terrain was mountainous and impassable without a large attacking force. Mussolini then told him there would be no resistance as Grazzi had bought off the Greek government. Badoglio said that he would not like to risk it.

Mussolini went ahead. On October 26, a communique issued by the official Italian news agency described an attack "by a band of Greeks armed with rifles and hand grenades on an Albanian outpost." Two Albanian soldiers were killed and three wounded. This was the pretext for invasion. The Greeks had provoked war by attacking Albania, Italian territory, they claimed. On October 28, Grazzi gave a most sumptuous reception in the Italian legation at Athens. The cream of Greek aristocracy was there. Cabinet ministers, bankers, editors and diplomats added greater dignity to the occasion. A while later, the chunky Italian go-between handed a three-hour ultimatum to Prime Minister John Metaxas, in the latter's private apartment.

The document demanded the use of Greek naval bases for the Italian fleet and the renunciation of all

British guarantees. Before the ultimatum expired, Italian troops were on the march. Six waves of Fascist planes bombed the harbor of Piraeus. The first days of the campaign showed the invincibility of Mussolini's legions. They pierced far into the Pindus mountains on Greek soil. On November 7, they crossed the Kalamas river. Gleefully, Mussolini held a conference with Hitler in Florence and assured him that Grazzi had done a superb job.

Suddenly, the Italians were stopped. The hardy Greek mountaineers had orders to beat them back. The pompous Italian tanks and big rumbling trucks were discourteously halted and thrown into confusion in the recesses of the craggy heights.

"We will throw them into the sea," proclaimed General Alexander Papagos, the Greek commander-in-chief, in his message to his troops. "We will write new and glorious pages in our history. Do not doubt that we shall win our cause."

There was a turn. The Greeks actually began driving the Italians into the sea. The mechanized units were rounded up by the Greek cavalry playing hide-and-seek with them around the rugged hills. It was plain that Grazzi's men who had taken the money would not or could not deliver.

The campaign was fought in the depth of winter with snow eight and ten feet deep. The Italians were ill-clad, some of them even wore their summer uniforms. As the need for greater forces increased, the equipment became less and less efficient. The Italian tanks could not stand up in the rough, mountainous terrain. Their construction was too haphazard to resist a campaign of such severity. They had been made for parade. Not alone were the men poorly clad and improperly fed but there were tragic shortages of munitions. Rifles were faulty. There was a shortage of mules for mountain artillery. What stocks of equipment and munitions remained were always the wrong size or weight.

Besides, very erroneous calculations were made in keeping the army in the field. First, the risk of transport from Italy was not foreseen since the campaign was to be a pushover. Then in the interior of Albania, where the roads were nothing but mere tracks through the passes, there was no place for mechanized units to operate. The only thing which could work with any degree of success was the mule. The Greeks had mules.

Here, too, were evidences of bravery of individual soldiers. Prisoners captured by the Greeks stated that in many battalions only a few survivors could be counted. One battalion entered the line with five hundred and fifty men and only thirty-six survived. With such deplorably poor staff work, it was inevitable that the morale of the soldiers and of the officers of the line should collapse. Here was the answer to the capture of whole regiments of Italians. The only alternative was surrender.

In the spring of 1941, Mussolini made a personal visit to the Greek front. He ordered General Cavallero, who by this time had assumed command, to start an offensive. The attack crumbled when the Italians were thrown back with heavy losses, a habit they had

been acquiring all winter. The Greeks claimed that
up to that moment they had put 120,000 Italians out
of action, had downed a hundred and thirty planes and
had captured twelve hundred field guns, fifteen hundred mortars, seven hundred machine-guns and enormous stores. This was the Italian campaign against
Greece.

On April 5, Hitler invaded Greece. It was another
story. He took Athens on April 27. Mussolini con-
gratulated Cavallero. Churchill called it a new record
in bluster.

While the Italians were being roughly handled in
the Pindus mountains, Marshal Graziani was awaiting a cool day, a full moon, a favorable wind, a hang-
ing fog or something for his projected invasion of
Egypt. His main force was still at Sidi Barrani. But
on December 9, General Wavell had given orders to
his new army reinforced by Australian and New Zea-
land units to jump off. They jumped and caught
Graziani's entire concentration completely unawares.

The attack was prepared with the greatest secrecy.
Wavell duped the Italian command with a force of
dummy tanks and trucks massed along the desert to
give the Italians the impression that his main force was
still held there. Instead, the real force had stealthily
advanced during the night and found the Italians leisurely eating their breakfast unaware that any attack
was in the offing. The main body remained in a semi-
circle about the town five miles from the forts. The
following day, the mechanized units smashed through

the barbed wire entanglements and the victory was complete. The British captured 40,000 prisoners, two thousand trucks, twelve hundred tanks and enormous amounts of equipment which had been assembled as the storehouse for the Italian campaign.

After the fall of Sidi Barrani, General Wavell advanced his army along the coast in cooperation with the British fleet. They pushed on Solum, Bardia, Tobruk and finally captured Benghazi. More than 150,000 prisoners fell into British hands during the advance. It meant the complete disintegration of Graziani's forces.

Graziani had adopted strategy which no military man has been able to understand. He heavily fortified Sidi Barrani. The rest of his forces were strewn along the coast road for a thousand miles, making transport between them very difficult and costly. Once the Army of the Nile had overcome the forces at Sidi Barrani, it went on to conquest after conquest.

The whole campaign showed that Italian equipment was façade. Mussolini wanted to give the world the impression of great power in mechanized units. It was like his navy, just a show. The tanks were built with inferior material. Italy does not have the facilities for the manufacture of millions of tons of armor plate and other special steels required by the exigencies of war. Besides, the British patrol of the Mediterranean had prevented supplies from reaching Graziani. The marshal blamed his defeat on Mussolini's failure to deliver more trucks and claimed his army had not been surprised. Mussolini replied he had given him the trucks.

The campaign reached an inevitable result. On the one hand there was superior generalship, expert staff work, every consideration for the troops, abundant supplies and efficient communications; on the other, there was deplorable generalship, inexistent staff work, disregard for the troops, poor equipment, insufficient supplies and an imperfect means of communications. One side was militarily efficient; the other, confused.

And to add to the woe, the Italian units which had been proceeding to victory after victory in East Africa now began meeting reverses. In Ethiopia, feats were being performed by the British which resembled very impressively those achieved by Lawrence of Arabia. Natives were dashing in and out of the mountain recesses and eluding Italian patrols to strike blow after blow on Fascist columns. Britishers familiar with Ethiopian natives had organized these bands in the Sudan and had sent them through ravine and jungle to harass the common enemy.

Simultaneously, the Army of the Nile began an invasion of Italian East Africa. The Italian forces on occasion put up considerable resistance. A strong British column advanced from the north on Asmara, the capital of Eritrea, and succeeded in capturing it. Five columns converged from the coast, from Kenya and from the Sudan to march on Addis Ababa. These came along with astonishing speed. In 1936, it had taken the Italians six months to overcome the poorly armed Ethiopians. These British columns had turned the original Italian advantage in East Africa to crushing defeat. From the start of their campaign in De-

cember they had taken less than four months. Addis
Ababa fell on April 5, 1941. Haile Selassie returned in
fanatical triumph on May 5, 1941, after five years of
exile and resumed his throne.

Symptomatic was the message of the Duke of Aosta,
Italian viceroy of Ethiopia, in his flight from the capital. It read :

"His Royal Highness, the Duke of Aosta, wishes to express his appreciation for the initiative taken by General
Wavell and General Cunningham for the protection of
women and children in Addis Ababa, demonstrating that
strong bonds of humanity and race still exist between our
nations."

This was not in harmony with the ruthlessness of Axis
blitzkrieg. The Duke of Aosta is pro-British, received
part of his education in England and naturally speaks
the language with academic perfection. He was married to Princess Anne of France and may yet become a
favorite with British diplomacy in the manipulation of
the exigencies of war.

Now, while these successive defeats were dealing
their crushing blows to Italian military prestige, what
was happening on the sea was equally humiliating.
We have seen how the fleet was lined up in parade for
Hitler to inspect. It was quite another task to send it
into action. With a fleet built for boast and not for
battle, what use could it serve now? Events proved it.
We have learned that most units were obsolete and
new units were built of inferior material. This was
bad enough but training was not up to combat inten-

sity. The crews received no grounding in the exacting demands of conditions approximating action. No gunnery school existed. The shortage of oil prevented sufficient submarine practice and maneuvers on the high seas. The lack of precise military discipline disorganized the personnel of the whole fleet. This was partly explained by the fact that the officers were discouraged because of insufficient supplies and also because they never knew what their military problems were going to be. In a foreign policy where in one period the nation would be in agreement with England and in another Germany, the naval command never knew for what eventuality they should prepare.

These inefficiencies and deficiencies brought the navy to grief almost immediately. On November 11, an attack was made with flying torpedoes from the British aircraft carriers *Eagle* and *Illustrious* on the Italian fleet concentrated at Taranto. One battleship, either the *Littorio* or *Vittorio Veneto*, the biggest in the Italian navy, was put out of commission. Two other battleships of the obsolete type were sunk together with numerous other smaller units.

A large Italian squadron ventured into the Ionian Sea on March 28. It was met by the British Eastern Mediterranean fleet. Five Italian cruisers were sunk and either the *Littorio* or *Vittorio Veneto*, since these two ships have not been identified, was seriously damaged. This action practically excluded any combat power from Italy on the sea. The British fleet returned to its base without a scar.

And where were the five thousand planes? During

the endless talk of disarmament in the late 1920s and early 1930s, Italy had the finest air force in the world. The morale was the very highest. Italian pilots were winning all the international records. They had developed the fastest pursuit plane and the best long distance bomber. Germany had no air force. Great Britain and France having no enemies to worry about then did not spend any money on the air.

The Ethiopian war found Italian machines more than equal to that task and the same could be said about the campaign in Spain. Following these two campaigns there has been no money available to build new planes. What Italy had for Ethiopia and for Spain she had for the present war and nothing more. The struts were of wood, the wings of fabric and the motors outdated. They had few, very few all metal planes.

Now when these machines went against Spitfires and Hurricanes, they were outmatched and shot down with relative ease. Their speed even though epochal at four hundred miles an hour in 1930 could not compare with the new British fighter planes hurtling between five and six hundred miles an hour. Spitfires and Hurricanes possessed an overwhelming superiority in armament. It was suicide for an Italian pilot. In the Lybian campaign alone, Italy lost twelve hundred planes. Three hundred were destroyed in Albania and another two hundred were shot down in the Mediterranean and over the English Channel. Her air force is now so crippled that it is virtually non-existent and besides cannot be replaced since anything done to such planes does not make them serviceable in modern combat.

What applied to the navy, also applied to the air force. Maneuvers, exercises, training and research was held down to the minimum because of the financial state of the country. Nothing could be afforded. The pilots had no chance for training under conditions approximating battle. There was no fuel, no spare parts, no weapons and finally no new planes. Under such conditions, the pilots were utterly unprepared. They had never learned any night-flying. They had never used a bomb sight and they were unequal in physical training to the exactions of active service. The Italian air force, just like the navy and army, had always looked well on parade.

And now with the whole of the African empire "torn to tatters," Il Duce faced the reckoning he never contemplated. The invincible army was only invincible in peace. The navy which was to claim the *Mare Nostrum* was master of the seas only when no enemy was in sight. The air force which was to darken the sky black was unconquerable when no others challenged. The words which once terrorized the plain taxpayers of the decadent democracies were now but blatant brass. The balloons of boast were flattened by the realities of enemy tanks, enemy flying and enemy gunnery.

At the fatal stab when France lay prostrate and Britain reeled with the battering blows of battle, he had raised the sword upon the balcony to rally his eight million bayonets, five thousand planes and three hundred men-of-war. He had declared the failing foes already crushed by his staggering might.   One stroke and it would all be over.   He had chosen the moment.   It was victory.   He knew it was his.

Writhing Britain rallied.   The fighting tenacity of the scorned and decadent democracy challenged his brassy emptiness.   The invincible conqueror had arms and feet of clay.   He had no gold, no guns, nothing.   And, the war had only begun.

CHAPTER XXI

AND, SO WHAT?

For Italy, any war was woe. It could only be out of it. Non-belligerency was belligerency. It forced blockade. Even a short war meant vassalage. A long war, for soldiers and civilians, for men, women and children, was starvation, torment, desperation, death and defeat.

To stamp out the stains of his flagrant duplicity, Mussolini must enter and win. The twisting trail of snare and delusion which he had hoped to make a path of glory led him to inextricable ambush, entangled in the battered debris of his boasted might. The opportunism on which he banked and which had served him well in eighteen years of rule deserted him in this decisive stroke of destiny. War was his undoing.

Condemnation stalks in the evil he did — to intimate friends, to colleagues, to his own people and to the nations, large and small. I can remember his solemn promises given publicly and privately in my presence to the Arabs, to the Jews, to the Ethiopians, to the Yugoslavs, to the Austrians, to the Albanians, to the Poles, to the French, and to the British and to all.

"Once I have given my word," he told me in emphatic and sober tones in a conversation at Venice palace, "that word will be fulfilled to the last scruple. Once I have put my name to paper, every letter will be executed even to the dots on the I's."

He always spoke with impressive sincerity declaiming his own impregnable rectitude. With all this display of faith in right, it was difficult to understand how in high position he could with such dramatic animation guarantee one thing in words and then do quite the opposite in acts whenever it suited his purpose. Of Alexander VI, the Borgia pope, Machiavelli said:

"No man ever had a more effective manner of sincere assertion or made promises with more solemn protestations and then observed them less. And yet, because he understood this side of human nature his frauds always succeeded."

And so did those of Mussolini. There is hardly a nation which has not been the victim of his deception. Lush and exuberant words had he given to Haile Selassie and then again to his son, the Crown Prince, on two different occasions in Rome.

He told the Arabs that he was a much wiser and more benevolent ruler than either Britain or France. He proclaimed himself, as we saw, the Protector of Islam and yet he did not hesitate to massacre them by the hundreds of thousands in the inhuman repression undertaken by Marshal Graziani. He befriended Zogu Mali Bey, then the Albanian chieftain who with Yugoslav support had risen to power in Albania. He induced him to desert his friendship for his first benefactors by offers of money and splendor. Royal honors were bestowed upon Zogu. He took the title of king. On that Good Friday of 1939, Il Duce decided he was "a grafter" and without warning invaded his country forcing even the queen to flee with her baby.

He befriended the Bolsheviks in 1924. Since the help he counted on did not materialize, he condemned them for their barbarity and Asiatic cruelty. He signed the Anti-Comintern Pact. But, when Russian friendship was needed in the present war, he maintained that there were many points in common between Fascism and Communism. He was a friend of the Poles and signed a treaty of friendship and commerce with them. Yet in their hour of despair, he told them that they had no reason for existence as a nation. He said the same thing of the Czechoslovaks.

He announced himself the protector of Austria. When the German invasion appeared imminent, he warned Chancellor Schuschnigg that he had better make the best terms with Hitler he could get. In 1929 he signed the Lateran Treaty with the Vatican ending the fifty-nine-year quarrel with the Holy See. In 1931 he started a new quarrel on the pretext that Catholics were interfering in politics. In 1939 he made the Pope believe him a man of peace and induced the Pontiff to make many personal allusions to his pacific intentions; yet he was preparing to enter the war all the time.

In 1934 he called Hitler a fool and the Nazis a nation of pederasts. In his proclamation of war against England and France he declared him a true and sincere friend. The German people he ranked as the cultural and military brothers of the Italians. He hurled at the Japanese the condemnatory epithet of yellow peril and charged them with plans to destroy the white race. Today, the common aims, ideals and comradeship of Japan and Italy are the binding cement of two great civilizations. The Japanese are everything to him but blood brothers.

In the war in Spain, it was officially announced by Italian ambassadors that Italy was in no way giving any military aid to Franco. They insisted the contrary was true — Mussolini was prohibiting any "volunteers" from serving in Spain. Whole divisions, however, were transferred to the civil war. Recruiting offices were set up all over Italy by militia officers. The pay for service in Spain was raised to five times the Italian. When it was all too self-evident, Mussolini admitted he had 100,000 troops there. When Franco finally entered Madrid, Il Duce claimed greater credit for the victory than El Caudillo.

He first insisted that Ethiopia should be admitted as a member of the League of Nations. Then in violation of Article 16, he made war on Ethiopia stating that the article was obsolete. In January, 1934, he signed a treaty of friendship with France regulating all outstanding Italo-French differences. In 1938 he repudiated the treaty and demanded Tunisia, Savoy, Corsica and Nice. In the present war, he feigned neutrality, then made the fatal stab.

With England he had been playing a series of betrayals. In 1925 he signed a treaty with England and France to respect the territorial independence of Ethiopia. When he violated the accord by invasion, he remarked that "Treaties are not eternal." In 1938 the gentlemen's agreement for the Mediterranean was reached. The status quo would be respected. Then he marched into Albania. When Hitler invaded Po-

land, he accepted orders for motors, airplanes and munitions from both France and England, evidently expecting to shop around for the best bid for his services.
When he felt the Germans had a good chance, he can-
celed the orders and began building up his own forces.

On October 31, 1939, he signed a treaty of friendship with the Greeks in order to keep them within his
own orbit and to strengthen whatever influence he had
in the Balkans. A year later, he invaded Greece intent
on subjugating the whole country to his rule. Similarly, he signed a treaty of friendship and goodwill
with Egypt, yet he prepared the enormous expedition
under Graziani to invade Egypt on the pretext that he
was attacking the Suez Canal though his chief purpose
was not alone to seize the canal but bring rich Egypt
under his sway and join his two African colonies.

Through his base penetration into the peaceful life
of freedom-loving peoples, he has brought nations to
writhing torment and millions to death. A half million
native dead in Lybia, another half million in Ethiopia
and still another half million in Spain indict him.
Hundreds of thousands suffered in Austria. And there
was Albania, Greece and Yugoslavia which had done
nothing to warrant his chastisement. The peaceful desire of being allowed to work and to flourish upon their
own soil was their only demand. And with these dead
go the hundreds and thousands of his own blood thrown
into the battle without even the knowledge of what
their fight was about. And his chicanery was just as
generously bestowed in his personal relations and indeed in his relations with his own people. In 1926 he

made a solemn vow that he would maintain the value of the Italian lira at a fixed level based on gold. This he did to create confidence in the currency. When the United States devaluated the dollar in 1934, he used it as a pretext for devaluating the lira forty per cent. He had always made the Italian industrialists feel that his first loyalty was to them. "Discipline, work and order," was the war-cry. To win the great mass of the workingclass, he deserted the industrialists and reformed the laws to suit his own political convenience. He gladdened the hearts of all Italians by his out-and-out neutrality pronouncements. He saddened their hearts by entering the war on the side of Germany.

The course of his entire political career is strewn with his duplicity. He started as a revolutionary and violent Socialist, as a sworn enemy of royalty and a wild antagonist of the Church. We have seen him attack the aristocracy and landed gentry and the military caste. He was a violent opponent of the capitalist class. And yet he submerged what he fought for as an ideal to make common cause with its opponents. He used the enemies of one period to fight the enemies of another. There was never a moment when one who had accepted him as a friend was not sure the next moment that he was going to be an enemy. His word in the ordinary activity of life would mean one thing today and another tomorrow, as was often shown in his relations with the greatest personalities of our times, among whom even the Sovereign Pontiff was not to be excepted.

Are Hitler and Mussolini friends?

"Scratch a German and there you will find a barbarian," viciously remarked Mussolini with curled lip to me in the midst of one of his periodic German hates.

This is his true heart. <u>He is a Latin.</u>

Even in the short span since they were first thrown together by the currents of international collusion, the dictators have tricked and betrayed one another with unfettered abandon when it suited. They are faithful while events are favorable to their union. When Hitler needed the Italian fleet, he gave Mussolini the promise of empire to the Indian Ocean. Now that the Italian fleet has shown its weakness, he owes him nothing. This is the friendship they respect. From my own personal observation, they disdain each other.

Both had dreams of world conquest. Both cannot rule the world. Each connived to use the other as a stepping stone. Whether Hitler has greater skill in his diplomatic chicanery is not much of a question; Mussolini possesses the same conniving dexterity. Where he overpowers Il Duce is in being in control of a disciplined people and a mighty industrial organization. Mussolini has neither. He could well boast of his armed might while Hitler had nothing, but once he had aided the building of Der Fuehrer's vast military establishment, it was inevitable that the bubble of Italian armed strength deflated to nothingness in comparison.

The world now wonders what Mussolini expected when Hitler became strong. No doubt, he expected his share, — domination of the Mediterranean and the empire to the Indian Ocean. This meant suzerainty over France and Spain. Hitler was to make England his vassal and with it all the rest of Europe and Russia. If such a dream had followed its course to reality, the world would have still had two dictators each eager for world conquest and a single rule. We can see how Hitler calculated. He could easily crush his weaker partner if that need be.

But how was Mussolini to project *his* dream of world domination? He counted surely on the fortune of destiny. Il Duce with his quick turns would return to his tirades against the barbarian Hun. His plan was to rally the Latins and the Anglo-Saxons against the common tyrant. He wanted a Latin world. It is a long, long distance away.

The course of events through the life of Il Duce have beat faster and brought him greater realization than he had ever hoped in the dingy offices of his newspaper as a debt ridden editor. Currents and occasions have turned in his favor, it is true. Now, he has struck a snag. The forces which have turned the world to play into his hand and to chart his destiny seem now to have deserted him. The great pronouncements of his unfailing prowess in victory demand a reckoning.

The great decision to enter the war was bound to uncover the emptiness of his boisterous boasts — eight million bayonets, five thousand planes and three hundred men-of-war. In his swagger, he had copied the late P. T. Barnum. In his way also, this was "the greatest show on earth." Unconsciously perhaps, he had also adopted the Barnum technique, for to him a dupe was born every minute. As an advance agent and barker, he terrorized the nations of Europe, from powerful Britain to helpless Egypt. He ranted over the air. He sent pictures of tanks and artillery, of airplanes in combat and of battleships in action in the bays of Naples and Taranto. His loud talk was published in the newspapers of the world. It was not that the military men were fooled. They knew. But in times of peace, the democracies spurn a soldier. Many, many ordinary souls believed him. France and England stroked him gently to keep him quiet. He thought it weakness and barked the more.

And with his unconquerable legions, with their tanks, airplanes and battleships, he met the Greeks. He met the Army of the Nile. He met the British Navy. Each had once shown respect for the "Greatest Show on Earth." Now it was scorn. No more did the air vibrate with terrorizing rants. No pictures of scampering legions left Rome to thrill a waiting world. No fiery speeches filled the press. But this was remembered : once he had a voice, a camera, a gullible international public — and little else.

When it is said that Italy could not make a shoestring without importing the material, it corresponds to fact. One may buy an electric light bulb of Italian manufacture but the parts come from abroad. The metal of the coffee-pot or frying-pan has been imported. Italian life geared to present-day civilization is stymied without recourse to goods from the outside. Italy begins without the bare essentials within her own frontiers — no coal, no oil, no cotton, no copper and, one might add, no steel, for what remains is negligible.

Even in time of peace, it is a hand to mouth existence. The course of Italian commerce and industry since the Ethiopian war has been to jump from pillar to post. It was necessary to relieve the country of its dependence on imports. There was no gold to pay for them. Research endeavored to produce synthetic coal, synthetic wool, synthetic oil and synthetic cotton. These experiments took billions in government funds but rendered little which could be of any practical use in solving the niggardliness of nature's stores.

Without gold it was convenient to go straight into the arms of Germany, though France and Britain would have come to Italy's aid with loans had Mussolini desired. The formation of the Axis permitted importations from Germany in exchange for Italian agricultural products, bauxite and sulphur. In their places, Italy received machinery, coal, steel and chemicals. In these exchanges, Germany sent about three billion lire worth of merchandise while Italy could muster only two billion lire to pay for it. And, in this strained effort, she was sending forty per cent of her fruit and eighty per cent of her vegetables. The deficit was accepted by the Germans in tourist due-bills, used to good advantage in strategically placed students, sightseers, engineers and Gestapo.

We should consider that 45,000,000 people live on the narrow Italian peninsula. It is not even as big as the State of Kansas and to lessen its fertility it is herringboned from top to bottom by the Alps and the Apennines. Of its 76,000,000 acres, only two fifths are cultivable; two fifths more are only partly cultivable and the remaining one fifth is completely barren. The peasant has brought to fruition every available inch of land and has kept it productive even when it has been necessary by back-breaking work to terrace the steep hillsides of the mountain ranges.

And with all the toil forced by the stubborn soil, Italy cannot grow enough grain to feed her prolific population. She needs annually two-hundred and fifty million bushels of wheat and her average year will yield her but one hundred and fifty million. To make up this difference and the other needs in raw materials, she must export vegetables, fruits, cheese, textiles, silk, hemp, wine, marble and automobiles. And these are not enough, she must entice hundreds of thousands of tourists, encourage freight in Italian steamers and urge her people living abroad to send their relatives their savings. It is the only way that Italy can make ends meet. When one job goes vacant in Italy, there are scores of hands always ready to fill it.

The national wealth reached between sixty and seventy billion lire in normal years. This was roughly between three hundred and three hundred and fifty million dollars. It is ordinarily a twentieth of our usual yearly income. But the budget of the Italian government runs to twenty-five billion lire, most of which is the interest on the national debt while fully one-third of the total is devoted to military expenditures. If local and municipal expenses are added, the governmental budgets are swelled to thirty-five billion lire. This means that the state takes half the national wealth. An Italian works every other day for the government.

We must recognize, too, despite this almost abject

poverty the potential genius of the Italian race. Historically, it used to be said that if one should take five of the greatest men in any branch of human activity, two of them were sure to be Italians. We scan the poets, the philosophers, the historians, the scientists, the inventors and the artists. History is studded with illustrious Italian names. In our day, we have witnessed the discovery of one of man's greatest achievements by Guglielmo Marconi. In the past fifteen years, Italy has furnished three of the Nobel prize winners. There is Toscanini, Respighi and Mascagni. Painting, sculpture and architecture are generously dotted, if not dominated, by Italian names.

Labor, skill and intellect working in a persistent tenacity had brought the country forward to a high degree of industrial and scientific progress. Ships like the *Rex* and *Conte di Savoia* could only be built by workmen and artisans who were the peers of any other shipbuilding peoples. The construction of the great works in the development of water power which has permitted Italy to claim the greatest network of electric railroads in Europe is testimony of a pioneering courage. The Italians held records in flying, both for speed and altitude. Italy possessed the fastest cruiser in the world. The fastest motorcars were made there. The world's longest tunnel runs under the Apennines. One of the world's greatest reclamation schemes succeeded when the Pontine marshes were drained. It was an undertaking bigger even than the Zuyder Zee. The hydraulic dams in Calabria and in Sardinia are the great-

est ever built in Europe.   It is in these things that
Mussolini might have said,

"This is the kind of war in which we excel."

As long as Mussolini kept to these pursuits, just as
long was he putting his nation on the road to progress
and even to greatness.   The Italians have never known
prosperity as it is enjoyed by the wealthier nations.   It
has been hard enough to live.   Had Il Duce kept to
his social and economic objectives he would have won
a more glorious and lasting gratitude, more profound
and basic, than the emphemeral cheers of the balcony,
occasioned by the artificial drumming of an unwelcome war.

The superman wanted to create himself a greater than
Caesar.   Caesar carried his campaigns amongst races
less developed than the Romans.   The war machines
of the barbarians both in men and contrivances were
inferior to his.   There was valor but there was also
might.   Mussolini in crushing defenseless blacks or
unarmed Arabs was within his military capabilities,
but to challenge the modern equipment of Britain and
the potential war machine of the United States was a
step in which Caesar would have been more discreet
and less valorous.   It was all part of the lure of self-
aggrandizement.   There would have been glory enough
for any man in successfully raising Italy to self-
sufficiency.

Before Mussolini was launched on his imperial mad-
ness, he had preached that in Italy there was enough
to give bread to every Italian.   He decried the spirit

which complained of the increasing population and said that the same arguments had been used when there were but half the number of people in Italy. Now with scientific and mechanical progress, he claimed, forty-five millions could make a living on the cultivable and partly cultivable lands. The country could be reforested and the water power still further developed, giving to industry the necessary impetus. This was his own story.

Italian patriotism burns with unquenchable ardor. Whether the nation has been classed amongst the five great powers or whether it has been listed in a secondary group has made no difference to the basic genius and industriousness of the race. Italians can think and can work. No nation condemns them in their zeal for national prestige and in racial pride. But, when efforts to keep up a first-class power front weigh down too heavily on the nation's potential wealth, then the façade of elaborate diplomatic and military undertakings should be simplified. The financial burden of government should be reduced. The Italian people would prosper were it not for the excessive taxation. One cannot work every other day for the government and have very much left for trips, movies or even a new suit.

And undoubtedly the greatest perfidy of all was to have misled rather than led on his own blustering impetuousness the nation into the "guerra fulmine" when it was a war of attrition. Winston Churchill charged him with being the "one man alone responsible." In his cupidity, he had connived not to fight but to get credit for fighting. Even at the moment he had so slyly chosen to be in at the kill, he committed the cardinal error of believing that Hitler would give him the palm of victory. Should the war have been as short as he himself had calculated, he would have gained nothing for Hitler would have promptly told him he had done nothing.

Aspersion has been cast upon the common soldier of Italy. The terrible defeats suffered were not due to lack of fighting fiber in the men. The peasant and the mountaineer are as hardy a stock as is found anywhere in all the world. Our every-day life in America uncovers constantly before us in commerce, in pioneering and in sports that the hardworking Italian is not a coward. Much discredit has been laid upon the common soldier for the failures of the staff and the government. At Caporetto, the fighting men had neither food, ammunition nor clothing. Guadalajara was not their cause and neither were Greece and Egypt. Bravery showed out in relief in the Battle of the Piave where an Italian army, greatly outnumbered, routed the flower of the Austrian empire. I heard the late Major-General Allen, U. S. A., say that it was the greatest display of heroism in the whole war.

Mussolini had been warned by Marshal Caviglia that wars today depend on industrial and economic resources. In his narrow military experience Il Duce may not have known what great resources meant. It is not conceivable. And much, much less is it conceivable that the head of a nation did not realize the almost complete impoverishment of his country in the very minimum of war essentials.

Few doubt the claims and no one condemns the right of the Italian nation for the living space necessary for its fullest capabilities, culturally and economically. To cry aloud for Fiume, a port of no utter use to Italy, and fail to ask for lands where wheat could grow or coal be mined is giving the child a rattle when it cries for milk. To add the title of emperor to that of king never made the grass grow nor caused the fruit to blossom. Il Duce chased an imperial phantom. Gold is only where you find it and it was not there.

And in those grandiose schemes of empire, where he aspired to possess Tunisia, Corsica, Savoy and Nice, the absolute control of the Mediterranean and the empire of Islam — with all of them, how could they be defended? There is not one of the lands in these aspirations which provides material to build his industries. The great resources are all outside this vast and cherished empire. In the turns of time, other aspirants could come again and take them all back, for the power to defend them would not reside in them.

And what is much more, had he succeeded now he would have owed it all to Hitler. The debt would have to be paid. In the decades to come, a Hitler defeat would be more advantageous for Italy than a victory. Within a German orbit, no sentimental quality of international friendship would rule their relationship. Whatever suited the schemes of German aggrandizement would be established policy. The "new order" would be a German order for Italian as well as Frenchman, for Spaniard as well as Briton, for Scandinavian as well as Slav. There would be a German but no Italian Empire.

Even the Mussolini dream of *Mare Nostrum* could only be subject to the exigencies of German expansion. German strategists have already said that their scheme for domination of the Mediterranean depended on the use of the Italian fleet. Since the Italian fleet has been swept from the seas what could Mussolini ask in the ordering of this important waterway? He could claim no credit for having mastered it or even policed it. The British fleet would either be scuttled, escape to the Americas or be held in German hands. Dominion would be to Germany alone. Italy would be a German vassal.

In British victory, on the other hand, Italy would be assured at least of freedom as a national entity. It would decisively mean the end of Fascism. Whatever internal blessings the bundles of combat have brought through the corporative state and the development of the nation's industrial and agricultural possibilities are part of the national heritage anyway and as fixed as the soil. These, after enjoying eighteen years of exploitation, Fascism could very well bequeath. There was much corruption in Italy before Fascism. There was much more during Fascism and both were unhealthy for the state. The cyclone of dictatorial severity being over, the sober calm and rugged spirit for vital reconstruction will prevail. It will be a political chastening It will be health for Italy.

Territorially, it would serve no purpose of lasting

peace to trim the frontiers and wrest from her the regions which by race and geographical nature are Italian.
All Italians can very well be left within strategic and
racially fixed boundaries. The region of the South Tyrol
with its 250,000 Austrians of German blood will undoubtedly return to a new Austria. The boundary will
be changed from the Brenner to the line fixed by Napoleon as the natural line of Italy, both strategic and
racial, when he created the Cisalpine Republic. It in-
cludes the historic city of Trent. In the East, some adjustments may be made to allot many thousands of
Croats now living under Italian rule to Yugoslavia.
The fate of Fiume may again be fought out.

Within those national lines, Italians can spur themselves forward to consolidate their industrial possibilities and to return to the great maxims of many of her
great statesmen who frowned on grandiose international undertakings. Agreements must be made with
all her neighbors. Industrial and agricultural life has
been too hard in the parsimonious soil. Economic concessions must be allowed her all over the world. Trade
barriers must be removed so that she can exchange her
products of agriculture, her textiles, her bauxite for
those essentials like coal, oil and steel which she so
much lacks. The economic ways of the world must
be made easier for her so that with her hardworking
population she may be able to prosper as other nations
prosper. The dictates of peace demand that those who
establish the next new order will give Italy a better
chance.

Whatever colonies are awarded to Italy will alone

depend on the generosity of England. As this conflict develops, it appears that the people of Great Britain feel no deep hatred for the people of Italy. The feeling of mutual trust which prevailed between the two peoples before Mussolini will easily return.

Since England proclaimed Haile Selassie as an ally, it is unthinkable that Italy should ever again try to possess his territory. In North Africa, Lybia does not offer a fertile land for development. Whatever the Italians have done there has been done at great cost and the returns have shown that the outlay has not warranted the expense. Some land to be developed should be assigned to Italy. A contented Italy with territory to be developed could be a powerful factor in the councils of world peace. The genius of her people recommends that Italy be made a partner in the work of restoring the world to sober living. The Italian people never wanted this war.

We can be sure that Italy's great recuperative powers will be evident. The country knows how to face hardships. The travail of reconstruction will be faced with the same determination to go on for eternity which has kept the race in the forefront of all man's greatest achievements in all the centuries. Italy will go on and resume her place as one of the dynamic nations in a new world community.

Italy has been forced into three wars since the advent of Fascism. The Ethiopian campaign was undertaken against the advice of her military experts and certainly without any consultation whatsoever with the people. The war fever created was generated by artificial stimulation, sword rattling and promises of glory when little was to be obtained. The expedition to Spain was a clandestine undertaking for which Mussolini again is responsible. Finally, the formation of the Rome-Berlin Axis and entrance into a struggle which Italians did not want and for which they had neither heart nor resources are placed against his name in the grand reckoning of history.

In all the betrayals of men and principles, of systems and theories, of dreams and ideals, the lust for military conquest at a cost in blood and suffering overloaded with grief is the challenging indictment of the misuse of the trust, so freely and generously given by his people. Ominously was he warned, persuasively was he entreated and prayerfully was he urged against the sword. He took it up in abject degradation against a prostrate neighbor.

As each successive blow turned against him slowly to crush his self-made magnitude, the words of Vincenzo Pareto, whose wisdom he acquired and adopted in shaping his internal policy, must rattle in his ears.

"No military enterprises," counseled the great Pareto.

He, too, was betrayed.

Italy was betrayed.

INDEX